Fourteenth Edition–1997

Recommendations on the Colleges

*Compiled and Edited by the College Staff of
Rugg's Recommendations*

by Frederick E. Rugg

Rugg's Recommendations • Atascadero, California

To
Barbara, Betsie, and Sue

TABLE OF CONTENTS

SOME NOTES FROM THE AUTHOR

WHY THIS BOOK?

As a secondary school college counselor, I heard the following question from a student or parent almost daily: "Can you please give us a list of quality colleges where one can major in psychology (or engineering or business or whatever)?"

For many years I pulled out the college handbooks and came up with a list of hundreds of colleges for each category and spent too much time with the student sifting through the multitude of schools, trying to narrow down the huge list.

I thought about a way out of this dilemma for a long time. People from Harvard would find an easy solution. They might tell the parents and student not to worry about a college major—just go to a fine liberal arts college (like Harvard) and everything will fall into place. After all, it's not the major and professors that count, it's the wonderful student body that makes a great college great. Right?

Well…over the years, I had trouble convincing parents of the merits of that argument. I guess they realize that all good universities are not good in every field.

Today, there's just so much pressure on young people to line up their careers and pick their occupations in life early. Career education seems to start in kindergarten these days. I've noticed that many parents pick right up on it and give Johnny the business if he hasn't chosen his career by the sophomore year of high school or earlier. No matter what I told Johnny and his parents, they still wanted a list of "the quality colleges with a good psychology (or whatever) department."

This book lists the quality departments at quality colleges and it will make the school counselor's job easier. For example, a public school counselor can use it constantly in January when juniors (and sometimes sophomores) line up outside his/her office, asking for a list of colleges to "go with" their PSAT scores. Probably a prep school counselor, a junior and community college transfer counselor, or a librarian might even find more use of this guide for college majors. Since this book is for the aid of the counselor, it is, then, also a guide for students and their parents in the college admissions process.

WHY THESE 760 COLLEGES?

From our experience in the college admissions process, we have chosen 760 quality four-year colleges (out of over 2000 that offer bachelor degrees) to study. We began with the 260 colleges that have survived the careful screening process involved in the granting of a Phi Beta Kappa chapter. The Phi Beta Kappa schools are listed in Appendix A. These colleges received chapters for superior undergraduate performance in the liberal arts and sciences.

To this list were added over 500 colleges—schools that our staff felt are as good (or better) as several of the Phi Beta Kappa colleges or have excellent specialized programs. We should also note that, in general, the more well-respected the college, the more departments and majors were included. Berkeley is listed under 24 departments while some others only under one. The typical school in the study was noted with 5.0 departments. A departmental page averages 100 recommended colleges.

WHY MOSTLY STUDENT INPUT?

After selecting the colleges to be placed in the study, I had to find a fair way of evaluating each college and its departments. I've always felt that students are usually very fair and objective in evaluating their courses. An article in the *Journal of Educational Psychology* caught my eye (*Journal of Educational Psychology*, 1979, Vol, 71, No. 2, pp. 149-160). Marsh, Overell, and Kesler did an exhaustive study at the University of Southern California in the spring of 1976. Students were allowed to evaluate their professors in 207 undergraduate courses taught by the social studies faculty. The findings were:

1. The correlations between student and faculty ratings on the same factors were quite high and statistically significant.

2. The results reaffirmed the validity of student evaluations of college courses and professors. Many other recent studies have also concluded that student evaluations are reliable tools in judging teachers.

Another interesting article on this subject appeared in the *Chronicle of Higher Education:* "Fair and Useful Evaluation of Professors by Students: Experts Say It Can Be Done," by Suzanne Perry, Dec. 1, 1982, pg. 19. This theme is also noted in Henry Rosovsky's *The University: An Owner's Manual* (W.W. Norton & Co., 1990). On July 21, 1993 the *Chronicle's* Book Page by Peter Seldin goes like this: "…student's appraisals of courses and professors can be invaluable when the questions asked are appropriate."

Thus, our staff decided that we would poll *students* at the 735 colleges and universities for our study. I've always found if you want a straight answer, the young folks seldom waver. So we began a campaign asking college students, "What departments at your college would you recommend most to high school seniors?" Our research staff of 20 made phone calls to random college dormitories, visited college campuses, always questioning students. We found students very willing to provide candid information about their college departments. Ten thousand students were contacted with a minimum of 12 students queried per college. This student input represents 70.0% of our recommendations with 20.0% divided between secondary school counselor input and college personnel participation. The remaining 10.0% comes from unsolicited "tips" from many individuals, frequently parents, some who have spent a hundred hours studying and visiting one department, trying to decide where (and if) to place their $100,000. Some of this latter information is excellent. This past year, we made a special effort to obtain college lists from school counselors who, during the past year, had an extra client—their own offspring. Most of their contributions we feel are outstanding. A counselor doing research for a student usually does a fine job, and comes up with a good list. A counselor doing research for their own son/ daughter does the best of jobs. And a final note; finally we reached a critical point a year and a half ago. The input coming to us, much of it voluntary, is better than the old method. Just this morning a counselor from Maine called, tipping us off on the greatness of Western Maryland. We knew it was good. We knew it was very good, but her call led us to investigate more closely. Also, an Ohio Dean of Admissions kept us honest with some input. And a nice lady parent from San Francisco called saying, "Are you sure there's Studio Art at Harvard?" (Yes, there is, but hidden under another department.)

HOW DO YOU USE THIS BOOK?

If you know what you want to major in at college—great!—just look it up. In most cases, you will find each departmental section organized into three groups of colleges:

Group I—Most Selective Colleges

Colleges here are among the 100 most selective colleges in America. They accept very few students with high school averages below 80 (top prep schools can, of course, lower this figure significantly) and College Board scores below (recentered)1200 (SAT-1 combined) and 27 (on the American College Test).

Group II—Very Selective Colleges

Many of the students at these colleges have "B" averages (80-90), and College Board scores between 1100 and 1200 (SAT-1 total) and ACTs between 24 and 26.

Group III—Selective Colleges

Although these colleges are, in general, easier to get into than Group I and II colleges, please keep in mind that they are, in our opinion at least, among the top 735 colleges in the country. Many students at these colleges have College Board scores just under 1100 (SAT-1 total), or just under 24 on the ACTs.

Now that we have an idea of the group breakdown, a student may need help deciding from which group(s) to select his/her colleges. The guidance counselor can help here—having knowledge of colleges and a student's grade point average, class rank, board scores, etc. Most students will want to start with a group of 8 to 10 colleges from the departmental major page. This "major page" is a starting point. Schools can be added to the student's list by his/her counselor—from the counselor's own knowledge of the student, and knowledge of other colleges that might "fit" the student. Schools can be eliminated from a student's list after reviewing the college catalogs (see Appendix F—The Get Going Form), checking out undesirable features (city vs. rural setting, etc.), visiting the colleges, and other personal preferences. If the student does *not* have a major in mind, he or she should go to a typical liberal arts (e.g., English or Math) page to get started. I've also included a letter code system for the college's enrollment figure. The enrollment letter appears beside each college name with the following code:

XL = Extra Large Enrollment (over 20,000 students)
L = Large Enrollment (from 8,000 to 20,000 students)
M = Medium Enrollment (from 3,000 to 8,000 students)
R = Moderate Enrollment (from 1,000 to 3,000 students)
S = Small Enrollment (under 1,000 students)

SOME PARTING SHOTS

I don't care to go into the argument of "Picking a college because it has a great Mathematics Department" vs. "Picking a school because the school overall is great (Yeah Harvard!) and you'll probably change your major anyway." The fact of the matter is that parents, career educators, and other educators are telling 16-year-olds (and younger) to have a career and a major all mapped out and I bet will continue to do so. I'm sure high school counselors will continue to be asked to help Suzy find a list of quality schools with "excellent majors in mathematics." Personally, I see nothing wrong with a high school senior, who loves mathematics, trying to pick a quality school where the math department at that institution is ranked by its students as one of the top majors at that school and is generally recognized as being top notch by college counselors. If Suzy changes her mind after a year or two, she's at least given it a good shot with a premier math department. And chances are excellent that if she changes her major, it was because another outstanding department at that school helped her grow and reassess her career goals. She'll probably stay with that department for her new major. No harm done.

A few other comments on this book and some random thoughts...

1. Some state universities, like Penn State, are very competitive for out-of-staters. A university such as this may be in Group II for in-staters, but, in reality, is a Group I school for "outsiders."

2. In general, a college that is competitive is that way for all majors—but there are some departments that are exceptions. For example, engineering is a tough major and must be considered "Group II" at a "Group III" school.

3. A knowledgeable observer of the college scene will note that some competitive "alternative" colleges do not appear in this work, e.g., Hampshire College (MA), St. John's (MD). The jury is not unanimous on these progressive schools, and they are not included in this book except under "Miscellaneous Majors Pages."

4. A few majors in this book, such as engineering, have *not* been broken down into subdivisions (Civil, Electrical, Mechanical, etc.). Students will have to research these majors more fully. Foreign Languages, however, is broken down.

5. Every year a few more colleges close their doors. Today, colleges are under pressure to compete and "Be Hot." We need a college guide to weed things out a bit, a consumer-oriented handbook. We hope this helps.

6. Don't overlook the *good* small liberal arts college. Too many large universities are too impersonal.

7. Keep in mind that weak departments at Harvard, Yale, Stanford, Princeton, etc. might be equal to or better than the strongest departments at many colleges and universities.

8. This book is an aid for counselors, parents, and kids—nothing more. It is not a guide for the colleges to compare themselves one with the other.

9. Do not be surprised if you discover that the best of the more expensive schools are actually least expensive—because they have financial aid, the part-time jobs, etc. They're able to meet a student's financial need in many cases.

10. Students should discuss with their counselors the socioeconomic factors of the colleges they are considering. Will the college of your choice have several students enrolled with your socioeconomic background?

11. When you visit a college, seek out the students who attend and ask them the following question: "When you sign up for classes, do you get 100% of your choices, or only 4 out of 10 courses, or...?"

12.   Most states have a "flagship" university, the leader of the system (e.g., The University of North Carolina at Chapel Hill). In this book it is listed as just "No. Carolina." The other members of the University system are listed as follows: No. Carolina (Asheville), No. Carolina (Charlotte), No. Carolina (Greensboro), No. Carolina (Wilmington).

13.   Some colleges do a great job with private school youngsters, others do a fantastic job with public school youngsters. Some colleges are outstanding with *both* groups. A very fine college with an outstanding record with public school youngsters is Virginia's Roanoke College.

14.   A tip for the high school senior: Don't ease up in your senior year. Take a tough course load with courses such as Physics. College admissions people aren't stupid. The first thing they look at when they review your high school record is the quality of your high school courses.

15.   To parents and counselors: Hang tough. The pieces will finally fit.

16.   If you review only one page in this book, make it the page near the back called "Appendix G (Fred Rugg's One Hundred Colleges...Just Darn Good Schools)." This is probably the most used and Xeroxed page in the U.S.A. on the colleges.

17.   This book is not perfect. It has never claimed to be perfect. But it is a good place to start and represents tens of thousands of contacts. We've even moved to many parts of the country to try to put together "the big picture." We do our best.

Frederick E. Rugg

Easthampton, Massachusetts
March, 1980 (1st Edition)

San Luis Obispo, California
January, 1997 (14th Edition)

SOME NOTES ON THE FOURTEENTH EDITION

The fourteenth edition contains over 750 entry changes since the thirteenth edition. All 80 majors have been revised and changed. All SAT scores are recentered.

Hispanic Studies and Jazz have been added to the "Miscellaneous Majors Pages."

The "Average SAT-1 Total/Recommended majors" pages are included mainly because of counselors' requests. School counselors wanted average score comparisons and an index of colleges showing recommended majors. In all cases, SAT-1 Total Scores are noted (ACT scores are converted). These scores are the best estimate by our staff for the entering fall class of 1997. Especially young counselors tell us this section is a quick ready reference—a marker for them.

The fourteenth edition still includes "The Counselors' Choice"—a star (★) indicating the top college for each major as selected by 388 secondary school counselors, chosen at random. Over 900 counselors received a brief survey and were asked to complete the following question: "Which college or university would you most recommend to a student who asks for an outstanding place to major in a given field—regardless of size, location, the nature of the student, etc.?"

The fourteenth edition still contains "One Hundred Just Darn Good Schools"—found in Appendix G. I hear more nice things about these schools than any others. All but seven of the colleges return from last year. As in the past, when a state university is noted like Wisconsin, we mean the flagship at Madison, if no other city follows in parenthesis.

Frederick E. Rugg

San Luis Obispo, California
January, 1997 (14th Edition)

ACKNOWLEDGMENTS

I would like to thank the following for their help in the preparation of this guidebook: Phi Beta Kappa Office, Bureau of Educational Statistics, our Research Aides, and especially the great number of secondary counselors who've filled out questionnaires and tip me off on quality departments to look at. I am independent of the colleges and these people are, too.

A "Thank You" also goes to the counselors and students I've worked with who have contributed each in their own way. At last count, I've worked 25,000 hours in five secondary school guidance cubicles with 30 counselors, and conducted over 250 workshops with over 3500 counselors. Of course I've learned from them. Together we've probably done the college admissions process a million times. Also I thank the counselors and students and university officials in the United States and abroad for their help, suggestions, and, yes, their complaints. I appreciate, too, those departments who have sent us vitae on their professors. College PR officers who write always get a reading.

I am also grateful to George Gibbs, Reg Alexander, Arvin R. Anderson, Howard Ahlskog, Hy Kleinman, Michele M. Charles, Gary Metras, Edward Field, Betty Rossie, Horacio Rodriquez, A.P. Stevens, Madeline Field, Cyrus Benson, John Barker, Fred Ames, Matthew Jagielski, Gilbert Field, Jeff Sheehan, Charles Doebler, Joan Girard, Mrs. Fran Fisher, Ralph Strycharz, Dennis Gurn, John DeBonnville, Kevin L. Miller, Hoover Sutton, Francona, J.R., and Rebecca Lou.

And finally, a special thanks to my wife, Barbara, for her patience and industry.

Inquiries and comments about this guide should be addressed to:

Rugg's Recommendations
7120 Serena Court
Atascadero, CA 93422

SECTION ONE

RECOMMENDED
UNDERGRADUATE PROGRAMS

AGRICULTURE

Author's Note: *Students in the schools of Agriculture, in general, tend to have median college test scores below the University's overall median.*

GROUP I
Most Selective

★ CORNELL (NY) L	Iowa State XL
Florida, U. of XL	Pennsylvania State XL
Illinois, U. of (Urbana-Champaign).....XL	Rutgers (NJ) L

GROUP II
Very Selective

Auburn (AL).................................L	Michigan Tech ....M
California, U. of (Davis)................L	Minnesota, U. of......................XL
Cal. Poly. State U. (San Luis Obispo)....L	Missouri, U. of.........................XL
Clemson (SC)..............................L	New Hampshire, U. of L
Connecticut, U. of L	North Carolina State L
Hawaii, U. of...............................L	Purdue (IN)...............................XL
Kansas State L	Texas A&M XL
Maine, U. of ....M	Vermont, U. of ....M
Maryland, U. of XL	Virginia Poly. Inst......................L
Michigan State.............................XL	Wisconsin, U. of.......................XL

GROUP III
Selective

Arizona, U. of XL	New Mexico State U. L
Arkansas, U. of..........................L	North Dakota State....................L
Berea (KY) ....R	Ohio State XL
Colorado State L	Oklahoma State........................L
Delaware Valley (PA) ....R	Oregon State............................L
Dordt (IA) ....S	Tennessee, U. of XL
Georgia, U. of XL	Texas Tech U. L
Idaho, U. of ....M	Tuskegee University (AL) ....M
Kentucky, U. of L	Utah State L
Louisiana State XL	Washington State......................L
Mississippi State L	Western Michigan L
Montana State L	Wilmington (OH) ....S
Nebraska, U. of...........................L	Wyoming, U. of L
Nevada, U. of (Reno) ....M	

Enrollment Code

S = Small (less than 1000 students)	**M** = Medium (3000-8000 students)	**XL** = Extra Large (over 20,000 students)
R = Moderate (1000-3000 students)	**L** = Large (8000-20,000 students)	

★ THE COUNSELORS' CHOICE ■ Men Only ▲ Women Only

AMERICAN STUDIES

GROUP I
Most Selective

American U. (DC)	M	★ PENNSYLVANIA, U. OF	L
Amherst (MA)	R	Pomona (CA)	R
Buffalo (SUNY) (NY)	L	▲ Smith (MA)	R
California, U. of (San Diego)	L	St. Olaf (MN)	R
Franklin & Marshall (PA)	R	Stanford (CA)	M
George Washington (DC)	M	Tulane (LA)	M
Georgetown (DC)	M	Virginia, U. of	L
Harvard (MA)	M	Wesleyan (CT)	R
Kalamazoo (MI)	R	William & Mary (VA)	R
Michigan, U. of	XL	Williams (MA)	R
North Carolina, U. of	L	Yale (CT)	M

GROUP II
Very Selective

Arizona, U. of	XL	Skidmore (NY)	R
California, U. of (Santa Cruz)	M	South Florida, U. of	L
George Mason (VA)	L	Texas, U. of	XL
Hobart & Wm. Smith (NY)	R	Washington College (MD)	S
▲ Hollins (VA)	S	▲ Wells (NY)	S
Mary Washington (VA)	R	Wyoming, U. of	L
Minnesota, U. of	XL		

Enrollment Code

S = Small (less than 1000 students)	**M** = Medium (3000-8000 students)	**XL** = Extra Large (over 20,000 students)
R = Moderate (1000-3000 students)	**L** = Large (8000-20,000 students)	

★ THE COUNSELORS' CHOICE　■ Men Only　▲ Women Only

ANTHROPOLOGY

GROUP I
Most Selective

Brandeis (MA) ....R	Macalester (MN) ....R
▲ Bryn Mawr (PA) ....S	Michigan, U. of XL
Buffalo (SUNY) (NY) L	New College (FL) ....S
California, U. of (Berkeley) XL	Northwestern (IL) ....M
California, U. of (Los Angeles) XL	Pennsylvania, U. of L
Case Western Reserve (OH) ....R	Pitzer (CA) ....S
★ CHICAGO, U. OF (IL) ....R	Pomona (CA) ....R
Columbia (NY) ....M	Rice (TX) ....R
Dartmouth (NH) ....M	Skidmore (NY) ....R
Duke (NC) ....M	▲ Smith (MA) ....R
Florida, U. of XL	South, U. of the (TN) ....R
Grinnell (IA) ....R	Stanford (CA) ....M
Lafayette (PA) ....R	Vanderbilt (TN) ....R
Harvard (MA) ....M	Washington U. (MO) ....M
Illinois, U. of (Urbana-Champaign).....XL	Yale (CT) ....M

GROUP II
Very Selective

Arizona, U. of XL	Maryland, U. of XL
Beloit (WI) ....R	Oregon, U. of L
California, U. of (Santa Cruz) ......M	Pittsburgh, U. of (PA) L
Colorado, U. of L	Tulsa, U. of (OK) ....M
Hamline (MN) ....R	Washington State L
Hofstra (NY) ....M	Washington, U. of XL
Kansas, U. of L	Wisconsin, U. of XL

GROUP III
Selective

Hawaii, U. of...............................L	Queens (CUNY) (NY) L
New Mexico State U. L	Tennessee, U. of XL
New Mexico, U. of.......................M	

Enrollment Code

S = Small (less than 1000 students)	**M** = Medium (3000-8000 students)	**XL** = Extra Large (over 20,000 students)
R = Moderate (1000-3000 students)	**L** = Large (8000-20,000 students)	

★ THE COUNSELORS' CHOICE ■ Men Only ▲ Women Only

ARCHITECTURE

GROUP I
Most Selective

Buffalo (SUNY) (NY)	L	Michigan, U. of	XL
California, U. of (Berkeley)	XL	MIT (MA)	M
Carnegie Mellon (PA)	M	Notre Dame (IN)	M
Columbia (NY)	M	★ PRINCETON (NJ)	M
Cooper Union (NY)	S	Rensselaer (NY)	M
Cornell (NY)	L	Rice (TX)	R
Florida, U. of	XL	Tulane (LA)	M
Georgia Inst. of Tech.	L	Virginia, U. of	L
Illinois Inst. of Tech.	R	Washington U. (MO)	M
Illinois, U. of (Urbana-Champaign)	XL	Yale (CT)	M
Miami U. (OH)	L		

GROUP II
Very Selective

Arizona State	XL	Montana State	L
Arizona, U. of	XL	Nebraska, U. of	L
Auburn (AL)	L	North Carolina State	L
Cal. Poly. State U. (San Luis Obispo)	L	Oklahoma, U. of	L
Catholic U. (DC)	M	Oregon, U. of	L
Cincinnati, U. of (OH)	L	Pennsylvania State	XL
Clemson (SC)	L	Rhode Island School of Design (RI)	R
Detroit Mercy, U. of (MI)	M	Southern California, U. of	L
Drury (MO)	S	Syracuse (NY)	L
Houston, U. of (TX)	L	Texas A&M	XL
Kansas State	L	Texas, U. of (Austin)	XL
Kansas, U. of	L	Virginia Poly. Inst.	L
Milwaukee Sch. of Engineering (WI)	R	Washington, U. of	XL

GROUP III
Selective

Arkansas, U. of	L	Pratt Inst. (NY)	R
City College (CUNY) (NY)	L	Roger Williams (RI)	R
Kent State (OH)	L	Texas, U. of (Arlington)	L
Louisiana State	XL	Tuskegee University (AL)	M
Nevada, U. of (Las Vegas)	M	Woodbury (CA)	S
Ohio State	XL		

Enrollment Code

S = Small (less than 1000 students) M = Medium (3000-8000 students) XL = Extra Large (over 20,000 students)
R = Moderate (1000-3000 students) L = Large (8000-20,000 students)

★ THE COUNSELORS' CHOICE ■ Men Only ▲ Women Only

ART (STUDIO)

GROUP I
Most Selective

Bard (NY)	R	New Jersey, College of	M
Bates (ME)	R	★ NEW YORK U.	L
Boston U. (MA)	L	Pennsylvania, U. of	L
Brown (RI)	M	R.I. School of Design	R
▲ Bryn Mawr (PA)	S	Rochester, U. of (NY)	M
Carnegie Mellon (PA)	M	▲ Scripps (CA)	S
Cooper Union (NY)	S	Skidmore (NY)	R
Cornell (NY)	L	▲ Smith (MA)	R
Dallas, U. of (TX)	R	Southwestern (TX)	R
Dartmouth (NH)	M	St. Olaf (MN)	R
Drew (NJ)	R	Trinity (TX)	R
Furman (SC)	R	Virginia, U. of	L
Harvard (MA)	M	Washington U. (MO)	M
Lafayette (PA)	R	▲ Wellesley (MA)	R
Macalester (MN)	R	Wesleyan (CT)	R
Middlebury (VT)	R	Williams (MA)	R
Michigan, U. of	XL	Yale (CT)	M

GROUP II
Very Selective

Arizona, U. of	XL	Houghton (NY)	S
Art Center College of Design (CA)	R	Hunter (CUNY) (NY)	L
Auburn (AL)	L	Knox (IL)	R
▲ Agnes Scott (GA)	S	Lake Forest (IL)	S
Alma (MI)	R	Loras (IA)	R
Augustana (IL)	R	Manhattanville (NY)	S
Birmingham-Southern (AL)	R	Marietta (OH)	R
Bowling Green (OH)	L	Maryland Institute–College of Art	S
California Institute of the Arts	S	Mass. College of Art	R
California, U. of (Irvine)	M	Messiah (PA)	R
California, U. of (Santa Barbara)	L	▲ Mills (CA)	S
Colorado State	L	Missouri, U. of (Kansas City)	M
▲ Converse (SC)	S	Moore College of Art (PA)	S
Delaware, U. of	L	Moravian (PA)	R
Hamline (MN)	R	Muhlenberg (PA)	R
Hofstra (NY)	M	Ohio State	XL
▲ Hollins (VA)	S		

GROUP II continues next page

Enrollment Code

S = Small (less than 1000 students) **M** = Medium (3000-8000 students) **XL** = Extra Large (over 20,000 students)
R = Moderate (1000-3000 students) **L** = Large (8000-20,000 students)

★ THE COUNSELORS' CHOICE ■ Men Only ▲ Women Only

ART (STUDIO), *continued*

GROUP II, *continued*

Ohio U.	L	Syracuse (NY)	L
Otis Art Institute (CA)	S	Temple (PA)	M
Parsons School of Design (NY)	R	Washington & Jefferson (PA)	S
Principia (IL)	S	Washington, U. of	XL
▲ Randolph-Macon Woman's Col. (VA)	S	▲ Wesleyan Col. (GA)	S
Redlands, U. of (CA)	R	Western Washington U. (WA)	L
▲ Rosemont (PA)	R	Wheaton (MA)	R
Salem College (NC)	S	Whitworth (WA)	R
Shepherd (WV)	R	Wittenberg (OH)	R
Southern Methodist (TX)	M		

GROUP III
Selective

Arizona State	XL	Mercyhurst (PA)	R
Belhaven (MS)	R	Millikin (IL)	R
Bloomsburg (PA)	M	Mount St. Joseph (OH)	R
California State U. (Long Beach)	L	New Mexico, U. of	L
California State U. (San Jose)	XL	North Carolina (Greensboro)	M
▲ Chatham Col. (PA)	S	Northern Iowa	L
Fairleigh Dickinson (NJ)	M	Old Dominion (VA)	L
Hawaii, U. of	L	Roanoke (VA)	R
Jacksonville (FL)	R	Rockford (IL)	S
Keene State (NH)	R	▲ Salem College (NC)	S
Kent State (OH)	L	Santa Fe, College of (NM)	S
Kutztown (PA)	M	▲ Seton Hill (PA)	S
▲ Mary Baldwin (VA)	S	Virginia Commonwealth U.	L
Massachusetts, U. of (Dartmouth)	M	West Virginia Wesleyan	R

ART HISTORY

GROUP I
Most Selective

Bowdoin (ME) ....R
Brown (RI) ....M
▲ Bryn Mawr (PA) ....S
California, U. of (Los Angeles)............XL
Case Western Reserve U. (OH)...............R
Chicago, U. of (IL) ....R
Columbia (NY) ....M
Harvard (MA) ....M
Johns Hopkins (MD) ....R
Michigan, U. of XL
▲ Mount Holyoke (MA)..............................R
★ **NEW YORK U.** L
North Carolina, U. of.................................L

Oberlin (OH)..R
Pennsylvania, U. of....................................L
Princeton (NJ) ....M
Rochester, U. of (NY) ....M
Skidmore (NY) ....R
▲ Smith (MA) ....R
Swarthmore (PA) ....R
Vassar (NY) ....R
Washington U. (MO) ....M
▲ Wellesley (MA) ....R
Williams (MA) ....R
Yale (CT)...M

GROUP II
Very Selective

California, U. of (Riverside)...................M
California, U. of (Santa Barbara) L
Colorado State L
Delaware, U. of..L
Florida State L
▲ Hollins (VA)...S
Kansas, U. of..L
Lake Forest (IL)...S
Manhattanville (NY)..................................S

Minnesota, U. of...XL
Missouri, U. of...XL
Oregon, U. of L
▲ Rosemont (PA)...S
▲ Salem College (NC) ....S
Southern Methodist (TX).........................M
▲ Sweet Briar (VA).......................................S
Wheaton (MA) ....R
Wooster (OH) ....R

Enrollment Code

S = Small (less than 1000 students)   **M** = Medium (3000-8000 students)   **XL** = Extra Large (over 20,000 students)
R = Moderate (1000-3000 students)   **L** = Large (8000-20,000 students)

★ **THE COUNSELORS' CHOICE**   ■ Men Only   ▲ Women Only

ASTRONOMY

GROUP I
Most Selective

Boston U. L
★ **CALIFORNIA INST. OF TECH.** ....S
California, U. of (Berkeley) XL
California, U. of (Los Angeles) XL
Case Western Reserve U. (OH) ....R
Cornell (NY) L
Harvard (MA) ....M
Haverford (PA) ....S
Illinois, U. of (Urbana-Champaign).....XL
Michigan, U. of XL

MIT (MA) ....M
North Carolina, U. of.............................L
Northwestern (IL) ....M
Pennsylvania, U. of.................................L
Pennsylvania State XL
Villanova (PA)..M
Virginia, U. of..L
Wesleyan (CT)...R
Williams (MA) ....R

GROUP II
Very Selective

Arizona, U. of XL
Colorado, U. of L
Hawaii, U. of L
Iowa, U. of..XL
Kansas, U. of..L

Maryland, U. of XL
Oklahoma, U. of......................................L
Texas, U. of (Austin)............................XL
Washington, U. of XL

GROUP III
Selective

Louisiana State XL
Lycoming (PA) ....R

Wyoming, U. of L

Enrollment Code

S = Small (less than 1000 students) **M** = Medium (3000-8000 students) **XL** = Extra Large (over 20,000 students)
R = Moderate (1000-3000 students) **L** = Large (8000-20,000 students)

★ **THE COUNSELORS' CHOICE** ■ Men Only ▲ Women Only

BIOCHEMISTRY (MOLECULAR BIOLOGY)

GROUP I
Most Selective

Binghamton (SUNY) (NY) L	Iowa, U. of...XL
Bowdoin (ME) ....R	Miami, U. of (FL)...................................L
Brandeis (MA) ....R	MIT (MA) ....M
Brown (RI) ....M	▲ Mount Holyoke (MA) ....R
California, U. of (Berkeley) XL	Pennsylvania, U. of L
California, U. of (Los Angeles)............XL	Princeton (NJ) ....M
California, U. of (San Diego) L	Rice (TX)..R
Columbia (NY) ....M	Rutgers (NJ) L
Cornell (NY) L	Rochester, U. of (NY) ....M
Dallas, U. of (TX)................................R	Swarthmore (PA) ....R
Geneseo (SUNY) (NY) ....M	Tulane (LA) ....M
★ HARVARD (MA)..............................M	Yale (CT)..M

GROUP II
Very Selective

Albright (PA) ....R	Muhlenberg (PA) ....R
Beloit (WI) ....R	Pennsylvania State XL
California, U. of (Davis)........................L	Pittsburgh, U. of (PA) L
California, U. of (Riverside).................M	Purdue (IN)...XL
Colorado, U. of L	Ripon (WI) ....R
Denison (OH)..R	Skidmore (NY) ....R
Florida Inst. of Tech............................R	St. Andrews Presbyterian (NC)...............S
Kansas State L	Stony Brook (SUNY) (NY) L
Lewis & Clark (OR) ....R	Virginia Poly. Inst................................L
Louisiana State XL	Wisconsin, U. of....................................XL
Michigan State......................................XL	

GROUP III
Selective

Ohio Northern......................................R	Sacred Heart (CT) ....R
Oregon State...L	Temple (PA) L

Enrollment Code

S = Small (less than 1000 students) M = Medium (3000-8000 students) XL = Extra Large (over 20,000 students)
R = Moderate (1000-3000 students) L = Large (8000-20,000 students)

★ THE COUNSELORS' CHOICE ■ Men Only ▲ Women Only

BIOLOGY

GROUP I
Most Selective

Albany (SUNY) (NY)	L	Miami, U. of (FL)	L
Amherst (MA)	R	Middlebury (VT)	R
Bates (ME)	R	Minnesota, U. of (Morris)	R
Bethany (WV)	S	MIT (MA)	M
Boston College (MA)	L	▲ Mount Holyoke (MA)	R
Bowdoin (ME)	R	New College (FL)	S
Brandeis (MA)	R	Occidental (CA)	R
Brown (RI)	M	Pomona (CA)	R
▲ Bryn Mawr (PA)	S	Princeton (NJ)	M
Bucknell (PA)	R	Reed (OR)	R
California Inst. of Tech.	S	Rhodes (TN)	R
California, U. of (Los Angeles)	XL	Rice (TX)	R
California, U. of (San Diego)	L	Rochester, U. of (NY)	M
Carleton (MN)	R	Rutgers (NJ)	L
Chicago, U. of (IL)	R	Skidmore (NY)	R
Claremont McKenna (CA)	S	▲ Smith (MA)	R
Colby (ME)	R	South, U. of the (TN)	R
Colgate (NY)	R	Southwestern (TX)	R
Colorado Col.	R	Stanford (CA)	M
Cornell (NY)	R	St. Mary's Col. of Maryland	R
Dallas, U. of (TX)	R	St. Olaf (MN)	R
Dartmouth (NH)	M	Swarthmore (PA)	R
Dickinson (PA)	R	Trinity (CT)	R
Duke (NC)	M	Tufts (MA)	M
Emory (GA)	R	Tulane (LA)	M
Franklin & Marshall (PA)	R	Ursinus (PA)	R
Geneseo (SUNY) (NY)	M	Union (NY)	R
Georgetown (DC)	M	Vassar (NY)	R
Gettysburg (PA)	R	Vermont, U. of	L
Grinnell (IA)	R	Villanova (PA)	M
Hamilton (NY)	R	Virginia, U. of	L
★ HARVARD (MA)	M	■ Wabash (IN)	S
Harvey Mudd (CA)	S	Wake Forest (NC)	M
Haverford (PA)	S	Washington U. (MO)	M
Holy Cross (MA)	R	▲ Wellesley (MA)	R
Illinois Wesleyan	R	Wesleyan (CT)	R
Johns Hopkins (MD)	R	Wheaton (IL)	R
Kalamazoo (MI)	R	Whitman (WA)	R
Kenyon (OH)	R	Willamette (OR)	R
Lafayette (PA)	R	William & Mary (VA)	M
Lawrence (WI)	R	Yale (CT)	M
Macalester (MN)	R	Yeshiva (NY)	R

BIOLOGY continues next page

BIOLOGY, *continued*

GROUP II
Very Selective

Albertson (ID) ....S	Loras (IA) ....R
Albright (PA) ....R	Loyola (IL) ....M
Allegheny (PA)..............................R	Loyola (MD) ....R
Alma (MI).....................................R	Marquette (WI) ....M
Berry (GA) ....R	Mary Washington (VA) ....R
California, U. of (Irvine) ....M	Michigan State XL
California, U. of (Riverside)............M	Millsaps (MS) ....S
California, U. of (Santa Cruz) ....M	Morningside (IA) ....S
Concordia (MN) ....R	Muhlenberg (PA) ....R
Connecticut, U. of.........................L	Nebraska Wesleyan ....R
Creighton (NE)..............................R	New Hampshire, U. of....................L
Delaware, U. of.............................L	North Central (IL)...........................R
Denison (OH).................................R	Ohio Northern................................R
Duquesne (PA)...............................M	Ohio Wesleyan ....R
Earlham (IN) ....R	Presbyterian (SC) ....S
Eckerd (FL) ....R	Randolph-Macon (VA)....................R
Erskine (SC) ....S	▲ Randolph-Macon Woman's Col. (VA) ...S
Fairfield (CT).................................M	Ripon (WI) ....R
Georgia, U. of XL	Roanoke (VA) ....R
Guilford (NC).................................R	Scranton, U. of (PA).......................M
Hamline (MN)................................R	▲ Scripps (CA) ....S
■ Hampden-Sydney (VA) ....S	Spring Hill (AL) ....R
Hendrix (AR) ....R	St. John's (MN) ....R
Hiram (OH)....................................R	St. Louis (MO)................................M
Hobart & William Smith (NY) ....R	Stony Brook (SUNY) (NY) L
▲ Hood (MD) ....S	Truman State (MO).........................M
Hope (MI)......................................R	Washington & Jefferson (PA) ....S
Houghton (NY)...............................S	Washington College (MD) ....S
Indiana U. XL	Western Maryland ....R
Juniata (PA) ....R	Westminster (PA)...........................R
Kansas State L	Wheaton (MA) ....R
Lake Forest (IL)..............................S	Wittenberg (OH) ....R
Lewis & Clark (OR) ....R	Wofford (SC) ....R
Linfield (OR)..................................R	Wooster (OH) ....R

BIOLOGY continues next page

BIOLOGY, *continued*

GROUP III
Selective

Blackburn (IL)	S	Puerto Rico (CAYEY), U. of	M
Carroll (MT)	R	▲ Spelman (GA)	R
Delaware Valley (PA)	R	St. Vincent (PA)	R
Houston Baptist (TX)	R	Temple (PA)	L
Jacksonville (FL)	R	Thomas More (KY)	S
Long Island U. (Southhampton Col.) (NY)	R	Tougaloo (MA)	S
▲ Meredith (NC)	R	Wartburg (IA)	R
Mount St. Mary's (CA)	R	Xavier University of Louisiana	R
Northland (WI)	S		

Enrollment Code

S = Small (less than 1000 students) **M** = Medium (3000-8000 students) **XL** = Extra Large (over 20,000 students)
R = Moderate (1000-3000 students) **L** = Large (8000-20,000 students)

★ THE COUNSELORS' CHOICE ■ Men Only ▲ Women Only

BOTANY

GROUP I
Most Selective

California, U. of (Berkeley) XL	Florida, U. of XL
Connecticut College ....R	Miami U. (OH) L
Cornell (NY) L	Michigan, U. of XL
★ DUKE (NC) ....M	

GROUP II
Very Selective

California, U. of (Davis) L	Ohio Wesleyan ....R
California, U. of (Riverside) ....M	Pennsylvania State XL
Connecticut, U. of L	Purdue (IN)..XL
Maine, U. of...M	Texas, U. of (Austin) XL
Maryland, U. of L	Washington, U. of XL
Michigan State XL	Wisconsin, U. of....................................XL
Montana, U. of..M	Vermont, U. of...L

GROUP III
Selective

Colorado State L	Oregon State..L
Hawaii, U. of...L	Tennessee, U. of XL
Humboldt State (CA) ....M	Wyoming, U. of...L
Louisiana State XL	

BUSINESS ADMINISTRATION

GROUP I
Most Selective

Albany (SUNY) (NY)	L	Lehigh (PA)	M
American (DC)	M	Miami U. (OH)	L
Binghamton (SUNY) (NY)	L	Michigan, U. of	XL
Boston College (MA)	L	MIT (MA)	M
Boston U. (MA)	L	Muhlenberg (PA)	R
Bucknell (PA)	R	New York U.	L
Buffalo (SUNY) (NY)	L	North Carolina, U. of	L
California, U. of (Berkeley)	XL	Notre Dame (IN)	M
Carnegie Mellon (PA)	M	Pennsylvania, U. of	L
Case Western Reserve U. (OH)	R	Rensselaer (NY)	M
Claremont McKenna (CA)	S	Richmond, U. of (VA)	R
Clarkson (NY)	M	Southwestern (TX)	R
➤ Colby (ME)	R	Syracuse (NY)	L
DePauw (IN)	R	Trinity (TX)	R
Emory (GA)	R	Tulane (LA)	M
Fairfield (CT)	R	U.S. Air Force Academy (CO)	M
Florida, U. of	XL	Vermont, U. of	L
Florida State	L	Villanova (PA)	M
Franklin & Marshall (PA)	R	Virginia Poly. Institute	L
Geneseo (SUNY) (NY)	M	Virginia, U. of	L
Georgetown (DC)	M	Wake Forest (NC)	M
Gettysburg (PA)	R	Washington U. (MO)	M
Gustavus Adolphus (MN)	R	Washington & Lee (VA)	M
★ ILLINOIS, U. OF (URBANA-		William & Mary (VA)	M
CHAMPAIGN	XL	Wisconsin, U. of	XL
Indiana U.	XL	Yeshiva (NY)	R

➤ *Administrative Science*

GROUP II
Very Selective

Alabama, U. of	L	Augustana (IL)	R
Albertson (ID)	S	Austin (TX)	R
Albright (PA)	R	Babson (MA)	R
Alfred (NY)	R	Baylor (TX)	M
Alma (MI)	R	Bentley (MA)	M
Arizona, U. of	XL	Birmingham Southern (AL)	R
Arizona State	XL	Bowling Green (OH)	L
Asbury (KY)	R		

GROUP II continues next page

Enrollment Code

S = Small (less than 1000 students) **M** = Medium (3000-8000 students) **XL** = Extra Large (over 20,000 students)
R = Moderate (1000-3000 students) **L** = Large (8000-20,000 students)

★ **THE COUNSELORS' CHOICE** ■ Men Only ▲ Women Only

BUSINESS ADMINISTRATION, *continued*

GROUP II, *Continued*

Bryant (RI)	R	Kentucky, U. of	L
Buena Vista (IA)	R	LaSalle (PA)	M
Butler (IN)	R	Lebanon Valley (PA)	R
California State (Fullerton)	L	LeMoyne (NY)	R
California, U. of (Santa Barbara)	L	Lewis & Clark (OR)	R
Capital U. (OH)	R	Longwood (VA)	R
Centenary (LA)	S	Loras (IA)	R
Christian Brothers (TN)	R	Lowell, U. of (MA)	L
Clark (MA)	R	Loyola (MD)	R
Coe (IA)	R	Loyola (LA)	R
Colorado, U. of (Col. Springs)	M	Loyola Marymount (CA)	M
Concordia (MN)	R	Luther (IA)	R
Delaware, U. of	L	Manhattan (NY)	M
Denver, U. of (CO)	M	Manhattanville (NY)	R
DePaul (IL)	M	Marietta (OH)	R
Drake (IA)	M	Marist (NY)	M
Eckerd (FL)	R	Marquette (WI)	M
Elizabethtown (PA)	R	Maryland, U. of	XL
Erskine (SC)	S	Massachusetts, U. of	L
Florida Atlantic	M	Michigan, U. of (Dearborn)	M
Florida Inst. of Tech.	R	Michigan State	XL
Florida International	M	Millersville (PA)	M
Fredonia (SUNY) (NY)	M	Millsaps (MS)	S
George Mason (VA)	L	Minnesota, U. of	XL
Gonzaga (WA)	R	Mississippi College	R
Goucher (MD)	S	Mississippi, U. of	M
Grove City (PA)	R	Mississippi U. for Women	R
Hampton (VA)	M	Monmouth (IL)	S
Hanover (IN)	S	Moravian (PA)	R
Hendrix (AR)	R	Nazareth (NY)	R
Hillsdale (MI)	R	New Paltz (SUNY) (NY)	M
Hofstra (NY)	M	North Carolina, U. of (Greensboro)	M
▲ Hood (MD)	S	North Dakota, U. of	M
Houston, U. of (TX)	L	Northeastern (MA)	XL
Indiana U. of Pennsylvania	L	North Florida	M
Iowa, U. of	XL	Ohio U.	L
James Madison (VA)	M	Oglethorpe (GA)	R
John Carroll (OH)	M	Oklahoma City U. (OK)	R
Juniata (PA)	R	Oklahoma State	L
Kansas Newman (KS)	S		

GROUP II continues next page

Enrollment Code

S = Small (less than 1000 students)　　**M** = Medium (3000-8000 students)　　**XL** = Extra Large (over 20,000 students)
R = Moderate (1000-3000 students)　　**L** = Large (8000-20,000 students)

★ **THE COUNSELORS' CHOICE**　■ Men Only　▲ Women Only

BUSINESS ADMINISTRATION, *continued*

GROUP II, *Continued*

Old Dominion (VA) L	St. Bonaventure (NY) .... R
Oregon, U. of L	▲ St. Catherine (MN) .... R
Oswego (SUNY) (NY) .... M	St. John's (MN) .... R
Pacific Lutheran (WA) .... R	St. Joseph's U. (PA) .... R
Pacific University (OR) .... S	St. Mary's Col. of CA .... R
Pennsylvania State XL	▲ St. Mary's Col. (IN) .... R
Pepperdine (CA) .... R	St. Mary's Col. (MN) .... R
Pittsburgh, U. of (PA) L	St. Michael's Col. (VT) .... R
Plattsburgh (SUNY) (NY) .... M	St. Norbert (WI) .... R
Presbyterian (SC) .... S	Stetson (FL) .... R
Principia (IL) .... S	Stockton State (NJ) .... M
Providence (RI) .... M	Stonehill (MA) .... R
Puerto Rico, U. of L	Susquehanna U. (PA) .... R
Puget Sound (WA) .... R	Texas A&M XL
Queens (NC) .... S	Texas A&M at Galveston .... S
Redlands, U. of (CA) .... R	Texas, U. of (Austin) XL
Ripon (WI) .... R	Texas Christian .... M
Roanoke (VA) .... R	Transylvania (KY) .... S
Rockhurst (MO) .... R	Truman State (MO) .... M
Rowan (NJ) .... M	▲ Trinity (DC) .... S
Salem College (NC) .... S	Ursinus (PA) .... R
Samford (AL) .... R	Valparaiso (IN) .... M
San Diego, U. of (CA) .... M	Virginia Military Inst. .... R
San Francisco, U. of (CA) .... M	Washington State L
Santa Clara, U. of (CA) .... M	Washington, U. of XL
Scranton, U. of (PA) .... M	▲ Wells (NY) .... S
Seton Hall (NJ) .... M	▲ Wesleyan College (GA) .... S
Shaw (NC) .... R	Western Maryland .... R
Shepherd (WV) .... M	Western Michigan L
Siena (NY) .... R	West Virginia U. L
▲ Simmons (MA) .... R	Wilberforce (OH) .... S
Skidmore (NY) .... R	William Jewell Col. (MO) .... R
Southern California, U. of L	Wittenberg (OH) .... R
Southern Methodist (TX) .... M	Wyoming, U. of L
Spring Hill (AL) .... R	

Enrollment Code

S = Small (less than 1000 students)   **M** = Medium (3000-8000 students)   **XL** = Extra Large (over 20,000 students)
R = Moderate (1000-3000 students)   **L** = Large (8000-20,000 students)

★ THE COUNSELORS' CHOICE   ■ Men Only   ▲ Women Only

BUSINESS ADMINISTRATION, *continued*

GROUP III
Selective

Alaska, U. of (Anchorage)	M	Hastings (NE) ... S
Alaska, U. of (Fairbanks)	M	Hawaii Pacific ... M
American International (MA)	R	Heidelberg (OH) ... S
Appalachian State (NC)	L	Hillsdale (MI) ... R
Arkansas, U. of	L	Howard (DC) ... M
Azusa Pacific (CA)	R	Illinois, U. of (Chicago) ... L
Baker (KS)	S	Indiana State U. ... L
Baldwin-Wallace (OH)	R	Iona (NY) ... M
Barry (FL)	R	Jacksonville (FL) ... R
Baruch (CUNY) (NY)	L	Kennesaw State (GA) ... R
Belmont Abbey (NC)	S	Kentucky Wesleyan (KY) ... S
Benedictine (KS)	S	King's (PA) ... R
▲ Bennett (NC)	S	LaVerne, U. of (CA) ... S
Bethel (MN)	R	Lenoir-Rhyne (NC) ... R
Bluffton (OH)	S	▲ Lesley (MA) ... S
Brockport (SUNY) (NY)	M	Linfield (OR) ... R
Caldwell (NJ)	S	Maine (Farmington) ... R
Carthage (WI)	R	Malone (OH) ... R
Canisius (NY)	M	Manchester (IN) ... R
Cedarville (OH)	R	▲ Mary Baldwin (VA) ... S
Catawba (NC)	S	Mercer (GA) ... R
Chapman (CA)	R	▲ Meredith (NC) ... R
▲ Chatham (PA)	S	Merrimack (MA) ... R
Colorado State	L	Milligan (TN) ... S
Delaware Valley (PA)	R	Mercyhurst (PA) ... R
Dillard (LA)	R	Montreat (NC) ... S
Doane (NE)	S	■ Morehouse (GA) ... R
Elmira (NY)	R	Mount Mercy (IA) ... S
Emory & Henry (VA)	S	Mount St. Joseph (OH) ... R
Eureka (IL)	S	Mount St. Mary's (CA) ... R
Fairleigh Dickinson (NJ)	M	Mount St. Mary's (MD) ... R
Ferris State (MI)	L	Mount Union (OH) ... S
Florida A&M	M	Muskingum (OH) ... R
Fisk (TN)	S	Nebraska, U. of ... L
Gannon (PA)	R	New Orleans, U. of ... L
Graceland (IA)	R	Niagara (NY) ... R
Green Mountain (VT)	S	North Carolina, U. of (Charlotte) ... L
Hartford, U. of (CT)	M	North Carolina, U. of (Wilmington) ... M
Hartwick (NY)	R	

GROUP III continues next page

Enrollment Code

S = Small (less than 1000 students)	**M** = Medium (3000-8000 students)	**XL** = Extra Large (over 20,000 students)
R = Moderate (1000-3000 students)	**L** = Large (8000-20,000 students)	

★ THE COUNSELORS' CHOICE   ■ Men Only   ▲ Women Only

BUSINESS ADMINISTRATION, *continued*

GROUP III, *Continued*

North Georgia	R	South Florida, U. of	XL
Northern Arizona	L	Southwest Texas State	L
Northern Illinois	L	St. Andrews Presbyterian (NC)	S
Northern Iowa, U. of	L	St. Francis (NY)	R
Northwood University (MI)	R	St. John Fisher (NY)	L
Nova Southeastern (FL)	R	St. John's (NY)	L
Ohio State	XL	St. Mary's (TX)	R
Ozarks, College of the (MO)	R	St. Rose (NY)	R
Pace (NY)	R	St. Thomas, Col. of (MN)	M
Phila. Col. of Textiles & Sci. (PA)	R	Tampa, U. of (FL)	R
Point Loma (CA)	R	Tennessee, U. of	L
Puerto Rico (CAYEY), U. of	M	Texas Wesleyan	R
Quinnipiac (CT)	R	Texas, U. of (San Antonio)	L
Phillips (OK)	R	Thomas More (KY)	S
Radford (VA)	M	Toledo, U. of	L
Regis (CO)	R	Towson State (MD)	L
Roosevelt (IL)	R	Utica College of Syracuse U. (NY)	R
Sacred Heart (CT)	R	Virginia Wesleyan	R
San Diego State (CA)	XL	Wagner (NY)	R
Schreiner (TX)	S	Washington & Jefferson (PA)	R
Seattle U. (WA)	R	West Chester (PA)	M
Seton Hall (NJ)	M	West Florida, U. of	M
Shippensburg (PA)	M	Western Connecticut State	M
Simpson (IA)	S	Western New England (MA)	R
Sonoma State (CA)	M	Whittier (CA)	R
South Carolina, U. of	L	Woodbury (CA)	S
South Dakota, U. of	M	Xavier (OH)	R
Southern Illinois	L	Xavier U. of Louisiana	R
Southern Mississippi	L		

Enrollment Code

S = Small (less than 1000 students)   M = Medium (3000-8000 students)   XL = Extra Large (over 20,000 students)
R = Moderate (1000-3000 students)   L = Large (8000-20,000 students)

★ THE COUNSELORS' CHOICE   ■ Men Only   ▲ Women Only

CHEMISTRY

GROUP I
Most Selective

Amherst (MA)	R	Lafayette (PA)	R
Bates (ME)	R	Lawrence (WI)	R
Bowdoin (ME)	R	MIT (MA)	M
Brown (RI)	M	▲ Mount Holyoke (MA)	R
▲ Bryn Mawr (PA)	S	New College (FL)	S
Bucknell (PA)	M	North Carolina, U. of	L
California Inst. of Tech.	S	Northwestern (IL)	M
California, U. of (Berkeley)	XL	Notre Dame (IN)	M
California, U. of (San Diego)	L	Oberlin (OH)	R
Carleton (MN)	R	Occidental (CA)	R
Carnegie Mellon (PA)	M	Pennsylvania State	XL
Case Western Reserve U. (OH)	R	Pomona (CA)	R
Centre (KY)	S	Princeton (NJ)	M
Colgate (NY)	R	Reed (OR)	R
Columbia (NY)	M	Rice (TX)	R
Dartmouth (NH)	M	Rochester, U. of (NY)	M
Davidson (NC)	R	Rutgers (NJ)	L
Drew (NJ)	R	Skidmore (NY)	R
Duke (NC)	M	Southwestern (TX)	R
Emory (GA)	R	St. Olaf (MN)	R
Franklin & Marshall (PA)	R	Stanford (CA)	M
Furman (SC)	R	Trinity (TX)	R
Grinnell (IA)	R	Tufts (MA)	M
Hamilton (NY)	R	Union (NY)	R
Harvard (MA)	M	▲ Wellesley (MA)	R
Haverford (PA)	S	Wesleyan (CT)	R
★ HARVEY MUDD (CA)	S	Wheaton (IL)	R
Illinois, U. of (Urbana-Champaign)	XL	Whitman (WA)	R
Johns Hopkins (MD)	R	Willamette (OR)	R
Kalamazoo (MI)	R	Williams (MA)	R
Kenyon (OH)	R		

CHEMISTRY continues next page

Enrollment Code

S = Small (less than 1000 students)   **M** = Medium (3000-8000 students)   **XL** = Extra Large (over 20,000 students)
R = Moderate (1000-3000 students)   **L** = Large (8000-20,000 students)

★ THE COUNSELORS' CHOICE   ■ Men Only   ▲ Women Only

CHEMISTRY, *continued*

GROUP II
Very Selective

Albertson (ID)	S	Marquette (WI)	M
Alma (MI)	R	Massachusetts, U. of	L
Baylor (TX)	M	Michigan State	XL
Birmingham-Southern (AL)	R	Minnesota, U. of (Morris)	R
California, U. of (Santa Cruz)	M	New Hampshire, U. of	L
Carroll (WI)	R	Ohio Northern	R
Centenary (LA)	S	Ohio University	L
Colorado, U. of	L	Ohio Wesleyan	R
Delaware, U. of	L	Oregon, U. of	L
Duquesne (PA)	M	Purdue (IN)	XL
Earlham (IN)	R	Ripon (WI)	S
Florida State	L	Rochester, U. of (NY)	M
Georgia, U. of	XL	Rockhurst (MO)	R
Goucher (MD)	S	St. John's (MN)	R
Hamline (MN)	R	St. Louis (MO)	M
Hendrix (AR)	R	St. Michael's (VT)	R
Hiram (OH)	R	▲ Spelman (GA)	R
Hobart & William Smith (NY)	R	Spring Hill (AL)	R
Hope (MI)	R	Stetson (FL)	R
Houghton (NY)	S	Stony Brook (SUNY) (NY)	L
Huntingdon (AL)	S	Texas A&M	XL
Indiana U.	XL	Truman State (MO)	M
Ithaca Col.	M	Ursinus (PA)	R
Juniata (PA)	R	Vermont, U. of	L
Kansas, U. of	L	Washington & Jefferson (PA)	S
Knox (IL)	R	Washington, U. of	XL
Lake Forest (IL)	S	Wofford (SC)	R
Linfield (OR)	R	Wooster (OH)	R
Louisiana State	XL		

GROUP III
Selective

Houston Baptist (TX)	R	Whittier (CA)	R
Louisiana State	XL	Wyoming, U. of	L
▲ Sweet Briar (VA)	S	Xavier U. of Louisiana	R
Temple (PA)	L		

Enrollment Code

S = Small (less than 1000 students)	**M** = Medium (3000-8000 students)	**XL** = Extra Large (over 20,000 students)
R = Moderate (1000-3000 students)	**L** = Large (8000-20,000 students)	

★ THE COUNSELORS' CHOICE   ■ Men Only   ▲ Women Only

CLASSICS

GROUP I
Most Selective

Brown (RI) ....M	Middlebury (VT) ....R
▲ Bryn Mawr (PA) ....S	New York U. ....M
Chicago, U. of (IL) ....R	North Carolina, U. of.................L
Columbia (NY) ....M	Northwestern (IL) ....M
Dallas, U. of (TX) ....R	Pennsylvania, U. of L
Duke (NC) ....M	Princeton (NJ)............................M
★ HARVARD (MA) ....M	Stanford (CA) ....M
Holy Cross (MA).........................R	Swarthmore (PA) ....R
Johns Hopkins (MD) ....R	Tufts (MA) ....M
Kalamazoo (MI) ....R	Williams (MA) ....R
Macalester (MN) ....R	Yale (CT) ....M
Michigan, U. of XL	

GROUP II
Very Selective

Beloit (WI) ....R	Fordham (NY).............................L
California, U. of (Santa Barbara) L	■ Hampden-Sydney (VA) ....S
Catholic U. (DC) ....M	Montana, U. of...........................L
Florida, U. of XL	▲ Randolph-Macon Woman's Col. (VA) ...S

COMPUTER SCIENCE

GROUP I
Most Selective

Brandeis (MA) ....R
Brown (RI) ....M
California, U. of (Berkeley) XL
California, U. of (Los Angeles) XL
Carnegie Mellon (PA) ....M
Case Western Reserve U. (OH) ....M
Cornell (NY) L
Dartmouth (NH) ....M
Furman (SC) ....R
Georgia Institute of Tech. ....M
Grinnell (IA) ....R
Haverford (PA) ....R
Illinois, U. of XL
Iowa State XL
Maryland, U. of (Baltimore County) .....M

Michigan, U. of XL
★ MIT (MA) ....M
Missouri, U. of (Rolla) ....M
Pennsylvania State XL
Rensselaer (NY) ....M
Rice (TX) ....R
Stanford (CA) ....M
Washington, U. of XL
Washington U. (MO) ....M
William & Mary (VA) ....M
Williams (MA) ....R
Wisconsin, U. of XL
Worcester Poly. Tech. (MA) ....R
Yeshiva (NY) ....R

GROUP II
Very Selective

Allegheny (PA) ....R
Alma (MI) ....R
Bradley (IL) ....M
Cal. Poly. State U. (San Luis Obispo) L
California, U. of (Irvine) L
California, U. of (Santa Barbara) L
Central (IA) ....R
Central Florida, U. of L
Clarke (IA) ....S
Clemson (SC) L
Drexel (PA) ....M
Goucher (MD) ....R
Hiram (OH) ....R
Hunter (CUNY) (NY) L
LaSalle (PA) ....M
Massachusetts, U. of L
Michigan, U. of (Dearborn) ....M
Minnesota, U. of (Morris) ....R
Montana, U. of ....M
Moravian (PA) ....R

North Central (IL) ....R
Oregon, U. of L
Pacific Lutheran (WA) ....R
Pepperdine (CA) ....R
Pittsburgh, U. of (Johnstown) ....R
Potsdam (SUNY) (NY) ....M
Regis (CO) ....R
Rhode Island, U. of L
Rochester, U. of (NY) ....M
Rochester Inst. of Tech. (NY) L
Rutgers (Camden) (NJ) ....M
Santa Clara U. (CA) ....M
St. Ambrose (IA) ....R
Stony Brook (SUNY) (NY) L
Texas, U. of XL
Transylvania (KY) ....S
Utah, U. of L
Westminster (PA) ....R
Wofford (SC) ....R

COMPUTER SCIENCE continues next page

Enrollment Code

S = Small (less than 1000 students)
R = Moderate (1000-3000 students)
M = Medium (3000-8000 students)
L = Large (8000-20,000 students)
XL = Extra Large (over 20,000 students)

★ THE COUNSELORS' CHOICE   ■ Men Only   ▲ Women Only

COMPUTER SCIENCE, *continued*

GROUP III
Selective

Arizona State	XL	
California State U. (Chico)	L	
Catawba (NC)	S	
Colorado, U. of (Col. Springs)	M	
Colorado, U. of (Denver)	M	
Eureka (IL)	S	
Evansville (IN)	R	
Ferris State (MI)	L	
Hawaii Pacific	M	
Louisiana State U.	XL	
Loyola U. (LA)	M	
Marygrove (MI)	R	

Monmouth (NJ)	M	
■ Morehouse (GA)	R	
Mount Union (OH)	S	
Muskingum (OH)	R	
Oakland U. (MI)	M	
Pittsburgh, U. of (Bradford)	S	
Quinnipiac (CT)	R	
Rider (NJ)	M	
▲ Spelman (GA)	R	
West Florida, U. of	M	
West Virginia Wesleyan	R	
Wisconsin (LaCrosse)	L	

DANCE/DRAMA/THEATER

GROUP I
Most Selective

American Acad. of Dramatic Arts (NY) S		▲ Mount Holyoke (MA)	R
Amherst (MA)	R	New York U.	L
Boston U. (MA)	L	North Carolina, U. of	L
Brandeis (MA)	R	Northwestern (IL)	M
California, U. of (Los Angeles)	XL	Princeton (NJ)	M
Carleton (MN)	R	Sarah Lawrence (NY)	S
★ CARNEGIE MELLON (PA)	M	Skidmore (NY)	R
Columbia (NY)	M	Southwestern (TX)	R
Cornell (NY)	L	Tufts (MA)	M
Dartmouth (NH)	M	Tulane (LA)	M
Drew (NJ)	R	Vassar (NY)	R
Illinois Wesleyan	R	Wesleyan (CT)	R
Juilliard (NY)	S	Whitman (WA)	R
Kenyon (OH)	R	William & Mary (VA)	R
Macalester (MN)	R	Yale (CT)	M
Miami, U. of (FL)	L		

GROUP II
Very Selective

Bard (NY)	R	Muhlenberg (PA)	R
Baylor (TX)	M	No. Carolina School of the Arts	S
Beloit (WI)	R	Ohio U.	L
Bennington (VT)	S	Oklahoma State	L
Butler (IN)	R	Purchase (SUNY) (NY)	R
California, U. of (Irvine)	M	Rollins (FL)	R
Catawba (NC)	S	▲ Scripps (CA)	S
Catholic U. (DC)	M	Southern Methodist (TX)	M
DePaul (IL)	M	Texas Christian	M
Florida State	L	Texas, U. of	XL
George Mason (VA)	L	Utah, U. of	L
Goucher (MD)	S	Virginia Commonwealth U.	L
Hofstra (NY)	M	Washington, U. of	XL
Indiana U.	XL	West Virginia U.	L
Kansas, U. of	L	Wheaton (MA)	R
Loyola (IL)	M	Wooster (OH)	R
Lyon (AR)	S		

DANCE/DRAMA/THEATER continues next page

Enrollment Code

S = Small (less than 1000 students) **M** = Medium (3000-8000 students) **XL** = Extra Large (over 20,000 students)
R = Moderate (1000-3000 students) **L** = Large (8000-20,000 students)

★ THE COUNSELORS' CHOICE ■ Men Only ▲ Women Only

DANCE/DRAMA/THEATER, *continued*

GROUP III
Selective

Alaska, U. of (Fairbanks)	M	Northwestern College (IA)	S
Allentown College (PA)	S	Ohio State	XL
Barry (FL)	R	Otterbein (OH)	R
Bethany (WV)	S	Point Park (PA)	R
Emerson (MA)	R	Rockford (IL)	S
Evansville (IN)	R	San Francisco State (CA)	L
Fontbonne (MO)	S	Santa Fe, College of (NM)	S
Franklin (IN)	S	▲ Seton Hill (PA)	S
Humboldt State (CA)	M	South Florida, U. of	L
Illinois State	L	St. Mary's (MN)	R
Jacksonville (FL)	R	Temple (PA)	L
Evansville (IN)	R	Webster (MO)	R
Niagara (NY)	R	Western Michigan	L

Enrollment Code

S = Small (less than 1000 students) **M** = Medium (3000-8000 students) **XL** = Extra Large (over 20,000 students)
R = Moderate (1000-3000 students) **L** = Large (8000-20,000 students)

★ THE COUNSELORS' CHOICE ■ Men Only ▲ Women Only

ECONOMICS

GROUP I
Most Selective

American U. (DC)	M	★MIT (MA)	M
Amherst (MA)	R	Middlebury (VT)	R
Bates (ME)	R	▲ Mount Holyoke (MA)	R
Boston University (MA)	L	Northwestern (IL)	M
Bowdoin (ME)	R	Occidental (CA)	R
Brandeis (MA)	R	Pennsylvania, U. of	L
▲ Bryn Mawr (PA)	S	Pomona (CA)	R
Bucknell (PA)	M	Princeton (NJ)	M
California, U. of (Los Angeles)	XL	Rhodes (TN)	R
California, U. of (San Diego)	L	Rochester, U. of (NY)	M
Chicago, U. of (IL)	R	▲ Smith (MA)	R
Claremont McKenna (CA)	S	South, U. of the (TN)	R
Colby (ME)	R	Stanford (CA)	M
Columbia (NY)	M	St. Olaf (MN)	R
Cornell (NY)	L	Swarthmore (PA)	R
Dallas, U. of (TX)	R	Trinity (CT)	R
Dartmouth (NH)	M	Trinity (TX)	R
Duke (NC)	M	Vanderbilt (TN)	M
Hamilton (NY)	R	Virginia, U. of	L
Harvard (MA)	M	Wake Forest (NC)	M
Haverford (PA)	S	Washington & Lee (VA)	R
Holy Cross (MA)	R	▲ Wellesley (MA)	R
Kalamazoo (MI)	R	Wesleyan (CT)	R
Kenyon (OH)	R	Whitman (WA)	R
Lafayette (PA)	R	Willamette (OR)	R
Macalester (MN)	R	Williams (MA)	R
Michigan, U. of	XL	Yale (CT)	M

ECONOMICS continues next page

Enrollment Code

S = Small (less than 1000 students) **M** = Medium (3000-8000 students) **XL** = Extra Large (over 20,000 students)
R = Moderate (1000-3000 students) **L** = Large (8000-20,000 students)

★ **THE COUNSELORS' CHOICE** ■ Men Only ▲ Women Only

ECONOMICS, *continued*

GROUP II
Very Selective

▲ Agnes Scott (GA) ....S
  Albion (MI) ....R
  Allegheny (PA)........................R
  Centre (KY) ....S
  Denison (OH) ....R
  George Mason (VA)..................L
  Hendrix (AR) ....R
  Hobart & William Smith (NY) ....R
  Illinois Col..............................S
  Lake Forest (IL) ....S
  Maryland, U. of XL
  Michigan State XL
  North Carolina State L
  Ohio Wesleyan (OH) ....R
  Oneonta (SUNY) (NY)..............M
  Randolph-Macon (VA)..............R

  Ripon (WI) ....S
▲ Salem Col. (NC) ....S
  San Francisco, U. of ....M
  St. John's (MN) ....R
  St. Lawrence (NY) ....R
  Texas A&M XL
  Ursinus (PA) ....R
  Virginia Military Inst. ....R
  Washington & Jefferson (PA) ....S
  Washington, U. of XL
  Westminster Col. (MO) ....S
  Westmont Col. (CA) ....R
  Wheaton (MA) ....R
  Wofford (SC) ....R
  Wooster (OH) ....R

GROUP III
Selective

  Heidelberg (OH) ....S
  St. Anselm (NH).......................R
  Washington State.....................L

  Whittier (CA)............................R
▲ Wilson (PA) ....S
  Wyoming, U. of L

EDUCATION

GROUP I
Most Selective

Boston U. (MA)	L	
Bucknell (PA)	R	
Buffalo (SUNY) (NY)	L	
Connecticut Col.	R	
Dallas, U. of (TX)	R	
Earlham (IN)	R	
Illinois, U. of	XL	
Iowa, U. of	XL	
Miami U. (OH)	L	
Michigan, U. of	XL	
New Jersey, College of	M	
North Carolina, U. of	L	
Occidental (CA)	R	
Pennsylvania, U. of	L	
Rutgers (NJ)	L	
Skidmore (NY)	R	
Swarthmore (PA)	S	
Trinity (TX)	R	
➤ Tufts (MA)	M	
★ VANDERBILT (TN)	M	
▲ Wellesley (MA)	R	
Wheaton (IL)	R	
William & Mary (VA)	M	

➤ *Child Study*

GROUP II
Very Selective

Adelphi (NY)	M	
Adrian (MI)	S	
Albertson (ID)	S	
Alfred (NY)	R	
Alma (MI)	R	
Arizona, U. of	XL	
Auburn (AL)	L	
Augustana (IL)	R	
Augustana (SD)	R	
Austin (TX)	R	
Baylor (TX)	L	
Berry (GA)	R	
Birmingham Southern (AL)	R	
Buena Vista (IA)	R	
Butler (IN)	R	
California, U. of (Santa Barbara)	L	
Calvin (MI)	M	
Capital U. (OH)	R	
Carroll (WI)	R	
Centenary (LA)	S	
Central (IA)	R	
Coe (IA)	R	
Connecticut, U. of	L	
Concordia (MN)	R	
Dayton, U. of (OH)	M	
Delaware, U. of	L	
Drake (IA)	M	
Erskine (SC)	S	
Florida State	L	
Fredonia (SUNY) (NY)	M	
Georgia, U. of	XL	
Goucher (MD)	R	
Guilford (NC)	R	
Hanover (IN)	S	
Hillsdale (MI)	R	
Hiram (OH)	R	
▲ Hood (MD)	S	
Houghton (NY)	S	
Hunter (CUNY) (NY)	L	
Indiana, U.	XL	
Indiana, U. of (PA)	L	
Iowa State	XL	
James Madison (VA)	M	
Juniata (PA)	R	
Kentucky, U. of	L	

GROUP II continues next page

Enrollment Code

S = Small (less than 1000 students)   **M** = Medium (3000-8000 students)   **XL** = Extra Large (over 20,000 students)
R = Moderate (1000-3000 students)   **L** = Large (8000-20,000 students)

★ **THE COUNSELORS' CHOICE**   ■ Men Only   ▲ Women Only

EDUCATION, *continued*

GROUP II, *continued*

Loras (IA)......................................R	▲ St. Mary's Col. (IN) ....R
Luther (IA)....................................R	St. Mary's Col. (MN) ....R
Lyon (AR) ....S	St. Michael's (VT) ....R
Manhattan (NY)............................M	Shepherd (WV) ....M
Manhattanville (NY) ....R	Shippensburg (PA) ....M
Maryland, U. of XL	Southwest Missouri L
Messiah (PA) ....R	Stetson (FL) ....R
Michigan State XL	Tennessee, U. of XL
▲ Mills (CA).................................S	Texas A&M XL
Minnesota, U. of XL	Texas, U. of (Austin).....................XL
Moravian (PA) ....R	Truman State (MO) ....M
Nazareth (NY) ....R	Ursinus (PA) ....R
New Paltz (SUNY) (NY) ....M	Washington & Jefferson (PA)..........R
North Carolina, U. of (Asheville)..........R	Washington, U. of XL
North Dakota, U. of ....M	▲ Wells (NY) ....S
North Florida ....M	Western Maryland College ....R
Ohio U. L	Western Michigan L
Oregon, U. of L	Western Washington U. L
Pennsylvania State XL	Whitworth (WA) ....R
Principia (IL).................................S	William Jewell Col. (MO) ....R
Puerto Rico, U. of L	Wisconsin, U. of............................XL
Queens (CUNY) (NY) L	Wisconsin, U. of (Milwaukee).........L
Redlands, U. of (CA) ....R	Wittenberg (OH) ....R
Regis (CO) ....R	Wofford (SC) ....R
St. Mary's Col. (CA) ....R	York (PA) ....M

GROUP III
Selective

Alaska, U. of (Anchorage) ....M	Bethel (MN) ....R
Appalachian State (NC) L	Bowling Green (OH)......................L
Arkansas, U. of................................L	Bloomsburg (PA) ....M
Arizona State XL	Brockport (SUNY) (NY)................M
Augsburg (MN) ....R	Caldwell (NJ) ....S
Averett (VA)...................................R	Catawba (NC).................................S
Baldwin-Wallace (OH) ....R	Cedarville (OH) ....R
▲ Bennett (NC) ....S	Central Michigan U. L
Berea (KY) ....R	City Col. (CUNY) (NY) L
Bethany (WV) ....S	*GROUP III continues next page*

GROUP III continues next page

Enrollment Code

S = Small (less than 1000 students)	**M** = Medium (3000-8000 students)	**XL** = Extra Large (over 20,000 students)
R = Moderate (1000-3000 students)	**L** = Large (8000-20,000 students)	

★ THE COUNSELORS' CHOICE   ■ Men Only   ▲ Women Only

EDUCATION, *continued*

GROUP III, *continued*

College of Charleston (SC) .... M	Nevada, U. of (Reno) .... M
▲ Converse (SC) .... S	New Mexico, U. of .... M
Dordt (IA) .... S	Northern Arizona L
Dubuque, U. of (IA) .... S	Northern Iowa L
Elmira (NY) .... R	Northwestern (IA) .... R
Flagler (FL) .... R	Northwestern (MN) .... R
Florida A&M U. .... M	Ohio State L
Florida Atlantic .... M	Oklahoma Baptist .... R
Franklin (IN) .... S	Ozarks, College of the (MO) .... R
George Fox (OR) .... S	Peru State (NE) .... R
Georgia Southern L	Puerto Rico (CAYEY), U. of .... M
Gordon (MA) .... R	Radford (VA) .... M
Graceland (IA) .... R	Saint Rose (NY) .... R
Huntingdon (AL) .... S	St. Joseph's (IN) .... S
Illinois State L	St. Joseph's (ME) .... S
Jacksonville State (AL) .... M	▲ St. Joseph's Col. (CT) .... S
Keene State (NH) .... R	Simpson (IA) .... S
Kent State (OH) L	Southern Oregon State College .... M
Kutztown (PA) .... M	Southwest Baptist (MO) .... R
▲ Lesley (MA) .... S	Texas Tech. U. L
Linfield (OR) .... R	Texas Wesleyan .... R
Lock Haven (PA) .... M	Tougaloo (MS) .... S
Longwood (VA) .... R	Utah State L
Mansfield (PA) .... R	Wagner (NY) .... R
Mass. St. Col. System .... M	Wartburg (IA) .... R
Millikin (IL) .... R	Westfield State (MA) .... M
Mississippi State L	West Florida, U. of .... M
Monmouth (IL) .... S	West Virginia Wesleyan .... R
Montevallo (AL) .... R	Western Kentucky L
Mount St. Joseph (OH) .... R	▲ Wheelock (MA) .... S
Muskingum (OH) .... R	Whittier (CA) .... R

ENGINEERING

GROUP I
Most Selective

Boston U. (MA) L	Missouri, U. of (Rolla) ....M
Brown (RI) ....M	New Mexico Inst. of Mining & Tech. ......S
Bucknell (PA) ....M	New Jersey, College of ....M
Buffalo (SUNY) (NY) L	Northwestern (IL) ....M
California Inst. of Tech. ....S	Notre Dame (IN) ....M
California, U. of (Berkeley) XL	Pennsylvania State XL
California, U. of (Davis) L	Pennsylvania, U. of L
California, U. of (Los Angeles)............XL	Princeton (NJ) ....M
California, U. of (San Diego) L	Rensselaer (NY) ....M
California, U. of (Santa Barbara) L	Rice (TX) ....R
Carnegie Mellon (PA) ....M	Rose-Hulman (IN) ....R
Case Western Reserve U. (OH) ....R	Rutgers (NJ) L
Clarkson (NY) ....M	Southern California, U. of L
Colorado School of Mines......................R	★STANFORD (CA)..................................M
Cooper Union (NY) ....S	Stevens Inst. of Tech. (NJ) ....R
Cornell (NY) L	Swarthmore (PA) ....R
Dartmouth (NH) ....M	Trinity (CT)...R
Duke (NC) ....M	Tufts (MA) ....M
General Motors Inst. (MI) ....R	Tulane (LA) ....M
Georgia Inst. of Tech. ....M	Union (NY) ....R
Harvey Mudd (CA)...................................S	U.S. Air Force Academy (CO)................M
Illinois Inst. of Tech..............................R	U.S. Coast Guard Academy (CT) ....S
Illinois, U. of (Urbana-Champaign).....XL	U.S. Military Academy (NY) ....M
Iowa State XL	U.S. Naval Academy (MD) ....M
Iowa, U. of...XL	Vanderbilt (TN) ....M
Johns Hopkins (MD) ....R	Villanova (PA)..M
Lafayette (PA) ....R	Virginia, U. of..L
Lehigh (PA) ....M	Washington U. (MO) ....M
MIT (MA) ....M	Washington, U. of L
Michigan, U. of XL	Worcester Poly. Tech. (MA)....................R

GROUP II
Very Selective

Alabama, U. of...L	California Maritime Academy.................S
Alfred (NY)..R	Cal. Poly. State U. (San Luis Obispo)....L
Arizona, U. of XL	Calvin (MI) ....M
Arizona State XL	Catholic U. (DC) ....M
Arkansas, U. of...L	Central Florida, U. of L
Auburn (AL)...L	Christian Brothers (TN) ....R
Bradley (IL) ....M	Cincinnati, U. of (OH) L
California, U. of (Irvine) ....M	Clemson (SC)..L
California, U. of (Riverside)...................M	

GROUP II continues next page

ENGINEERING, *continued*

GROUP II, *continued*

Colorado, U. of	L	New Orleans, U. of	L
Colorado, U. of (Col. Springs)	R	North Carolina State	L
Dayton, U. of (OH)	M	North Dakota State	L
Delaware, U. of	L	Northeastern (MA)	XL
Detroit Mercy (MI)	M	Oakland U. (MI)	M
Florida Inst. of Tech.	R	Ohio State	XL
Gannon (PA)	R	Ohio U.	L
Geneva (PA)	R	Oklahoma, U. of	L
Grove City (PA)	R	Oklahoma State	L
Houston, U. of (TX)	L	Pacific, U. of the (CA)	R
Kansas, U. of	L	Pennsylvania State	XL
Kansas State	L	Pittsburgh, U. of	L
Kentucky, U. of	L	Pittsburgh, U. of (Johnstown)	R
Letourneau College (TX)	S	Polytechnic Univ. of NY	R
Louisville (KY)	L	Portland, U. of (OR)	R
Lowell, U. of (MA)	L	Purdue (IN)	XL
Loyola (MD)	R	Rhode Island, U. of	L
Loyola Marymount (CA)	M	Rochester Inst. of Tech. (NY)	L
Maine, U. of	M	Santa Clara, U. of (CA)	M
Manhattan (NY)	M	Seattle Pacific (WA)	R
Marquette (WI)	M	South Carolina, U. of	L
Massachusetts, U. of	L	So. Dakota School of Mines	R
Massachusetts, U. of (Lowell)	M	Southern Maine, U. of	M
Mass. Maritime Academy	S	Texas A&M	XL
Michigan State	XL	Texas, U. of (Arlington)	L
Michigan Tech.	M	Tulsa, U. of (OK)	R
Michigan, U. of (Dearborn)	M	Tuskegee University (AL)	M
Milwaukee Sch. of Eng, (WI)	R	Utah, U. of	L
Minnesota, U. of	XL	Virginia Military Inst.	R
Mississippi State	L	Virginia Poly. Inst.	L
Montana College of Min. Sci. & Tech.	R	Washington State	L
Montana State	L	Wayne State (MI)	L
Nevada, U. of (Las Vegas)	M	Western New England (MA)	R
New Jersey Inst. of Tech.	M	Wisconsin, U. of	XL
New Mexico State U.	L	Wyoming, U. of	L

Enrollment Code

S = Small (less than 1000 students)   M = Medium (3000-8000 students)   XL = Extra Large (over 20,000 students)
R = Moderate (1000-3000 students)   L = Large (8000-20,000 students)

★ THE COUNSELORS' CHOICE   ■ Men Only   ▲ Women Only

ENGLISH

GROUP I
Most Selective

Amherst (MA).................................R	Macalester (MN) ....R
Bard (NY)......................................R	Middlebury (VT) ....R
Boston Col. (MA)...........................L	▲ Mount Holyoke (MA).....................R
Bowdoin (ME)................................R	North Carolina, U. of.....................L
Brandeis (MA)...............................R	New Jersey, College of ....M
▲ Bryn Mawr (PA) ....S	Northwestern (IL) ....M
Buffalo (SUNY) (NY) L	Oberlin (OH)..................................R
California, U. of (Berkeley) XL	Pennsylvania, U. of.......................L
California, U. of (Los Angeles)............XL	Pomona (CA) ....R
Carleton (MN) ....R	Princeton (NJ)...............................M
Chicago, U. of (IL) ....R	Reed (OR).....................................R
Claremont McKenna (CA) ....S	Rhodes (TN)..................................R
Colby (ME) ....R	Richmond, U. of (VA).....................R
Colgate (NY)..................................R	Rutgers (NJ) L
Colorado College ....R	Sarah Lawrence (NY) ....S
Columbia (NY)...............................M	Skidmore (NY)...............................R
Connecticut Col.............................R	▲ Smith (MA) ....R
★ CORNELL (NY) L	South, U. of the (TN) ....R
Dallas, U. of (TX)...........................R	Southwestern (TX).........................R
Dartmouth (NH) ....M	Stanford (CA) ....M
Davidson (NC)...............................R	St. Olaf (MN) ....R
Dickinson (PA)...............................R	Swarthmore (PA) ....R
Duke (NC) ....M	Trinity (TX) ....R
Emory (GA) ....R	Tufts (MA) ....M
Florida, U. of XL	Vanderbilt (TN)..............................M
Franklin & Marshall (PA) ....R	Vassar (NY) ....R
Georgetown (DC)...........................M	Virginia, U. of................................L
Gettysburg (PA) ....R	Wake Forest (NC) ....M
Grinnell (IA)...................................R	Washington & Lee (VA)...................R
Hamilton (NY)................................R	Washington U. (MO).......................M
Haverford (PA) ....S	▲ Wellesley (MA) ....R
Holy Cross (MA)............................R	Wesleyan (CT)...............................R
Iowa, U. of.....................................XL	Wheaton (IL)..................................R
Kalamazoo (MI) ....R	Whitman (WA)................................R
Kenyon (OH) ....R	Willamette (OR) ....R
Knox (IL)...R	Williams (MA) ....R
Lafayette (PA) ....R	Wisconsin, U. of............................XL
Lawrence (WI)................................R	Yale (CT).......................................M

ENGLISH continues next page

Enrollment Code

S = Small (less than 1000 students)	**M** = Medium (3000-8000 students)	**XL** = Extra Large (over 20,000 students)
R = Moderate (1000-3000 students)	**L** = Large (8000-20,000 students)	

★ **THE COUNSELORS' CHOICE** ■ Men Only ▲ Women Only

ENGLISH, *continued*

GROUP II
Very Selective

▲ Agnes Scott (GA) .... S	Marquette (WI) .... M
Albany (SUNY) (NY) L	Massachusetts, U. of L
Albion (MI) .... R	Millsaps (MS) .... S
Alfred (NY) .... R	Mississippi, U. of .... M
Arizona, U. of XL	New Hampshire, U. of L
Baylor (TX) .... M	Ohio U. L
Beloit (WI) .... R	Oklahoma, U. of L
Bennington (VT) .... S	Pittsburgh, U. of (PA) L
Birmingham-Southern (AL) .... R	Presbyterian (SC) .... S
California, U. of (Davis) L	Principia (IL) .... S
Cal Poly State U. (San Luis Obispo) L	Puget Sound (WA) .... R
Calvin (MI) .... M	Purchase (SUNY) (NY) .... R
Cornell Col. (IA) .... R	Queens (NC) .... S
Denison (OH) .... R	Randolph-Macon (VA) .... R
Denver, U. of (CO) .... M	▲ Randolph-Macon Woman's Col. (VA) ... S
Emmerson (MA) .... R	Redlands, U. of (CA) .... R
Fordham (NY) L	Ripon (WI) .... S
George Mason (VA) L	Rochester, U. of (NY) .... M
Georgia, U. of XL	Rollins (FL) .... R
Gonzaga (WA) .... R	Rutgers (Camden) NJ .... M
Goucher (MD) .... R	Salem College (NC) .... S
Grand Valley (MI) L	▲ Scripps (CA) .... S
Guilford (NC) .... R	Spring Hill (AL) .... R
Hamline (MN) .... R	St. Lawrence (NY) .... R
■ Hampton-Sydney (VA) .... S	▲ St. Mary's Col. (IN) .... R
Hiram (OH) .... R	Stetson (FL) .... R
Hobart & Wm. Smith (NY) .... R	Stony Brook (SUNY) (NY) L
▲ Hollins (VA) .... S	Washington & Jefferson (PA) .... R
Hunter (CUNY) (NY) L	▲ Wells (NY) .... S
Lake Forest (IL) .... S	Wheaton (MA) .... R
Loras (IA) .... R	Wittenberg (OH) .... R
Marietta (OH) .... R	Wofford (SC) .... S

ENGLISH continues next page

Enrollment Code

S = Small (less than 1000 students)	**M** = Medium (3000-8000 students)	**XL** = Extra Large (over 20,000 students)
R = Moderate (1000-3000 students)	**L** = Large (8000-20,000 students)	

★ THE COUNSELORS' CHOICE   ■ Men Only   ▲ Women Only

ENGLISH, *continued*

GROUP III
Selective

Adrian (MI) ....S	Rockford (IL) ....S
Arkansas, U. of...L	St. Mary (KS) ....S
Baldwin-Wallace (OH) ....R	▲ Salem Col. (NC) ....S
▲ Chestnut Hill (PA).............................S	San Francisco State (CA)...........................L
Fairleigh Dickinson (NJ) ....M	▲ Spelman (GA) ....R
Fort Lewis (CO) ....M	Temple (PA) L
Montevallo (AL) ....R	Tennessee, U. of XL
Niagara (NY) ....R	Utah, U. of L
North Carolina, U. of (Wilmington) ......M	Whittier (CA)...R
Rhode Island, U. of...................................L	Wisconsin, U. of (Milwaukee)................R

FOREIGN LANGUAGES

GROUP I
Most Selective

Bowdoin (ME) ....R
Brown (RI) ....M
▲ Bryn Mawr (PA) ....S
California, U. of (Berkeley) XL
California, U. of (Los Angeles) XL
Carleton (MN) ....R
Colby (ME) ....R
Columbia (NY) ....M
Dallas, U. of ....R
Dartmouth (NH) ....M
Dickinson (PA) ....R
Drew (NJ) ....R
Emory (GA) ....R
Georgetown (DC) ....M
Grinnell (IA) ....R
Gustavus Adolphus (MN) ....R
Harvard (MA) ....M
Illinois, U. of (Urbana-Champaign).....XL
Kalamazoo (MI) ....R
Lawrence (WI)...R
Michigan, U. of XL

Middlebury (VT) ....R
▲ Mt. Holyoke (MA) ....R
New York U. ....M
North Carolina, U. of...............................L
Pennsylvania, U. of...................................L
Pomona (CA) ....R
Princeton (NJ)..M
Rochester, U. of (NY) ....M
Rutgers (NJ) L
Skidmore (NY) ....R
▲ Smith (MA) ....R
South, U. of the (TN) ....R
Southwestern (TX).....................................R
Tulane (LA)...M
Wake Forest (NC) ....M
Washington & Lee (VA)............................R
Washington U. (MO) ....M
▲ Wellesley (MA) ....R
Whitman (WA) ....R
Yale (CT)..M

FOREIGN LANGUAGES continues next page

Enrollment Code

S = Small (less than 1000 students)   **M** = Medium (3000-8000 students)   **XL** = Extra Large (over 20,000 students)
R = Moderate (1000-3000 students)   **L** = Large (8000-20,000 students)

★ **THE COUNSELORS' CHOICE**   ■ Men Only   ▲ Women Only

FOREIGN LANGUAGES, *continued*

GROUP II
Very Selective

▲ Agnes Scott (GA) ....S
Beloit (WI) ....R
Boston College (MA) L
Brigham Young (UT)...............................XL
California, U. of (Santa Barbara) L
Calvin (MI) ....M
Catholic (DC)...M
Central (IA) ....R
Clark (MA) ....R
Drake (IA) ....M
Earlham (IN) ....R
Eckerd (FL) ....R
Georgia, U. of XL
Hawaii, U. of...L
▲ Hollins (VA)..S
★ INDIANA U..XL
Iowa, U. of..XL
James Madison (VA) L

Kansas, U. of...L
Lewis & Clark (OR) ....R
Linfield (OR) ....R
▲ Mills (CA)..S
Minnesota, U. of (Morris) ....R
Moravian (PA) ....R
Pacific University (OR) ....S
Pepperdine (CA) ....R
▲ Sweet Briar (VA)......................................S
Texas, U. of (Austin) XL
▲ Trinity (DC)..S
Truman State (MO) ....M
Utah, U. of L
Vermont, U. of L
▲ Wells (NY) ....S
Wheaton (MA) ....R
Wisconsin, U. of.......................................XL
Wofford (SC) ....R

GROUP III
Selective

Bethany (WV) ....S
Emory & Henry (VA) ....S
Montana State L
New Mexico, U. of....................................L

Southern Oregon State College ....M
South Florida, U. of L
Wayne State (MI) L

FOREIGN LANGUAGES continues next page

FOREIGN LANGUAGES, *continued*

Some Recommendations by Specific Departments
Compiled with the help of Minnesota's Jeff Sheehan, Secondary School Counselor.

FRENCH

California, U. of (Berkeley) ... XL	▲ Mills (CA) ... S
Columbia (NY) ... M	▲ Mount Holyoke (MA) ... R
Dartmouth (NH) ... M	Northwestern (IL) ... M
Emory (GA) ... R	Tufts (MA) ... M
Georgetown (DC) ... M	Tulane (LA) ... M
Harvard (MA) ... M	Washington U. (MO) ... M
Indiana U. ... XL	▲ Wellesley (MA) ... R

GERMAN

Brown (RI) ... M	Pennsylvania, U. of ... L
California, U. of (Santa Barbara) ... L	Stanford (CA) ... M
Illinois, U. of (Urbana-Champaign) ... XL	Texas, U. of (Austin) ... XL
Indiana U. ... XL	Williams (MA) ... R
Michigan State ... XL	Wisconsin, U. of ... XL
Penn State ... XL	Wofford (SC) ... R

JAPANESE

Brigham Young (UT) ... XL	Oregon, (U. of ?) ... L
Harvard (MA) ... M	Pennsylvania, U. of ... L
Hawaii, U. of (Manoa) ... L	Pittsburgh, U. of (PA) ... L
Ohio State ... L	Washington, U. of ... XL

SPANISH

Buffalo (SUNY) (NY) ... L	Kansas, U. of ... L
California, U. of (Irvine) ... M	Pittsburgh, U. of ... L
California, U. of (San Diego) ... L	Rutgers (NJ) ... L
California, U. of (Santa Barbara) ... L	Utah, U. of ... L
Indiana U. ... XL	Wisconsin, U. of ... XL

Enrollment Code

S = Small (less than 1000 students)   **M** = Medium (3000-8000 students)   **XL** = Extra Large (over 20,000 students)
R = Moderate (1000-3000 students)   **L** = Large (8000-20,000 students)

★ THE COUNSELORS' CHOICE ■ Men Only ▲ Women Only

FORESTRY

GROUP I
Most Selective

California, U. of (Berkeley) XL

Florida, U. of XL

Michigan, U. of XL

★ NORTH CAROLINA STATE L

SUNY Coll. of Env. Sci. & Forestry ......R

GROUP II
Very Selective

Arizona, U. of XL

Auburn (AL)...L

Berry (GA) ....R

Clemson (SC) L

Colorado State L

Georgia, U. of L

Iowa State XL

Maine, U. of ....M

Michigan State XL

Michigan Tech ....M

Minnesota, U. of XL

Missouri, U. of XL

Montana State L

Pennsylvania State XL

Purdue (IN)...XL

Syracuse (NY)...L

Texas A&M XL

Virginia Poly. Inst....................................L

Washington, U. of XL

West Virginia U. L

Wisconsin, U. of.....................................XL

GROUP III
Selective

Humboldt State (CA)...............................M

Idaho, U. of ....M

Montana, U. of...M

Northern Arizona....................................XL

Oregon State L

Stephen F. Austin (TX) L

Utah State L

GEOGRAPHY

GROUP I
Most Selective

Buffalo (SUNY) (NY) L
California, U. of (Berkeley) XL
California, U. of (Los Angeles) XL
Chicago, U. of (IL) ....R
★ **CLARK (MA)** ....R
Colgate (NY)...R
Dartmouth (NH) ....M

Florida, U. of XL
George Washington (DC) ....M
Johns Hopkins (MD) ....R
Macalester (MN) ....R
Michigan, U. of XL
Middlebury (VT) ....R
Minnesota, U. of....................................XL

GROUP II
Very Selective

Arizona State XL
Bemidji State (MN) ....M
California, U. of (Santa Barbara) L
Colorado, U. of L
Colorado, U. of (Colorado Springs) ......M
Indiana U. XL
Kansas, U. of..L
Louisiana State XL
Mary Washington (VA) ....R

Michigan State XL
Ohio State XL
Oregon, U. of L
Pennsylvania State XL
Radford (VA) ....M
Texas, U. of (Austin).............................XL
Vermont, U. of L
Wisconsin, U. of (Madison) XL
Wittenberg (OH) ....R

GROUP III
Selective

California State U. (Chico) L
Mansfield (PA) ....R

Salem State (MA)...................................M

GEOLOGY

GROUP I
Most Selective

Amherst (MA)	R	Furman (SC)	R
Bates (ME)	R	Geneseo (SUNY) (NY)	M
Brown (RI)	M	Harvard (MA)	M
Bowdoin (ME)	R	Lafayette (PA)	R
▲ Bryn Mawr (PA)	R	Lehigh (PA)	M
California Inst. of Tech.	S	MIT (MA)	M
★ CARLETON (MN)	R	Pennsylvania, U. of	L
Chicago, U. of (IL)	R	Pomona (CA)	R
Colgate (NY)	R	Princeton (NJ)	M
Colorado Col.	R	Rochester, U. of (NY)	M
Colorado School of Mines	R	Washington & Lee (VA)	R
Columbia (NY)	M	Washington U. (MO)	M
Dartmouth (NH)	M	William & Mary (VA)	M
Franklin & Marshall (PA)	R		

GROUP II
Very Selective

Albany (SUNY) (NY)	L	Michigan Tech	M
Alabama, U. of	L	Millsaps (MS)	S
Allegheny (PA)	R	Minnesota, U. of	XL
Arizona, U. of	XL	New Mexico Inst. of Mining & Tech.	S
Beloit (WI)	R	Oklahoma, U. of	L
California, U. of (Davis)	L	Purdue (IN)	XL
California, U. of (Santa Barbara)	L	St. Lawrence (NY)	R
Centenary College (LA)	S	Stony Brook (SUNY) (NY)	L
Colorado State	L	Texas A&M	XL
Colorado, U. of	L	Texas Christian	M
Cornell Col. (IA)	R	Texas, U. of (Austin)	XL
Denison (OH)	R	Tulsa, U. of (OK)	M
Earlham (IN)	R	Vermont, U. of	M
Guilford (NC)	R	Washington,U. of	XL
Hope (MI)	R	Wisconsin, U. of	XL
Indiana U.	XL	Wooster, College of (OH)	R

GROUP III
Selective

Brooklyn Col. (CUNY) (NY)	L	Louisiana State	XL
Fort Lewis (CO)	M	Wyoming, U. of	L
Hartwick (NY)	R		

HISTORY

GROUP I
Most Selective

Albion (MI) ....R	Lafayette (PA) ....R
Amherst (MA)...........................R	Lawrence (WI)...........................R
Bates (ME) ....R	Macalester (MN) ....R
Boston Col. (MA)......................L	Middlebury (VT) ....R
Boston U. (MA).........................L	▲ Mount Holyoke (MA)................R
Bowdoin (ME) ....R	North Carolina, U. of................L
Brandeis (MA) ....R	Northwestern (IL) ....M
Brown (RI) ....M	Pennsylvania, U. of...................L
▲ Bryn Mawr (PA) ....S	Pomona (CA) ....R
Bucknell (PA) ....M	Princeton (NJ)...........................M
California, U. of (Berkeley) XL	Reed (OR)..................................R
California, U. of (Los Angeles)............XL	Rice (TX)...................................R
Carleton (MN) ....R	▲ Smith (MA) ....R
Chicago, U. of (IL) ....R	South, U. of the (TN) ....R
Claremont McKenna (CA) ....S	Southwestern (TX)....................R
Colgate (NY)............................R	Stanford (CA) ....M
Colorado Col. ....R	Swarthmore (PA) ....R
Columbia (NY) ....M	Texas Christian U. (TX) ....M
Connecticut Col........................R	Trinity (TX) ....R
Cornell (NY) L	Tufts (MA) ....M
Dallas, U. of (TX) ....R	Tulane (LA) ....M
Davidson (NC) ....R	Union (NY) ....R
Dickinson (PA) ....R	Vanderbilt (TN) ....R
Drew (NJ) ....R	Vassar (NY) ....R
Duke (NC) ....M	Virginia, U. of...........................L
Emory (GA)...............................R	■ Wabash (IN) ....S
George Washington (DC) ....M	Wake Forest (NC) ....M
Georgetown (DC) ....M	Washington & Lee (VA).............R
Gettysburg (PA) ....R	▲ Wellesley (MA) ....R
Grinnell (IA) ....R	Wesleyan U. (CT) ....R
Hamilton (NY) ....R	Whitman (WA) ....R
★ HARVARD (MA)........................M	Williams (MA) ....R
Haverford (PA) ....S	William & Mary (VA).................M
Holy Cross (MA)........................R	Yale (CT)...................................M
Kalamazoo (MI) ....R	Yeshiva (NY) ....R
Kenyon (OH).............................R	

HISTORY continues next page

Enrollment Code

S = Small (less than 1000 students) **M** = Medium (3000-8000 students) **XL** = Extra Large (over 20,000 students)
R = Moderate (1000-3000 students) **L** = Large (8000-20,000 students)

★ **THE COUNSELORS' CHOICE** ■ Men Only ▲ Women Only

HISTORY, *continued*

GROUP II
Very Selective

▲ Agnes Scott (GA) ....S
  Albion (MI) ....R
  Allegheny (PA).......................................R
  Alma (MI)...R
  Baylor (TX)..M
  Birmingham-Southern (AL) ....R
  California, U. of (Davis) L
  Calvin (MI) ....M
  Coe (IA) ....R
  Covenant (GA) ....S
  Denison (OH)..R
  Erskine (SC) ....S
  Goucher (MD) ....S
■ Hampden-Sydney (VA) ....S
  Hillsdale (MI) ....R
  Hiram (OH) ....R
  Hobart & William Smith (NY) ....R
  Kansas, U. of..L
  Kentucky, U. of L
  Knox (IL)..R
  Lake Forest (IL).....................................S
  Marquette (WI).......................................M
  Maryland, U. of XL

  Mary Washington (VA) ....R
  Massachusetts, U. of...............................L
  Miami, U. of (FL) ....M
  Millersville (PA) ....M
  Missouri, U. of.......................................XL
  Muhlenberg (PA) ....R
  North Carolina (Asheville)......................R
  Ohio U. L
  Oklahoma, U. of L
  Queens (NC) ....S
  Rutgers (Camden) (NJ) ....M
  Spring Hill (AL) ....R
  Stetson (FL) ....R
  Texas, U. of (Austin)............................XL
  Vermont, U. of L
  Washington College (MD) ....S
▲ Wells (NY) ....S
  Wheaton (MA) ....R
  Wisconsin, U. of.....................................XL
  Wittenberg (OH) ....R
  Wofford (SC) ....R
  Wooster (OH) ....R

GROUP III
Selective

  Alabama, U. of.......................................L
  Charleston, U. of (WV) ....S
  New Mexico, U. of..................................L

  St. Mary's (MN) ....R
  Toledo, U. of..L

Enrollment Code

S = Small (less than 1000 students)   **M** = Medium (3000-8000 students)   **XL** = Extra Large (over 20,000 students)
R = Moderate (1000-3000 students)   **L** = Large (8000-20,000 students)

★ THE COUNSELORS' CHOICE   ■ Men Only   ▲ Women Only

HOME ECONOMICS

GROUP I
Most Selective

★ CORNELL (NY) L

Illinois, U. of (Urbana-Champaign).....XL

Iowa State XL

GROUP II
Very Selective

Brigham Young (UT).............................XL

California, U. of (Davis)..........................L

Connecticut, U. of L

Delaware, U. of.......................................L

Drexel (PA) ....M

Florida State L

Georgia, U. of XL

▲ Hood (MD) ....S

Indiana U. (PA) L

James Madison (VA) L

➤ Kansas State L

Kentucky, U. of L

Maine, U. of...M

Maryland, U. of XL

Massachusetts, U. of...............................L

Michigan State.......................................XL

Minnesota, U. of....................................XL

Oneonta (SUNY) (NY)..........................M

Pennsylvania State XL

Purdue (IN)..XL

Rockhurst (MO) ....R

Rowan (NJ)...M

St. Olaf (MN)..R

Seattle Pacific (WA)................................R

Western Washington U. L

Wisconsin, U. of....................................XL

GROUP III
Selective

Arizona State XL

Berea (KY) ....R

Central Michigan.....................................L

Fontbonne (MO) ....S

Herbert Lehman (CUNY) (NY) L

▲ Judson (AL) ....S

Linfield (OR) ....R

Mass. State College (Framingham)........M

▲ Meredith (NC) ....R

Montevallo (AL) ....R

Nebraska, U. of..L

North Carolina, U. of (Greensboro).......M

Ohio State XL

Oregon State..L

Point Loma (CA)......................................R

Rosary College (IL) ....S

▲+ Seton Hill (PA) ....S

Texas Tech. U. L

➤ *Nutritional & Exercise Sciences*

+ *Family Studies*

JOURNALISM/COMMUNICATIONS

GROUP I
Most Selective

American U. (DC) ....M	North Carolina, U. of L
Boston U. (MA) L	★ NORTHWESTERN (IL) ....M
California, U. of (Los Angeles)............XL	Ohio U. L
Creighton (NE) ....R	Southwestern (TX) ....R
Florida, U. of XL	Stanford (CA) ....M
Gettysburg (PA) ....R	Trinity (TX) ....R
Illinois, U. of (Urbana-Champaign).....XL	Villanova (PA).....................................M
Miami, U. of (FL) L	Wheaton (IL).......................................R
Michigan, U. of XL	Wisconsin, U. of................................XL

GROUP II
Very Selective

Arizona State XL	Moravian (PA) ....R
Arizona, U. of XL	Muhlenberg (PA).................................R
Central Florida, U. of L	Nevada, U. of (Reno) ....M
Colorado, U. of L	New Hampshire, U. of L
Delaware, U. of L	North Central (IL)................................R
Drake (IA) ....M	Ohio Wesleyan ....R
Duquesne (PA)....................................M	Pepperdine (CA)..................................R
Fairfield (CT).......................................M	▲ Randolph-Macon Woman's Col. (VA) ...S
Georgia, U. of XL	Santa Clara U. (CA) ....M
Gonzaga (WA) ....R	Scranton, U. of (PA)...........................M
Hanover (IN) ....S	▲ Simmons (MA) ....R
Illinois College ....S	South Carolina, U. of L
Indiana U. XL	Southern California.............................L
Iowa, U. of...XL	Southern Methodist (TX)....................M
John Carroll (OH) ....M	Spring Hill (AL) ....R
Kansas, U. of.......................................L	St. Ambrose (IA)................................R
Kansas State L	St. Bonaventure (NY).........................R
Kentucky, U. of L	St. Michael's (VT) ....R
Louisiana State XL	Susquehanna U. (PA) ....R
Loyola Marymount (CA) ....M	Syracuse (NY).....................................L
Marist (NY)..M	Texas A&M (Galveston) ....S
Maryland, U. of XL	Texas Christian U. ....M
Massachusetts, U. of L	Texas, U. of (Austin)..........................XL
Michigan State L	Tulsa, U. of (OK)................................R
Minnesota, U. of XL	West Virginia U. L
Mississippi, U. of ....M	Western Washington U. L
Missouri, U. of.....................................XL	Winona State U. (MN) L

JOURNALISM/COMMUNICATIONS continues next page

JOURNALISM/COMMUNICATIONS, *continued*

GROUP III
Selective

Appalachian State (NC)	L	Loyola (IL)	M
Arkansas, U. of	L	Loyola U. (LA)	M
Augsburg (MN)	R	Lynchburg (VA)	R
Bemidji State (MN)	M	Lyndon State (VT)	R
Bethany (WV)	S	Montana, U. of	M
Buena Vista (IA)	R	Morningside (IA)	S
Butler (IN)	R	Montevallo (AL)	R
California State U. (Fullerton)	L	Nebraska, U. of	L
California State U. (Long Beach)	L	North Carolina, U. of (Greensboro)	M
Chapman (CA)	R	Oakland U. (MI)	M
Elon (NC)	R	Regis (CO)	R
Flagler (FL)	R	St. John Fisher (NY)	R
Florida Southern	R	St. Mary's College (MN)	R
Franklin (IN)	S	Samford (AL)	R
Hofstra (NY)	M	San Diego State (CA)	XL
Howard (DC)	M	Santa Fe, College of (NM)	S
Hunter (CUNY) (NY)	L	Seton Hall (NJ)	M
Jacksonville (FL)	R	Tampa, U. of (FL)	R
Johnson C. Smith (NC)	R	Texas Wesleyan	R
Kent State (OH)	L	Xavier (OH)	R

Enrollment Code

S = Small (less than 1000 students)	**M** = Medium (3000-8000 students)	**XL** = Extra Large (over 20,000 students)
R = Moderate (1000-3000 students)	**L** = Large (8000-20,000 students)	

★ THE COUNSELORS' CHOICE   ■ Men Only   ▲ Women Only

MATHEMATICS

GROUP I
Most Selective

American U. (DC) ....M	▲ Mount Holyoke (MA) ....R
Bates (ME) ....R	New College (FL) ....S
Binghamton (SUNY) (NY) L	New York U. L
Bowdoin (ME) ....R	Northwestern (IL) ....M
Bucknell (PA) ....M	Occidental (CA) ....R
California Inst. of Tech. ....S	Pomona (CA) ....R
California, U. of (Berkeley) XL	Princeton (NJ) ....M
California, U. of (Los Angeles)...........XL	Rensselaer (NY) ....M
California, U. of (San Diego) L	Rice (TX) ....R
Carleton (MN) ....R	Stanford (CA) ....M
Case Western Reserve U. (OH) ....R	St. Mary's Col. of Maryland ....R
Chicago, U. of (IL) ....R	St. Olaf (MN)...R
Colgate (NY)..R	Trinity (CT) ....R
Columbia (NY) ....M	Tulane (LA) ....M
Dartmouth (NH) ....M	Union (NY) ....R
Davidson (NC)..R	■ Wabash (IN) ....S
Duke (NC) ....M	Washington U. (MO) ....M
Florida, U. of XL	▲ Wellesley (MA) ....R
★ HARVARD (MA)...................................M	Wesleyan (CT) ....R
Harvey Mudd (CA)..................................S	Wheaton (IL) ....R
Holy Cross (MA) ....R	Whitman (WA) ....R
Illinois Inst. of Tech. ....R	Willamette (OR) ....R
Illinois, U. of (Urbana-Champaign).....XL	Wisconsin, U. of XL
Kenyon (OH) ....R	Yale (CT) ....M
MIT (MA) ....M	

MATHEMATICS continues next page

Enrollment Code

S = Small (less than 1000 students)   **M** = Medium (3000-8000 students)   **XL** = Extra Large (over 20,000 students)
R = Moderate (1000-3000 students)   **L** = Large (8000-20,000 students)

★ THE COUNSELORS' CHOICE   ■ Men Only   ▲ Women Only

MATHEMATICS, *continued*

GROUP II
Very Selective

Albion (MI)	R	Muhlenberg (PA)	R
Arizona State	XL	North Carolina State	L
Birmingham-Southern (AL)	R	Ohio U.	L
California, U. of (Irvine)	L	Oregon, U. of	L
California, U. of (Riverside)	M	Potsdam (SUNY) (NY)	R
California, U. of (Santa Cruz)	M	▲ Simmons (MA)	R
Cincinnati, U. of (OH)	L	Southern California, U. of	L
Colorado, U. of	L	Southwest Missouri	L
Concordia (MN)	R	Stetson (FL)	R
Earlham (IN)	R	▲ Sweet Briar (VA)	S
Fairfield (CT)	M	Texas, U. of (Austin)	XL
Hiram (OH)	R	▲ Trinity (DC)	S
Kansas State	L	Valparaiso (IN)	M
Knox (IL)	S	Washington, U. of	XL
Lebanon Valley (PA)	R	Wofford (SC)	R
Michigan State	XL	Wooster (OH)	R
Millsaps (MS)	S		

GROUP III
Selective

Fisk (TN)	S	Malone (OH)	R
Fontbonne (MO)	S	Texas Tech. U.	L
Louisiana State	XL		

Enrollment Code

S = Small (less than 1000 students)   **M** = Medium (3000-8000 students)   **XL** = Extra Large (over 20,000 students)
R = Moderate (1000-3000 students)   **L** = Large (8000-20,000 students)

★ THE COUNSELORS' CHOICE   ■ Men Only   ▲ Women Only

MUSIC

GROUP I
Most Selective

Boston U. (MA)	L	Juilliard (NY)	S
Bowdoin (ME)	R	Lawrence (WI)	R
Brandeis (MA)	R	Miami, U. of (FL)	L
Bucknell (PA)	R	Michigan, U. of	XL
California, U. of (Berkeley)	XL	New York U.	L
California, U. of (Los Angeles)	XL	Northwestern (IL)	M
California, U. of (San Diego)	L	★ OBERLIN (OH)	R
Carnegie-Mellon (PA)	M	Princeton (NJ)	M
Case Western Reserve U. (OH)	R	Rice (TX)	R
Cleveland Inst. of Music (OH)	S	Rochester, U. of (NY)	M
Columbia (NY)	M	Skidmore (NY)	R
Connecticut College	R	▲ Smith (MA)	R
DePauw (IN)	R	Southwestern (TX)	R
Furman (SC)	R	Stanford (CA)	M
Geneseo (SUNY) (NY)	M	St. Mary's College of Maryland	R
Gustavus Adolphus (MN)	R	St. Olaf (MN)	R
Harvard (MA)	M	Vassar (NY)	R
Hofstra (NY)	M	Wheaton (IL)	R
Illinois, U. of (Urbana-Champaign)	XL	Whitman (WA)	R
Illinois Wesleyan	R	Willamette (OR)	R
Iowa, U. of	XL	Yale (CT)	M

GROUP II
Very Selective

Augustana (IL)	R	Colorado, U. of	L
Bard (NY)	R	▲ Converse (SC)	S
Birmingham-Southern (AL)	R	Curtis Institute of Music (PA)	S
Boston Conservatory	S	Drury (MO)	S
Butler (IN)	R	Florida State	L
Cal. Inst. of the Arts	S	Fredonia (SUNY) (NY)	M
California, U. of (Riverside)	M	Hope (MI)	R
California, U. of (Santa Barbara)	L	Indiana U.	XL
California, U. of (Santa Cruz)	M	Ithaca (NY)	M
Capital (OH)	R	James Madison (VA)	L
Catholic U. (DC)	M	▲ Judson (AL)	S
Clark (MA)	R	Lake Forest (IL)	S
Coe (IA)	R		

GROUP II continues next page

Enrollment Code

S = Small (less than 1000 students)	**M** = Medium (3000-8000 students)	**XL** = Extra Large (over 20,000 students)
R = Moderate (1000-3000 students)	**L** = Large (8000-20,000 students)	

★ THE COUNSELORS' CHOICE   ■ Men Only   ▲ Women Only

MUSIC, *continued*

GROUP II, *continued*

Lebanon Valley (PA)	R	Purchase (SUNY) (NY)	R
Louisiana State	XL	Rowan (NJ)	M
Luther (IA)	R	San Francisco Conservatory (CA)	S
Manhattanville (NY)	R	Santa Clara, U. of (CA)	M
Manhattan School of Music (NY)	S	Shepherd (WV)	R
▲ Mills (CA)	S	Southern California, U. of	L
Millsaps (MS)	S	▲ St. Catherine (MN)	R
Missouri, U. of (Kansas City)	M	Stetson (FL)	R
Moravian (PA)	R	West Chester (PA)	M
New England Consevatory (MA)	S	West Virginia, U. of	L
North Florida	M	William Jewell Col. (MO)	R
North Texas	L	Wittenberg (OH)	R
Ohio U.	L	Whitworth (WA)	R
Pacific, U. of the (CA)	R	Wooster, College of (OH)	R
Potsdam (SUNY) (NY)	M		

GROUP III
Selective

Arkansas, U. of	L	Jacksonville (FL)	R
Baldwin-Wallace (OH)	R	Keene State (NH)	R
Belhaven (MS)	S	Kent State (OH)	L
➤ Belmont (TN)	R	Loyola (LA)	M
Bethany (WV)	R	Massachusetts, U. of (Lowell)	M
Bowling Green (OH)	L	Memphis, U. of (TN)	L
Central Washington	L	▲ Meredith (NC)	R
Duquesne (PA)	M	Rider (NJ)	M
➤ Five Towns College (NY)	S	▲ Seton Hill (PA)	S
Hartford, U. of (CT)	M	Southwest Baptist (MO)	R
Hartwick (NY)	R	Tampa, U. of (FL)	R
Humboldt State (CA)	M		

➤ *Music Business*

Enrollment Code

S = Small (less than 1000 students)   **M** = Medium (3000-8000 students)   **XL** = Extra Large (over 20,000 students)
R = Moderate (1000-3000 students)   **L** = Large (8000-20,000 students)

★ THE COUNSELORS' CHOICE   ■ Men Only   ▲ Women Only

NURSING

GROUP I
Most Selective

Binghamton (SUNY) (NY) L	Illinois, U. of XL
Boston Col. (MA)...L	New York U. L
Case Western Reserve U. (OH) ....R	★ **PENNSYLVANIA, U. OF** L
Colorado, U. of L	Rochester, U. of (NY) ....M
Columbia (NY) ....M	St. Olaf (MN) ....R
DePauw (IN) ....R	Vanderbilt (TN) ....M
Duke (NC) ....M	Villanova (PA)...M
Emory (GA) ....R	Virginia, U. of L
Florida, U. of XL	Wisconsin, U. of L
Gustavus Adolphus (MN) ....R	

GROUP II
Very Selective

Adelphi (NY) ....M	Iowa, U. of..XL
Arizona, U. of XL	Lebanon Valley (PA)..............................R
Augustana (SD) ....R	Loyola (IL) ....M
Barry (FL) ....R	Luther (IA) ....R
Baylor (TX)..M	Marquette (WI) ....M
Bethel (MN) ....R	➤ Maryland, U. of (Baltimore County) .....M
Capital (OH) ....R	Massachusetts, U. of................................L
Carroll (WI) ....R	Michigan, U. of XL
Catholic U. (DC) ....M	Minnesota, U. of XL
Creighton (NE) ....R	▲ Mississippi U. for Women ....R
Daemen (NY) ....R	Morningside (IA) ....S
Delaware, U. of...L	Mount Mercy (IA) ....S
Detroit Mercy (MI) ....M	New Jersey, College of ....M
Duquesne (PA)..M	Pacific Lutheran (WA)............................R
Evansville (IN) ....R	Pennsylvania State XL
Fairfield (CT)..M	Pittsburgh, U. of (PA) L
George Mason (VA) ....M	Samford (AL)..R
Georgetown (DC) ....M	San Diego, U. of (CA)............................M
Gwynedd Mercy (PA) ....S	San Francisco, U. of (CA) ....M
Hunter (CUNY) (NY) L	*GROUP II continues next page*

Enrollment Code

S = Small (less than 1000 students)   M = Medium (3000-8000 students)   XL = Extra Large (over 20,000 students)
R = Moderate (1000-3000 students)   L = Large (8000-20,000 students)

★ THE COUNSELORS' CHOICE ■ Men Only ▲ Women Only

NURSING, *continued*

GROUP II, *continued*

Seattle Pacific (WA)..................................R
▲ Simmons (MA) ....R
▲ St. Catherine (MN) ....R
St. Louis (MO)..M
▲ St. Mary's College (IN) ....R
Texas Christian U. ....M

Truman State (MO)..............................M
Valparaiso U. (IN) ....M
Washington, U. of................................XL
William Jewell (MO).............................R
Wisconsin, U. of (Milwaukee)..............XL
York (PA) ....M

➤ *Health Policy, also*

GROUP III
Selective

Alaska, U. of (Fairbanks) ....M
Arizona State XL
Azusa Pacific (CA) ....R
Bellarmine (KY) ....R
Berea (KY) ....R
California State U. (Chico) L
Carroll (MT)...R
▲ Cedar Crest (PA) ....S
Cedarville (OH).......................................R
D'Youville (NY) ....R
Goshen (IN)..R
Graceland (IA)..R
Hartwick (NY) ....R
Howard (DC)...M
Jacksonville (FL) ....R
MacMurray (IL) ....S
Marycrest (IA) ....S
Maryville (St. Louis) (MO).....................R
Massachusetts, U. of (Dartmouth) ....M
Mercy (NY) ....M
Misericordia, College (PA)......................S
Mississippi College ....R
Mount St. Joseph (OH) ....R

Mount St. Mary's (CA) ....S
Mount St. Mary's (NY) ....S
North Carolina, U. of (Charlotte)............L
North Carolina, U. of (Greensboro).......M
Northeast Louisiana...............................L
Northern Illinois U. L
Ohio State..XL
Pace (NY) ....M
Pennsylvania State XL
Point Loma (CA) ....R
Rhode Island, U. of................................L
Russell Sage (The Sage Colleges) (NY) ......R
St. Scholastica (MN) ....R
St. Joseph's (ME) ....S
Seattle U. (WA)......................................R
South Dakota, U. of...............................M
South Florida, U. of...............................L
Southern Maine, U. of...........................M
St. Anselm (NH).....................................R
Tuskegee University (AL) ....M
Western Connecticut State ....M
Western Kentucky...................................L
Widener (PA)..R

Enrollment Code

S = Small (less than 1000 students)　M = Medium (3000-8000 students)　XL = Extra Large (over 20,000 students)
R = Moderate (1000-3000 students)　L = Large (8000-20,000 students)

★ THE COUNSELORS' CHOICE　■ Men Only　▲ Women Only

PHARMACY

GROUP I
Most Selective

Buffalo (SUNY) (NY) L	Michigan, U. of XL
Butler (IN)...R	North Carolina, U. of.............................L
Creighton (NE) ....R	Purdue (IN)..XL
Florida, U. of XL	★ RUTGERS (NJ) L
Illinois, U. of XL	

GROUP II
Very Selective

Albany Col. of Pharmacy (NY) ....S	Ohio Northern U. ....R
Connecticut, U. of L	Pacific, U. of the (CA) ....R
Drake (IA) ....M	Philadelphia Col. of Pharm. & Science .R
Duquesne (PA).....................................M	Pittsburgh, U. of L
Ferris State (MI)..................................L	Rhode Island, U. of L
Georgia, U. of L	Samford (AL)..R
Kansas, U. of.......................................L	South Carolina, U. of...........................L
Kentucky, U. of L	Southern California, U. of L
Maryland, U. of XL	St. John's (NY) L
Mass. College of Pharmacy...................R	St. Louis Col. of Pharmacy (MO) ....S
Mercer (GA)...R	Temple (PA)..M
Minnesota, U. of..................................XL	Texas, U. of (Austin)............................XL
Mississippi, U. of.................................M	Toledo, U. of..L
Montana, U. of.....................................M	Virginia Commonwealth U.......................L
New Mexico, U. of.................................M	Washington State L
Northeast Louisiana L	Wayne State (MI) L
North Dakota State...............................L	Wyoming, U. of L
Ohio State XL	

PHILOSOPHY

GROUP I
Most Selective

Bates (ME)	R	Johns Hopkins (MD)	R
Boston Col. (MA)	L	Kenyon (OH)	R
Boston U. (MA)	L	Macalester (MN)	R
Bowdoin (ME)	R	Michigan, U. of	XL
Bucknell (PA)	M	New College (FL)	S
California, U. of (Berkeley)	XL	New York U.	L
California, U. of (Los Angeles)	XL	Oberlin (OH)	R
Chicago, U. of (IL)	R	Pennsylvania, U. of	L
Claremont McKenna (CA)	S	Pittsburgh, U. of (PA)	L
Colgate (NY)	R	Pomona (CA)	R
Colorado Col.	R	★ PRINCETON (NJ)	M
Columbia (NY)	M	Reed (OR)	R
Connecticut Col.	R	Rochester, U. of (NY)	M
Cornell (NY)	L	▲ Smith (MA)	R
Davidson (NC)	R	St. Olaf (MN)	R
Duke (NC)	M	Swarthmore (PA)	R
Florida State	L	Trinity (CT)	R
Florida, U. of	XL	Trinity (TX)	R
George Washington (DC)	M	Tulane (LA)	M
Georgetown (DC)	M	Washington U. (MO)	M
Hamilton (NY)	R	Wheaton (IL)	R
Harvard (MA)	M	Whitman (WA)	R
Haverford (PA)	S	Yale (CT)	M
Holy Cross (MA)	R		

GROUP II
Very Selective

Allegheny (PA)	R	Milligan (TN)	S
Asbury (KY)	R	Muhlenberg (PA)	R
Biola (CA)	R	Regis (CO)	R
Cornell Col. (IA)	R	St. Andrews Presbyterian (NC)	S
Denison (OH)	R	St. Bonaventure (NY)	R
Fordham (NY)	L	St. Louis (MO)	M
Franciscan U. of Steubenville (OH)	R	Skidmore (NY)	R
▲ Hood (MD)	S	Stony Brook (SUNY) (NY)	L
Indiana U.	XL	Wofford (SC)	R
Loyola (LA)	M		

Enrollment Code

S = Small (less than 1000 students)
R = Moderate (1000-3000 students)
M = Medium (3000-8000 students)
L = Large (8000-20,000 students)
XL = Extra Large (over 20,000 students)

★ THE COUNSELORS' CHOICE ■ Men Only ▲ Women Only

PHYSICS

GROUP I
Most Selective

Amherst (MA)	R	Haverford (PA)	S
Bates (ME)	R	Illinois, U. of (Urbana-Champaign)	XL
Binghamton (SUNY) (NY)	L	Kalamazoo (MI)	R
Boston U. (MA)	L	Lawrence (WI)	R
▲ Bryn Mawr (PA)	S	MIT (MA)	M
★ CALIFORNIA INST. OF TECH.	S	New College (FL)	S
California, U. of (Berkeley)	XL	New Mexico Inst. of Mining & Tech.	S
California, U. of (San Diego)	L	Occidental (CA)	R
Carleton (MN)	R	Princeton (NJ)	M
Case Western Reserve U. (OH)	R	Reed (OR)	R
Centre (KY)	S	Rensselaer (NY)	M
Chicago, U. of (IL)	R	Rice (TX)	R
Colorado School of Mines	R	▲ Smith (MA)	R
Columbia (NY)	M	Stanford (CA)	M
Cornell (NY)	L	Swarthmore (PA)	R
Dartmouth (NH)	M	Wake Forest (NC)	M
Florida, U. of	XL	Washington U. (MO)	M
Franklin & Marshall (PA)	R	▲ Wellesley (MA)	R
Geneseo (SUNY) (NY)	M	Wheaton (IL)	R
Georgia Inst. of Tech.	M	Whitman (WA)	R
Grinnell (IA)	R	William & Mary (VA)	M
Gustavus Adolphus (MN)	R	Worcester Poly. Inst. (MA)	R
Harvard (MA)	M	Yeshiva (NY)	R
Harvey Mudd (CA)	S		

PHYSICS continues next page

PHYSICS

GROUP II
Very Selective

Adelphi (NY) ....M	Loyola (IL) ....M
Beloit (WI) ....R	Mississippi, U. of ....M
California, U. of (Irvine) ....M	Ohio State XL
California, U. of (Santa Barbara) L	Ohio U. L
California, U. of (Santa Cruz) ....M	Oregon State L
Colorado, U. of...........................L	Rollins (FL) ....R
Colorado, U. of (Colorado Springs) ......M	St. John's (MN) ....R
Denver, U. of (CO) ....M	Stony Brook (SUNY) (NY) L
Evansville, U. of (IN) ....R	Texas, U. of (Austin).................XL
Fairfield (CT)...............................M	Ursinus (PA) ....R
Guilford (NC) ....R	Vermont, U. of............................M
Lewis & Clark (OR) ....R	Wisconsin, U. of..........................XL

GROUP III
Selective

Brooklyn Col. (CUNY) (NY) L	Jacksonville (FL) ....R
City Col. (CUNY) (NY) L	Louisiana State XL
Goshen (IN)...................................R	Wyoming, U. of L

Enrollment Code

S = Small (less than 1000 students)   **M** = Medium (3000-8000 students)   **XL** = Extra Large (over 20,000 students)
R = Moderate (1000-3000 students)   **L** = Large (8000-20,000 students)

★ THE COUNSELORS' CHOICE   ■ Men Only   ▲ Women Only

POLITICAL SCIENCE

GROUP I
Most Selective

American U. (DC) .... M
Amherst (MA) .... R
Boston U. (MA) L
Brandeis (MA) .... R
Brown (RI) .... M
California, U. of (Los Angeles) XL
California, U. of (San Diego) L
Centre (KY) .... S
Chicago, U. of (IL) .... R
Claremont McKenna (CA) .... S
Colby (ME) .... R
Colgate (NY) .... R
Colorado Col. .... R
Columbia (NY) .... M
Connecticut Col. .... R
Dartmouth (NH) .... M
Dickinson (PA) .... R
Drew (NJ) .... R
Duke (NC) .... M
Emory (GA) .... R
Franklin & Marshall (PA) .... R
Furman (SC) .... R
George Washington (DC) .... M
Georgetown (DC) .... M
Grinnell (IA) .... R
Hamilton (NY) .... R
★ HARVARD (MA) .... M
Johns Hopkins (MD) .... R
Kenyon (OH) .... R

Macalester (MN) .... R
MIT (MA) .... M
Middlebury (VT) .... R
▲ Mount Holyoke (MA) .... R
Northwestern (IL) .... M
Nortre Dame (IN) .... M
Occidental (CA) .... R
Pennsylvania, U. of L
Princeton (NJ) .... M
Rochester, U. of (NY) .... M
Rhodes (TN) .... R
▲ Smith (MA) .... R
South, U. of the (TN) .... R
Southwestern (TX) .... R
Stanford (CA) .... M
Swarthmore (PA) .... R
Trinity (TX) .... R
Tufts (MA) .... M
Union (NY) .... R
Ursinus (PA) .... R
■ Wabash (IN) .... S
▲ Wellesley (MA) .... R
Washington & Lee (VA) .... R
Whitman (WA) .... R
Willamette (OR) .... R
Williams (MA) .... R
Yale (CT) .... M
Yeshiva (NY) .... R

POLITICAL SCIENCE continues next page

Enrollment Code
S = Small (less than 1000 students)
R = Moderate (1000-3000 students)
M = Medium (3000-8000 students)
L = Large (8000-20,000 students)
XL = Extra Large (over 20,000 students)
★ THE COUNSELORS' CHOICE   ■ Men Only   ▲ Women Only

POLITICAL SCIENCE, *continued*

GROUP II
Very Selective

Austin (TX) ....R	Ohio Wesleyan ....R
California, U. of (Davis).........................L	Presbyterian (SC) ....S
California, U. of (Riverside)..................M	Providence (RI) ....M
California, U. of (Santa Barbara)...........L	Randolph Macon (VA).....................R
Cal. Poly. State U. (San Luis Obispo)....L	Redlands, U. of (CA) ....R
Creighton (NE) ....R	Ripon (WI)...S
Denison (OH)....................................R	Siena (NY) ....R
DePaul (IL) ....M	Spring Hill (AL)...............................R
Drake (IA) ....M	St. Bonaventure (NY)......................R
Hawaii, U. of....................................L	St. John's (MN) ....R
Hobart & William Smith (NY) ....R	St. Lawrence (NY)............................R
Hofstra (NY) ....M	Stonehill (MA) ....R
Hope (MI) ....R	Syracuse (NY)...................................L
Knox (IL) ....R	▲ Trinity (DC)..................................S
Marquette (WI) ....M	Vermont, U. of L
Maryland, U. of (Baltimore County) .....M	Wheaton (MA) ....R
Minnesota, U. of XL	Wilberforce (OH) ....S
North Central (IL)............................R	Wittenberg (OH) ....R
Oglethorpe (GA)...............................S	

GROUP III
Selective

Adrian (MI) ....S	Radford (VA) ....M
Albright (PA) ....R	Rhode Island, U. of.........................L
Belmont Abbey (NC) ....S	St. Mary's (TX) ....R
▲ Chatham (PA)................................S	▲ Spelman (GA)...............................R
Hartwick (NY) ....R	Virginia Wesleyan ....R
Michigan State...............................XL	Whittier (CA)....................................R
Mt. St. Mary's (MD) ....R	

PRE-LAW

Author's Note: *Law School Associations usually recommend that a student choose a major dependent upon one's own individual intellectual interests and upon "the quality of undergraduate education" provided by various departments and colleges. The above recommended colleges have been taken primarily from our recommended departments in English, Economics, and Political Science.*

GROUP I
Most Selective

Albany (SUNY) (NY)	L	Franklin & Marshall (PA)	R
Allegheny (PA)	R	Furman (SC)	R
American U. (DC)	M	George Washington (DC)	M
Amherst (MA)	R	Georgetown (DC)	M
Bard (NY)	R	Gettysburg (PA)	R
Bates (ME)	R	Grinnell (IA)	R
Binghamton (SUNY) (NY)	L	Hamilton (NY)	R
Boston Col. (MA)	L	★ HARVARD (MA)	M
Boston U. (MA)	L	Haverford (PA)	S
Bowdoin (ME)	R	Holy Cross (MA)	R
Brandeis (MA)	R	Iowa, U. of	XL
Brown (RI)	M	Johns Hopkins (MD)	R
▲ Bryn Mawr (PA)	S	Kalamazoo (MI)	R
Bucknell (PA)	M	Kenyon (OH)	R
Buffalo (SUNY) (NY)	L	Lafayette (PA)	R
California, U. of (Berkeley)	XL	Macalester (MN)	R
California, U. of (Los Angeles)	XL	Maryland, U. of (Baltimore County)	M
California, U. of (San Diego)	L	MIT (MA)	M
Carleton (MN)	R	Michigan, U. of	XL
Centre (KY)	S	Middlebury (VT)	R
Chicago, U. of (IL)	R	▲ Mount Holyoke (MA)	R
Claremont McKenna (CA)	S	Muhlenberg (PA)	R
Clark (MA)	R	New Jersey, College of	M
Colby (ME)	R	North Carolina, U. of	L
Colgate (NY)	R	Northwestern (IL)	M
Colorado Col.	R	Notre Dame (IN)	M
Columbia (NY)	M	Oberlin (OH)	R
Connecticut Col.	R	Occidental (CA)	R
Dallas, U. of (TX)	R	Pennsylvania, U. of	L
Dartmouth (NH)	M	Pomona (CA)	R
Davidson (NC)	R	Princeton (NJ)	M
Dickinson (PA)	R	Providence (RI)	M
Drew (NJ)	R	Reed (OR)	R
Duke (NC)	M	Rhodes (TN)	R
Emory (GA)	R	Richmond, U. of (VA)	M
Florida, U. of	XL		

GROUP I continues next page

Enrollment Code

S = Small (less than 1000 students) **M** = Medium (3000-8000 students) **XL** = Extra Large (over 20,000 students)
R = Moderate (1000-3000 students) **L** = Large (8000-20,000 students)

★ **THE COUNSELORS' CHOICE** ■ Men Only ▲ Women Only

PRE-LAW, *continued*

GROUP I, *continued*

Richmond, U. of (VA).............M
Rochester, U. of (NY).............M
Rutgers (NJ)............L
Sarah Lawrence (NY)............S
Skidmore (NY)............R
▲ Smith (MA)............R
South, U. of the (TN)............R
Southwestern (TX)............R
Stanford (CA)............M
St. Olaf (MN)............R
Swarthmore (PA)............R
Trinity (CT)............R
Trinity (TX)............R
Tufts (MA)............M

Union (NY)............R
Ursinus (PA)............R
Vanderbilt (TN)............M
Vassar (NY)............R
Virginia, U. of............L
▲ Wabash (IN)............S
Wake Forest (NC)............M
Washington & Lee (VA)............R
Washington U. (MO)............M
▲ Wellesley (MA)............R
Wesleyan U. (CT)............R
Wheaton (IL)............R
Whitman (WA)............R

GROUP II
Very Selective

▲ Agnes Scott (GA)............S
Albany (SUNY) (NY)............L
Albion (MI)............R
Alfred (NY)............R
Alma (MI)............R
Arizona, U. of............XL
Baylor (TX)............R
Bennington (VT)............S
Birmingham-Southern (AL)............R
Butler (IN)............R
California, U. of (Davis)............L
California, U. of (Riverside)............M
California, U. of (Santa Barbara)............L
Calvin (MI)............M
Cornell Col. (IA)............R
Creighton (NE)............R
Denison (OH)............R
Denver, U. of (CO)............M
DePaul (IL)............M
Drake (IA)............M
Evansville (IN)............R

Fordham (NY)............L
George Mason (VA)............L
Georgia, U. of............XL
Gonzaga (WA)............R
Goucher (MD)............R
Grand Valley (MI)............L
Guilford (NC)............R
Hamline (MN)............R
■ Hampden-Sydney (VA)............S
Hartwick (NY)............R
Hobart & Wm. Smith (NY)............R
Hofstra (NY)............M
Hope (MI)............R
Hunter (CUNY) (NY)............L
Illinois College............S
Knox (IL)............S
Lake Forest (IL)............R
Lawrence (WI)............R
Loras (IA)............R
Marietta (OH)............R

GROUP II continues next page

Enrollment Code

S = Small (less than 1000 students) | **M** = Medium (3000-8000 students) | **XL** = Extra Large (over 20,000 students)
R = Moderate (1000-3000 students) | **L** = Large (8000-20,000 students)

★ THE COUNSELORS' CHOICE ■ Men Only ▲ Women Only

PRE-LAW, *continued*

GROUP II, *continued*

Marquette (WI)	M	San Francisco, U. of (CA)	M
Massachusetts, U. of	L	Santa Clara (CA)	R
Michigan State	XL	▲ Scripps (CA)	S
Millersville (PA)	M	Siena (NY)	R
Millsaps (MS)	S	Spring Hill (AL)	R
Minnesota, U. of	XL	St. Bonaventure (NY)	R
Minnesota, U. of (Morris)	R	St. John's (MN)	R
Mississippi, U. of	M	St. Lawrence (NY)	R
New Hampshire, U. of	L	▲ St. Mary's Col. (IN)	R
North Carolina State	L	Stetson (FL)	R
North Central (IL)	R	Stonehill (MA)	R
Oglethorpe (GA)	S	Stony Brook (SUNY) (NY)	L
Ohio U.	L	Syracuse (NY)	L
Ohio Wesleyan	R	▲ Trinity (DC)	S
Oklahoma, U. of	L	Ursinus (PA)	R
Oneonta (SUNY) (NY)	M	Vermont, U. of	L
Pittsburgh, U. of (PA)	L	Virginia Commonwealth U.	L
Presbyterian (SC)	S	Virginia Military Inst.	R
Principia (IL)	S	Washington, U. of	XL
Puget Sound (WA)	R	Washington & Jefferson (PA)	S
Purchase (SUNY) (NY)	R	▲ Wells (NY)	S
Queens (NC)	S	Westminster Col. (MO)	S
Randolph-Macon (VA)	R	Westmont (CA)	R
▲ Randolph-Macon Woman's Col. (VA)	S	Wheaton (MA)	R
Redlands, U. of (CA)	R	Wilberforce (OH)	S
Ripon (WI)	S	Wittenberg (OH)	R
Rutgers (Camden) (NJ)	M	Wofford (SC)	R
▲ Salem College (NC)	S	Wooster (OH)	R

PRE-LAW continues next page

Enrollment Code

S = Small (less than 1000 students)	**M** = Medium (3000-8000 students)	**XL** = Extra Large (over 20,000 students)
R = Moderate (1000-3000 students)	**L** = Large (8000-20,000 students)	

★ THE COUNSELORS' CHOICE　　■ Men Only　　▲ Women Only

PRE-LAW, *continued*

GROUP III
Selective

Adrian (MI)	S	Niagara (NY)	R
Albright (PA)	R	North Carolina, U. of (Wilmington)	M
Arkansas, U. of	L	Radford (VA)	M
Baldwin-Wallace (OH)	R	Roanoke (VA)	R
Belmont Abbey (NC)	S	Rhode Island, U. of	L
▲ Bennett (NC)	S	Rockford (IL)	S
▲ Chatham (PA)	S	San Francisco State (CA)	L
▲ Chestnut Hill (PA)	S	▲ Spelman (GA)	R
Emerson (MA)	R	St. Anselm (NH)	R
Fairleigh Dickinson (NJ)	M	Temple (PA)	L
Fisk (TN)	S	Tennessee, U. of	XL
Florida A&M	M	Utah, U. of	L
Fort Lewis (CO)	M	Virginia Wesleyan	R
Hawaii, U. of	L	Whittier (CA)	R
Heidelberg (OH)	S	▲ Wilson (PA)	S
▲ Hollins (VA)	S	Wisconsin, U. of (Milwaukee)	L
Mt. St. Mary's (MD)	R	Wyoming, U. of	L

Enrollment Code

S = Small (less than 1000 students)   M = Medium (3000-8000 students)   XL = Extra Large (over 20,000 students)
R = Moderate (1000-3000 students)   L = Large (8000-20,000 students)

★ THE COUNSELORS' CHOICE   ■ Men Only   ▲ Women Only

PRE-MED/PRE-DENTAL

Author's Note: *In addition to general college requirements and requirements of their major department, premedical and predental students must usually pass with a good grade the following: general chemistry, zoology, organic chemistry, general biology, English composition or literature, and general physics.*

Other required or highly recommended courses are: advanced biology, psychology or sociology, physical chemistry, calculus, and quantitative chemistry. Of course, the wise path to follow is to consult the exact course requirements of the school you expect to apply to. The recommended colleges below are taken primarily from our recommended departments in biology and chemistry.

GROUP I
Most Selective

Albany (SUNY) (NY)	L	Franklin & Marshall (PA)	R
Allegheny (PA)	R	Furman (SC)	R
Amherst (MA)	R	Geneseo (SUNY) (NY)	M
Bates (ME)	R	Georgetown (DC)	M
Binghamton (SUNY) (NY)	L	Gettysburg (PA)	R
Boston Col. (MA)	L	Grinnell (IA)	R
Bowdoin (ME)	R	Hamilton (NY)	R
Brandeis (MA)	R	Harvard (MA)	M
Brown (RI)	M	Harvey Mudd (CA)	S
▲ Bryn Mawr (PA)	S	Haverford (PA)	S
Bucknell (PA)	M	Holy Cross (MA)	R
Buffalo (SUNY) (NY)	L	Illinois, U. of (Urbana-Champagne)	XL
California Inst. of Tech.	S	Illinois Wesleyan	R
California, U. of (Berkeley)	XL	Iowa, U. of	XL
California, U. of (San Diego)	L	★ JOHNS HOPKINS (MD)	R
Carleton (MN)	R	Kalamazoo (MI)	R
Carnegie-Mellon (PA)	M	Kenyon (OH)	R
Case Western Reserve U. (OH)	R	Knox (IL)	R
Centre (KY)	S	Lafayette (PA)	R
Chicago, U. of (IL)	R	Lawrence (WI)	R
Claremont McKenna (CA)	S	Macalester (MN)	R
Clark (MA)	R	Miami, U. of (FL)	L
Colby (ME)	R	MIT (MA)	M
Colgate (NY)	R	Michigan, U. of	XL
Colorado Col.	R	Middlebury (VT)	R
Cornell (NY)	L	▲ Mount Holyoke (MA)	R
Dallas, U. of (TX)	R	New College (FL)	S
Dartmouth (NH)	M	New Jersey, College of	M
Davidson (NC)	R	North Carolina, U. of	L
Dickinson (PA)	M	Northwestern (IL)	M
Duke (NC)	R	Notre Dame (IN)	M
Emory (GA)	R	Oberlin (OH)	R
Fairfield (CT)	M		

GROUP I continues next page

PRE-MED/PRE-DENTAL, *continued*

GROUP I, *continued*

Occidental (CA) ....R	Tufts (MA) ....M
Pomona (CA) ....R	Tulane (LA) ....M
Princeton (NJ) ....M	Union (NY) ....R
Reed (OR).................................R	Ursinus (PA) ....R
Rhodes (TN).................................R	Vanderbilt (TN) ....M
Rice (TX).................................R	Villanova (PA) ....M
Rochester, U. of (NY) ....M	■ Wabash (IN) ....S
Rutgers (NJ) L	Wake Forest (NC) ....M
Skidmore (NY) ....R	Washington U. (MO) ....M
▲ Smith (MA) ....R	▲ Wellesley (MA) ....R
South, U. of the (TN) ....R	Wesleyan (CT) ....R
Southwestern (TX) ....R	Wheaton (IL) ....R
Stanford (CA) ....M	Whitman (WA) ....R
Stetson (FL) ....R	Willamette (OR) ....R
St. Mary's College of Maryland.............R	Williams (MA) ....R
St. Olaf (MN).................................R	William & Mary (VA)..................................M
Swarthmore (PA) ....S	Yale (CT) ....M
Trinity (CT).................................R	Yeshiva (NY) ....R
Trinity (TX) ....R	

GROUP II
Very Selective

Albertson (ID)................................S	Creighton (NE) ....R
Albright (PA)................................R	Delaware, U. of...L
Alma (MI)................................R	Denison (OH) ....R
Arizona State XL	Duquesne (PA)...M
Austin (TX) ....R	Earlham (IN) ....R
Baylor (TX)................................M	Eckerd (FL) ....R
Bethany (WY) ....S	Erskine (SC) ....S
Berry (GA) ....R	Florida State L
Birmingham-Southern (AL) ....R	Georgia, U. of XL
Butler (IN)................................R	Guilford (NC) ....R
California, U. of (Davis)................L	Hamline (MN) ....R
California, U. of (Irvine) ....M	■ Hampden-Sydney (VA) ....S
California, U. of (Riverside)................M	Heidelberg (OH)...R
California, U. of (Santa Cruz) ....M	Hendrix (AR) ....R
Carroll (WI) ....R	Hiram (OH)..R
Colorado, U. of................................L	Hobart & Wm. Smith (NY) ....R
Concordia (MN) ....R	*GROUP II continues next page*

GROUP II continues next page

Enrollment Code

S = Small (less than 1000 students)	M = Medium (3000-8000 students)	XL = Extra Large (over 20,000 students)
R = Moderate (1000-3000 students)	L = Large (8000-20,000 students)	

★ THE COUNSELORS' CHOICE ■ Men Only ▲ Women Only

PRE-MED/PRE-DENTAL, *continued*

GROUP II, *continued*

▲ Hood (MD) ....S	Presbyterian (SC) ....S
Hope (MI)..R	Randolph-Macon (VA)..............................R
Houghton (NY) ....S	▲ Randolph-Macon Woman's Col. (VA) ...S
Houston Baptist (TX) ....R	Regis (CO) ....R
Huntingdon (AL) ....S	Ripon (WI) ....S
Indiana U. XL	San Francisco, U. of (CA) ....M
Ithaca Col. (NY) ....M	Scranton, U. of (PA) ....M
Juniata (PA) ....R	▲ Scripps (CA) ....S
Kansas, U. of L	Siena (NY) ....R
Kansas State L	Spring Hill (AL) ....R
Kentucky, U. of L	St. John's (MN) ....R
Lake Forest (IL)..............................S	St. Louis (MO)...M
Lewis & Clark (OR) ....R	Saint Thomas, U. of (MN) ....S
Loyola (IL) ....M	Stetson (FL) ....R
Marquette (WI) ....M	Stony Brook (SUNY) (NY) L
Mary Washington (VA) ....R	Transylvania (KY).....................................S
Massachusetts, U. of L	Truman State (MO) ....M
Michigan State...............................XL	Texas A&M...XL
Minnesota, U. of (Morris) ....R	Vermont, U. of L
Morningside (IA)............................S	Washington & Jefferson (PA) ....S
Muhlenberg (PA) ....R	Washington, U. of XL
Nebraska Wesleyan........................R	▲ Wells (NY) ....S
New Hampshire, U. of L	Western Maryland ....R
New York U. L	Westminster (PA)......................................R
North Central (IL)..........................R	Westmont (CA)...R
Ohio State XL	Wheaton (MA) ....R
Ohio Wesleyan ....R	Wittenberg (OH) ....R
Pacific Lutheran (OR) ....R	Wofford (SC) ....R
Pennsylvania State XL	Wooster (OH) ....R
Pittsburgh, U. of (PA) L	Wyoming, U. of L

GROUP III
Selective

American International (MA) ....R	Mt. St. Mary's (MD) ....R
▲ Bennett (NC) ....S	▲ Spelman (GA) ....R
Blackburn (IL) ....S	St. Mary's (TX) ....R
Carroll (MT) ....R	St. Vincent (PA) ....R
Florida A&M.......................................M	Temple (PA) L
Florida Southern................................R	Thomas More (KY) ....S
Heidelberg (OH) ....S	Wartburg (IA) ....R
Jacksonville (FL) ....R	Wayne State (MI) L
Louisiana State XL	Xavier U. of Louisiana..............................R

PSYCHOLOGY

GROUP I
Most Selective

Allegheny (PA)..R	▲ Mount Holyoke (MA)...............................R
Amherst (MA)...R	New College (FL)..S
Bates (ME) ....R	New Jersey, College of ....M
Binghamton (SUNY) (NY) L	New York U. L
Boston U. (MA)..L	North Carolina, U. of...............................L
Brandeis (MA) ....R	Occidental (CA) ....R
▲ Bryn Mawr (PA) ....S	Pennsylvania, U. of..................................L
Bucknell (PA) ....M	Pitzer (CA) ....S
California, U. of (Berkeley).................XL	Reed (OR)..R
California, U. of (Los Angeles)............XL	Rhodes (TN)..R
California, U. of (San Diego) L	Rochester, U. of (NY) ....M
Carnegie-Mellon (PA) ....M	▲ Simmons (MA) ....R
Chicago, U. of (IL)....................................R	▲ Smith (MA) ....R
Claremont McKenna (CA) ....S	Southwestern (TX)....................................R
Colby (ME) ....R	★ STANFORD (CA) ....M
Connecticut Col..R	St. Mary's College of Maryland.............R
Drew (NJ) ....R	St. Olaf (MN)...R
Duke (NC) ....M	Swarthmore (PA) ....R
Emory (GA)..R	Tufts (MA) ....M
Furman (SC)...R	Union (NY) ....R
George Washington (DC) ....M	Vanderbilt (TN)..M
Gettysburg (PA) ....R	Vassar (NY) ....R
Grinnell (IA) ....R	Virginia, U. of..L
Gustavus Adolphus (MN) ....R	■ Wabash (IN) ....S
Harvard (MA) ....M	Wake Forest (NC) ....M
Haverford (PA) ....S	Wesleyan (CT)..R
Illinois, U. of (Urbana-Champagne)....XL	Whitman (WA) ....R
Kenyon (OH)...R	Willamette (OR)...R
Lafayette (PA) ....R	Williams (MA) ....R
Macalester (MN) ....R	Yale (CT)...M
Michigan, U. of XL	Yeshiva (NY)...M

PSYCHOLOGY continues next page

Enrollment Code

S = Small (less than 1000 students)	**M** = Medium (3000-8000 students)	**XL** = Extra Large (over 20,000 students)
R = Moderate (1000-3000 students)	**L** = Large (8000-20,000 students)	

★ **THE COUNSELORS' CHOICE**   ■ Men Only   ▲ Women Only

PSYCHOLOGY, *continued*

GROUP II
Very Selective

▲ Agnes Scott (GA) ....S
   Albany (SUNY) (NY) L
   Alfred (NY) ....R
   Arizona, U. of XL
   Beloit (WI) ....R
   Berry (GA) ....R
   Colorado State L
   California, U. of (Riverside).................M
   California, U. of (Santa Cruz) ....M
   Carroll (WI) ....R
   Clark (MA) ....R
   Colorado State L
   Concordia (MN) ....R
   Cornell Col. (IA) ....R
   Denison (OH)..R
   Denver, U. of (CO) ....M
   Earlham (IN) ....R
   Fairfield (CT)...M
   Florida Inst. of Tech.............................R
   Florida International L
   Florida State L
   George Mason (VA)..................................L
   Grand Valley (MI) L
   Hamline (MN)...R
   Hanover (IN) ....S
   Herbert Lehman (CUNY) (NY) L
   Hobart & Wm. Smith (NY) ....R
   Houghton (NY) ....S
   Hunter (CUNY) (NY) L
   Indiana U. XL
   Iowa, U. of..XL
   Lake Forest (IL)......................................S
   Lebanon Valley (PA)................................R
   Louisiana State U. L
   Loyola (IL) ....M
   Luther (IA) ....R
   Manhattanville (NY) ....R
   Marist (NY) ....M
   Mary Washington (VA) ....R
   Michigan State.......................................XL

▲ Mills (CA)...S
   Minnesota, U. of...................................XL
   New Paltz (SUNY) (NY) ....M
   North Carolina (Asheville)....................R
   Ohio U. L
   Oregon, U. of L
   Oswego (SUNY) (NY) ....M
   Pittsburgh, U. of (PA) L
   Queens (CUNY) (NY) L
   Randolph-Macon (VA)..............................R
   Roanoke (VA) ....R
▲ Randolph-Macon Woman's Col. (VA) ...S
   Rollins (FL) ....R
   Salisbury State (MD) ....M
   San Francisco, U. of (CA) ....M
   Santa Clara, U. of (CA) ....M
   Shepherd (WV) ....R
   Southern California L
   St. Lawrence (NY) ....R
   Stetson (FL) ....R
   Stonehill (MA) ....R
   Stony Brook (SUNY) (NY) L
▲ Sweet Briar (VA)......................................S
   Syracuse (NY)..L
   Texas, U. of (Austin)............................XL
   Tulsa, U. of (OK) ....R
   Virginia Poly. Inst..................................L
   Washington College (MD) ....S
   Washington & Jefferson (PA) ....S
   Washington, U. of XL
   Webster (MO) ....R
▲ Wells (NY) ....S
   Western Michigan L
   Westminster (MO) ....S
   Westmont (CA)..R
   Wheaton (MA) ....R
   Wisconsin, U. of XL
   Wittenberg (OH) ....R
   Wofford (SC) ....M

PSYCHOLOGY continues next page

Enrollment Code

S = Small (less than 1000 students)   **M** = Medium (3000-8000 students)   **XL** = Extra Large (over 20,000 students)
R = Moderate (1000-3000 students)   **L** = Large (8000-20,000 students)

★ THE COUNSELORS' CHOICE   ■ Men Only   ▲ Women Only

PSYCHOLOGY, *continued*

GROUP III
Selective

American International (MA) ....R	▲ Mary Baldwin (VA) ....S
Aquinas (MI)...R	Northern Arizona...............................L
Baker (KS) ....S	North Carolina (Wilmington) ....M
Bethel (MN) ....R	Otterbein (OH) ....R
Biola (CA) ....R	Ozarks, College of the (MO) ....R
Blackburn (IL) ....S	Pace (NY) ....M
Caldwell (NJ) ....S	Palm Beach Atlantic (FL).......................R
Canisius (NY) ....M	Purchase (SUNY) (NY) ....R
Carthage (WI) ....R	Regis (CO) ....R
▲ Cedar Crest (PA) ....S	Sacred Heart (CT) ....R
Chapman (CA) ....R	St. Joseph's (IN).................................S
Colorado, U. of (Colorado Springs) ......M	St. Vincent (PA) ....R
Elmira (NY) ....R	Seton Hall (NJ) ....M
Franciscan U. of Steubenville (OH) ....R	Sonoma State (CA) ....M
▲ Hollins (VA)..S	Taylor (IN) ....R
▲ Judson (AL) ....S	Virginia Commenwealth U. L
Lindenwood (MO) ....S	Virginia Wesleyan ....R
Longwood (VA) ....R	Western New England (MA)...................R
Lyon (AR)..S	Wyoming, U. of L
Manchester (IN) ....R	Xavier University of Louisiana ....R

RELIGIOUS STUDIES

GROUP I
Most Selective

Bates (ME) ....R	Lawrence (WI) ....R
Brown (RI) ....M	Northwestern (IL) ....M
California, U. of (Berkeley) XL	Oberlin (OH) ....R
Chicago, U. of (IL) ....M	Occidental (CA) ....R
Colgate (NY).............................R	Pomona (CA) ....R
Columbia (NY) ....M	Princeton (NJ) ....M
Dartmouth (NH) ....M	South, U. of the (TN) ....R
Davidson (NC)............................R	Stanford (CA) ....M
Dickinson (PA) ....R	Trinity (CT) ....R
Duke (NC) ....M	★ VIRGINIA, U. OF L
Emory (GA) ....R	Wake Forest (NC) ....M
Furman (SC)...............................R	▲ Wellesley (MA) ....R
Georgetown, (DC) ....M	Wesleyan (CT) ....R
Hamilton (NY) ....R	Wheaton (IL) ....R
Haverford (PA) ....S	William & Mary (VA) ....M
Kenyon (OH) ....R	Yale (CT)..................................M

GROUP II
Very Selective

Arizona State XL	Houghton (NY) ....S
Baylor (TX)................................M	Iowa, U. of................................XL
Birmingham-Southern (AL) ....R	Loyola (LA) ....M
Brigham Young (UT).....................XL	Roanoke (VA) ....R
California, U. of (Santa Barbara) L	Southern Methodist (TX) L
Catholic U. (DC) ....M	St. Bonaventure (NY)................R
Florida State L	Stony Brook (SUNY) (NY) L
Fordham (NY)..............................M	Texas Christian U. ....M
Gordon (MA) ....R	Westmont (CA)..........................R
Hendrix (AR) ....R	Whitworth (WA) ....R
Hiram (OH) ....R	Wooster (OH) ....R

GROUP III
Selective

Franciscan U. of Steubenville (OH) ....R	Taylor (IN) ....R
King (TN) ....S	▲ St. Catherine (MN) ....R
Milligan (TN)...............................S	Southwest Baptist (MO) ....R
Mississippi College ....R	Virginia Commonwealth U. L
Regis (CO) ....R	

Enrollment Code

S = Small (less than 1000 students)   M = Medium (3000-8000 students)   XL = Extra Large (over 20,000 students)
R = Moderate (1000-3000 students)   L = Large (8000-20,000 students)

★ THE COUNSELORS' CHOICE   ■ Men Only   ▲ Women Only

SOCIOLOGY

GROUP I
Most Selective

Amherst (MA)..R	Illinois, U. of (Urbana-Champaign) XL
▲ Bryn Mawr (PA) ....S	Kalamazoo (MI) ....R
California, U. of (Berkeley) XL	Michigan, U. of XL
California, U. of (Los Angeles) XL	North Carolina, U. of...............................L
★ CHICAGO, U. OF (IL) ....R	Northwestern (IL) ....M
Clarkson (NY) ....M	Oberlin (OH)..R
Columbia (NY) ....M	Pennsylvania, U. of..................................L
Dartmouth (NH) ....M	Pitzer (CA) ....S
Florida, U. of XL	Southwestern (TX)....................................R
Franklin & Marshall (PA) ....R	Stanford (CA) ....M
Gettysburg (PA) ....S	Wheaton (IL)..R

GROUP II
Very Selective

Asbury (KY) ....R	▲ Salem Col. (NC) ....S
Beloit (WI) ....R	St. Lawrence (NY)....................................R
Concordia (MN) ....R	St. Mary's Col. (CA) ....R
Cornell Col. (IA) ....R	Syracuse (NY)..L
Covenant (GA) ....S	▲ Trinity (DC)..S
Earlham (IN) ....R	▲ Wells (NY) ....S
Hamline (MN)...R	Westminster (PA)......................................R
Hendrix (AR) ....R	Western Maryland College......................R
Hofstra (NY) ....M	Western Washington U. L
Lewis & Clark (OR) ....R	Wheaton (MA)...R
Minnesota, U. of....................................XL	Winona State U. (MN) ....M
Moravian (PA) ....R	Wisconsin, U. of....................................XL
North Carolina (Asheville).....................R	Wooster (OH) ....R
Roanoke (VA)..R	

SOCIOLOGY continues next page

Enrollment Code

S = Small (less than 1000 students)   M = Medium (3000-8000 students)   XL = Extra Large (over 20,000 students)
R = Moderate (1000-3000 students)   L = Large (8000-20,000 students)

★ THE COUNSELORS' CHOICE   ■ Men Only   ▲ Women Only

SOCIOLOGY, *continued*

GROUP III
Selective

Adrian (MI) ....S	North Carolina, U. of (Wilmington) ......M
Belmont Abbey (NC) ....S	Northern Colorado L
Benedictine (KS) ....S	Quincy (IL) ....R
Biola (CA) ....R	▲ St. Catherine (MN) ....R
D'Youville (NY) ....R	San Francisco State (CA).................L
Fisk (TN)................................S	▲ Spelman (GA) ....R
George Fox (OR) ....S	St. Anselm (NH)..........................R
Hartwick (NY) ....R	St. Mary's U. of San Antonio (TX) ....R
Johnson C. Smith (NC) ....R	Temple (PA) L
Lenoir-Rhyne (NC) ....R	Virginia Wesleyan ....R
Lynchburg (VA) ....R	Wagner (NY)..............................R
▲ Mary Baldwin (VA) ....S	Whitman (WA) ....R
Massachusetts, U. of (Dartmouth) ....M	▲ Wilson (PA) ....S
Michigan State XL	

ZOOLOGY

GROUP I
Most Selective

California, U. of (Berkeley) XL
★ **CORNELL (NY)** ....**L**
Florida, U. of XL
Miami, U. of (OH) L

Michigan, U. of XL
North Carolina, U. of...............................L
Pennsylvania State XL
Wisconsin, U. of......................................XL

GROUP II
Very Selective

Albertson (ID) ....S
California, U. of (Davis).........................L
Connecticut, U. of L
Georgia, U. of L
Indiana U. XL
Iowa State XL
Kansas, U. of...L
Kentucky, U. of XL
Maryland, U. of XL

Massachusetts, U. of...............................L
North Carolina State L
Ohio U...L
Oklahoma, U. of L
Texas A&M XL
Vermont, U. of L
Washington State.....................................L
Washington, U. of XL

GROUP III
Selective

Colorado State L
Howard (DC)..M
Montana, U. of...M
Oregon State..L

Southern Illinois U. (Carbondale)...........L
Tennessee, U. of XL
Wyoming, U. of L

SECTION TWO

MISCELLANEOUS MAJORS

AFRO-AMERICAN STUDIES

Bates (ME)
California, U. of (Berkeley)
California, U. of (Santa Barbara)
Chicago, U. of (IL)
Columbia (NY)
Denison (OH)
Duke (NC)
Earlham (IN)
Emory (GA)
Harvard (MA)
Howard (DC)
Kalamazoo (MI)
Loyola Marymount (CA)
Luther (IA)
Mercer (GA)
New York U.
North Carolina (Chapel Hill)
Oberlin (OH)

Ohio State U.
Pennsylvania, U. of
Pomona (CA)
Princeton (NJ)
Rutgers (NJ)
San Diego State (CA)
San Francisco State (CA)
▲ Spelman (GA)
Stanford (CA)
Tuskegee University (AL)
Washington U. (MO)
▲ Wellesley (MA)
Wesleyan (CT)
Wooster (OH)
Wisconsin, U. of
Xavier (LA)
Yale (CT)

ALTERNATIVE COLLEGES *(see page ix)*

Antioch (OH)
Atlantic, College of the (ME)
Deep Springs (CA)
Eugene Lang (NY)
Evergreen (WA)
Hampshire (MA)

Marlboro (VT)
New College (FL)
St. John's (MD)
Shimer (IL)
Simon's Rock (MA)

ARCHAEOLOGY

Baylor (TX)
Brown (RI)
▲ Bryn Mawr (PA)
Cornell (NY)
Dartmouth (NH)
Evansville (IN)
Haverford (PA)
Hunter (CUNY) (NY)
Kansas, U. of

Michigan, U. of
Missouri, U. of
New York U.
Pennsylvania, U. of
Texas, U. of
Washington U. (MO)
Washington, U. of
Wheaton (IL)

ATMOSPHERIC SCIENCES

Albany (SUNY) (NY)
California, U. of (Davis)
Colorado State
Cornell (NY)
Florida Inst. of Tech.
Florida State
Hawaii
Iowa State
Kansas
Lyndon State (VT)
Massachusetts (Lowell)
Metropolitan State (CO)
North Carolina State

Northern Illinois
Oklahoma, U. of
Oneonta (SUNY) (NY)
Pennsylvania State
Purdue (IN)
San Jose State (CA)
St. Louis University (MO)
Texas A&M
Utah, U. of
Washington, U. of
Western Connecticut
Wisconsin, U. of

■ Men Only
▲ Women Only

AUDIOLOGY/SPEECH

Arizona	No. Colorado
Arizona State	Oklahoma
Boston U.	Purdue (IN)
California, U. of (Santa Barbara)	Rhode Island
Florida	S. Dakota, U. of
Florida State	SUNY-Buffalo
Geneseo (SUNY) (NY)	Tennessee
George Washington	Texas
Hawaii	Tulsa (OK)
Hofstra (NY)	Utah State
James Madison (VA)	Vanderbilt (TN)
Kansas	Washington, U. of
Longwood (VA)	Wayne State (MI)
Michigan State	Western Washington
Montana	Worcester State (MA)
Montevallo (AL)	Wisconsin
Nebraska	Wyoming

BUSINESS STATISTICS

Arizona State	Indiana U.
Baylor (TX)	New Hampshire College
Cleveland State (OH)	Pennsylvania State
Cornell (NY)	Tennessee, U. of
Illinois (Chicago)	Wright State (OH)
Illinois, U. of	

CERAMICS

Alfred (NY)	Maryland Inst. College of Art
California State U. (Long Beach)	Massachusetts College of Art
Cleveland Institute of Art (OH)	Otis/Parsons School of Art & Design (CA)
Clemson (SC)	Parsons School of Design (NY)
East Carolina (NC)	Rhode Island School of Design
Florida, U. of	Ringling School of Art & Design (FL)
Hartford, U. of (CT)	Temple (PA)
Iowa State	Washington, U. of
Illinois, U. of	
Kansas City Art Institute (MO)	

CINEMATOGRAPHY/FILM STUDIES

Boston U. (MA)	Kansas
Brooks Institute of Photography (CA)	Massachusetts College of Art
California, U. of (Berkeley)	Memphis State (TN)
California, U. of (Irvine)	New York U.
California, U. of (Santa Barbara)	Northwestern (IL)
California, U. of (Santa Cruz)	Pennsylvania State
California Institute of the Arts	Pittsburgh, U. of (PA)
Colorado, U. of	Purdue (IN)
Cincinnati, U. of (OH)	Rutgets (NJ)
Columbia (NY)	Santa Fe (NM)
Delaware, U. of	Southern California
Emerson (MA)	Texas, U. of
Florida State	Wayne State (MI)
Ithaca (NY)	Webster (MO)

■ Men Only
▲ Women Only

CREATIVE WRITING

Alabama, U. of	North Carolina State
Bard (NY)	Northwestern (IL)
Beloit (WI)	Oberlin (OH)
Bennington (VT)	Pittsburgh, U. of (PA)
Brown (RI)	Redlands (CA)
Carnegie Mellon (PA)	St. Andrews (NC)
Columbia (NY)	Santa Fe, College of (NM)
Creighton (NE)	Sarah Lawrence (NY)
Eckerd (FL)	▲ Stephens (MO)
Emerson (MA)	Susquehanna (PA)
Florida State	▲ Sweet Briar (VA)
Grinnell (IA)	Temple (PA)
Hamilton (NY)	Washington College (MD)
Iowa	Webster (MO)
Johns Hopkins (MD)	Wheaton (MA)
Michigan, U. of	Wittenberg (OH)

CRIMINAL JUSTICE

Albany (SUNY) (NY)	Massachusetts State College
Bowling Green (OH)	(Westfield)
California State U. (Fresno)	Mercy (NY)
California State U. (Fullerton)	Mercyhurst (PA)
California State U. (Los Angeles)	Michigan State
California State U. (Sacramento)	North Carolina (Chapel Hill)
California, U. of (Irvine)	North CarolinaWesleyan
Dayton, U. of (OH)	Northeastern (MA)
Delaware, U. of	No. Florida
Eastern Kentucky	Ohio Northern
Elmira (NY)	Regis (CO)
Florida Southern	Ripon (WI)
Florida State	Rowan (NJ)
George Washington (DC)	St. Edward's (TX)
Guilford (NC)	Salve Regina—The Newport
Indiana	College (RI)
Iona (NY)	St. John's (NY)
Kentucky Wesleyan	St. Leo (FL)
Loyola (LA)	San Diego State (CA)
Lycoming (PA)	Seton Hall (NJ)
Madonna (MI)	Southern Oregon
Mansfield (PA)	Wilmington (OH)
Marist (NY)	Youngstown State

DESIGN/COMMERCIAL ART

Alfred (NY)	Illinois Institute of Technology
Bradley (IL)	Illinois, U. of
Brigham Young (UT)	Kansas City Art Institute (MO)
Calif. Inst. of the Arts	Kendall Coll. of Art & Design
California State U. (Long Beach)	(MI)
California, U. of (Davis)	Maryland, U. of
California, U. of (Los Angeles)	Massachusetts College of Art
Columbia (IL)	Massachusetts, U. of
Cincinnati, U. of (OH)	(Dartmouth)
Cornish (WA)	Memphis College of Art
Drake (IA)	Moravian (PA)
Flagler (FL)	

■ Men Only
▲ Women Only

DESIGN/COMMERCIAL ART continues next page

DESIGN/COMMERCIAL ART, *CONTINUED*

Morningside (IA)
North Carolina State
North Florida, U. of
Ohio State
Otis Art Institute/Parsons (CA)
Parsons School of Design (NY)
Pratt Institute (NY)

Rhode Island School of Design
Rochester Inst. of Tech. (NY)
St. Mary's (MN)
Shepherd (WV)
Southern Illinois U.
Texas Christian
West Virginia Wesleyan

EAST ASIAN STUDIES

Bryn Mawr (PA)
Bucknell (PA)
California, U. of (San Diego)
Columbia (NY)
Cornell (NY)
DePauw (IN)
Furman (SC)
Harvard (MA)
Indiana
Lawrence (WI)
Lewis & Clark (OR)
Macalester (MN)
Manhattanville (NY)

Middlebury (VT)
Oberlin (OH)
Pennsylvania, U. of
Redlands (CA)
Stanford (CA)
Trinity (TX)
Ursinus (PA)
Vassar (NY)
Washington & Lee (VA)
Washington, U. of
▲ Wellesley (MA)
Wesleyan (CT)
Wittenberg (OH)

ENTREPRENEUR STUDIES

Arizona, U. of
Babson (MA)
Ball State U. (IN)
Baylor (TX)
Boise State U. (ID)
Colorado, U. of
Ferris State U. (MI)
Georgia, U. of
Indiana U.
Illinois

Kennesaw (GA)
Michigan
Muhlenberg (PA)
New York U.
Ohio University
Pennsylvania, U. of
Southern California, U. of
Texas, U. of
Washington & Jefferson (PA)

ENVIRONMENTAL STUDIES

Adelphi (NY)
Allegheny (PA)
Bethany (WV)
Bowdoin (ME)
Brown (RI)
▲ Bryn Mawr (PA)
California, U. of (Davis)
California, U. of (Irvine)
California, U. of (Riverside)
California, U. of (Santa Barbara)
California, U. of (Santa Cruz)
California State U. (Humboldt)
Centenary (LA)
Chicago, U. of (IL)
Clemson (SC)
Colby (ME)
Colorado, U. of
Cornell (NY)

Delaware Valley (PA)
Denison (OH)
Dickinson (PA)
Earlham (IN)
Eckerd (FL)
Findlay (OH)
Florida, U. of
Florida Institute of Technology
Harvard (MA)
Kalamazoo (MI)
Kentucky Wesleyan
Lake Forest (IL)
Macalester (MN)
Michigan, U. of
Michigan State
Middlebury (VT)
Millsaps (MS)

■ Men Only
▲ Women Only

ENVIRONMENTAL STUDIES continues next page

ENVIRONMENTAL STUDIES, *continued*

Minnesota, U. of
Monmouth (IL)
Moontreat (NC)
New Hampshire, U. of
New Mexico State
North Carolina (Asheville)
Northland (WI)
Oberlin (OH)
Ohio Wesleyan
Oregon State
Pennsylvania State
Pennsylvania, U. of
Pittsburgh (Bradford)
Pitzer (CA)
Ramapo (NJ)
Rutgers (NJ)
Sacred Heart (CT)
Santa Fe, College of (NM)
Sarah Lawrence (NY)
St. Lawrence (NY)

St. Michael's (VT)
San Francisco State (CA)
South Florida
Stanford (CA)
Stockton State (NJ)
SUNY Coll. of Env. Sci. &
  Forestry
Susquehanna (PA)
Tufts U. (MA)
Vermont, U. of
Washington State
Washington, U. of
Webster (MO)
Wesleyan (CT)
Western Washington
West Virginia Wesleyan
Whitman (WA)
Wisconsin, U. of (Stevens Point)
Wyoming, U. of
Yale (CT)

EQUESTRIAN STUDIES

Averett (VA)
Bluefield College (VA)
Centenary (NJ)
Colorado State
Findlay (OH)
Lake Erie (OH)

Otterbein (OH)
St. Andrews (NC)
▲ Stephens (MO)
Truman State (MO)
William Woods (MO)
▲ Wilson (PA)

FASHION DESIGN/MERCHANDISING

Arkansas, U. of
Auburn (AL)
Baylor (TX)
Bradley (IL)
Cincinnati (OH)
Delaware, U. of
Florida State
Indiana (PA)
Iowa State
Kent State (OH)
Madonna (MI)
▲ Meredith (NC)
New Hampshire College

Ohio U.
Philadelphia Col. Tex. & Sci. (PA)
Pratt (NY)
Purdue (IN)
Rhode Island School of Design
Rhode Island, U. of
Sanford (AL)
▲ Stephens (MO)
Texas Christian
Valparaiso (IN)
Vermont, U. of
Virginia Commonwealth
Wisconsin, U. of

HEALTH SERVICES ADMINISTRATION

Alfred (NY)
Appalachian State (NC)
Augustana (SD)
Baylor (TX)
Detroit Mercy (MI)
Eastern Michigan
Fisk (TN)
Herbert Lehman (CUNY) (NY)
Kentucky

Missouri, U. of
North Carolina (Chapel Hill)
Northeastern (MA)
Northern Michigan
Oregon State
Pennsylvania State
Providence College (RI)
Quinnipiac (CT)

■ Men Only
▲ Women Only

HEALTH SERVICES ADMIN. continues next page

HEALTH SERVICES ADMINISTRATION, *continued*

Saint Scholastica (MN)
Scranton (PA)
Stonehill (MA)

Washington, U. of
Winona State (MN)

HISPANIC STUDIES

Arizona, U. of
California, U. of (Berkeley)
California, U. of (Santa Barbara)
CUNY (Hunter)
Northridge State (CA)
Northwestern (IL)

Rutgers (NJ)
San Francisco State (CA)
Scripps (CA)
Sonoma State (CA)
Wheaton (MA)
Willamette (OR)

HOTEL AND RESTAURANT MANAGEMENT

Auburn (NY)
Cal Poly (Pomona)
Cornell (NY)
Delaware
Denver, U. of (CO)
Florida International U.
Florida Stat
Hawaii, U. of
Houston, U. of (TX)
Illinois, U. of
Iowa State
James Madison (VA)
Kansas State
Massachusetts, U. of
Michigan State

Nevada (Las Vegas)
New Hampshire College
New Hampshire, U. of
Niagara (NY)
Northern Arizona
Ohio U.
Penn State
Purdue (IN)
Rochester Inst. of Tech. (NY)
St. Leo (FL)
Texas Tech
Transylvania (KY)
Virginia Poly. Inst.
Washington State
Widener (PA)

HUMAN RESOURCES

American (DC)
Bethel (KS)
Boise State (ID)
Bowling Green (OH)
Cal Poly (Pomona)
Duquesne (PA)
Florida State
George Washington (DC)
Indiana U.
LeMoyne (NY)
Massachusetts, U. of (Dartmouth)
Muhlenberg (PA)

New Mexico, U. of
Northeastern (MA)
Ohio State
Ohio University
Rockhurst (MO)
Susquehanna (PA)
Washington & Jefferson (PA)
Wayne State (MI)
Wilmington (OH)
Winona State (MN)
Wisconsin (Milwaukee)

INDUSTRIAL ARTS

Berea (KY)
California (PA)
Cheyney (PA)
Clemson (SC)
Ferris State (MI)
Fitchburg (MA)
Idaho
Nebraska, U. of
Northern Illinois

Oswego (SUNY) (NY)
Pittsburgh, U. of (PA)
Purdue (IN)
Southern Illinois
Texas A&M
Western Michigan
Wisconsin, U. of (Stout)
Wyoming

■ Men Only
▲ Women Only

INTERNATIONAL RELATIONS/STUDIES

▲ Agnes Scott (GA)
Alma (MI)
American U. (DC)
Beloit (WI)
Boston U. (MA)
Brown (RI)
▲ Bryn Mawr (PA)
Bucknell (PA)
California State U. (Los Angeles)
California State U. (Sacramento)
California, U. of (Davis)
Claremont McKenna (CA)
Colby (ME)
Colgate (NY)
Colorado
Connecticut College
Dartmouth (NH)
Denison (OH)
DePaul (IL)
☎ Drake (IA)
☎ Eckerd (FL)
☎ Elizabethtown (PA)
☎ Elmira (NY)
Emory (GA)
☎ Florida International
George Washington (DC)
Georgetown (DC)
Goucher (MD)
Hamline (MN)
☎ Hawaii
☎ Hiram (OH)
Johns Hopkins (MD)
Juniata (PA)
☎ Illinois
Indiana
Kalamazoo (MI)
Kenyon (OH)
☎ Lenoir-Rhyne (NC)
Lewis & Clark (OR)
Macalester (MN)
Manhattanville (NY)
Miami, U. of (FL)
Middlebury (VT)
☎ Moravian (PA)
Mt. Holyoke (MA)

Mt. St. Mary's (MD)
Nebraska
North Carolina (Chapel Hill)
Oglethorpe (GA)
Ohio Wesleyan
Pacific, U. of the (CA)
Pennsylvania, U. of
Pepperdine (CA)
Pittsburgh, U. of
Pitzer (CA)
Pomona (CA)
Princeton (NJ)
▲ Randolph-Macon Woman's Col.
   (VA)
Redlands (CA)
Rhodes (TN)
☎ Rochester Inst. of Tech. (NY)
San Diego, U. of (CA)
☎ Santa Clara U. (CA)
Scranton, U. of (PA)
▲ Scripps (CA)
☎ South Carolina, U. of
Southwestern (TX)
Spring Hill (AL)
☎ St. Andrews (NC)
▲ St. Catherine (MN)
☎ St. Mary's (MN)
☎ St. Norbert (WI)
St. Olaf (MN)
▲ Sweet Briar (VA)
▲ Trinity (DC)
Tufts (MA)
Tulane (LA)
U. S. Air Force Academy (CO)
U. S. Military Academy (NY)
Vassar (NY)
Washington College (MD)
Westminster (MO)
Wheaton (MA)
Whittier (CA)
William & Mary (VA)
Wisconsin, U. of
Wittenberg (OH)
          ☎ *International Business*

JAPANESE STUDIES

Bucknell (PA)
California, U. of (Los Angeles)
California, U. of (Santa Barbara)
Earlham (IN)
Georgetown (DC)
Hawaii, U. of
Macalester (MN)

Minnesota, U. of
North Central (IL)
Pacific, U. of the (CA)
San Francisco State (CA)
Stanford (CA)
Washington, U. of
Washington U. (MO)

■ Men Only
▲ Women Only

JAZZ

Arizona State
Arizona, U. of
Auburn (AL)
Augustana (IL)
Bennington College (VT)
Berklee College of Music (MA)
California State U. (Los Angeles)
Cincinnati
Delaware
DePaul U. (IL)
Duquesne U. (PA)
Five Towns College (NY)
Hampshire College (MA)
Hartford (CT)
Iowa
Indiana U. (PA)
Loyola U. (New Orleans) (LA)
Manhattan School of Music (NY)
Mannes College of Music (NY)

Marlboro College (VT)
Miami (FL)
New England Conservatory of
   Music (MA)
New York U. (NY)
North Florida
North Texas
Oberlin College (OH)
Ohio State U. (OH)
Rochester (NY)
Rutgers (NJ)
Shenandoah U. (VA)
Temple U. (PA)
Tennessee
Washington, U. of
Webster U. (MO)
Western Michigan U.
Westfield State (MA)

MARINE SCIENCE

Barry (FL)
California State U. (Long Beach)
California State U. (Sonoma)
California U. of (Santa Barbara)
California U. of (Santa Cruz)
College of Charleston (SC)
Eckerd (FL)
Florida Inst. of Technology
Jacksonville U. (FL)
Juniata (PA)
Long Island U. (Southampton)
   (NY)
Miami, U. of (FL)

New College (FL)
North Carolina, U. of
   (Wilmington)
Occidental (CA)
South Carolina, U. of
Spring Hill (AL)
Tampa, U. of (FL)
Texas A&M
Texas A&M (Galveston)
U. S. Coast Guard Academy (CT)
Washington, U. of
Wittenberg (OH)

MEDICAL TECHNOLOGY

Bradley (IL)
Buffalo (SUNY) (NY)
California State U. (Bakersfield)
California, U. of (Davis)
Case Western Reserve U. (OH)
Creighton (NE)
Detroit Mercy (MI)
Florida State
Florida, U. of
▲ Hood (MD)
Humboldt (CA)
Maine, U. of
▲ Mary Baldwin (VA)
Mercy (NY)
Miami U. (OH)
Michigan State

Minnesota, U. of
Moravian (PA)
North Carolina (Chapel Hill)
North Dakota State
North Dakota, U. of
Northeastern (MA)
Quinnipiac (CT)
St. Leo (FL)
▲ St. Mary's (IN)
San Francisco State (CA)
Texas Tech
Virginia Commonwealth
Washington & Jefferson (PA)
Washington, U. of
Wisconsin, U. of

■ Men Only
▲ Women Only

NAVAL ARCHITECTURE

California Maritime Academy
Iowa State
Michigan, U. of
Texas A&M (Galveston)
U. S. Coast Guard Academy (CT)

U. S. Merchant Marine Academy (NY)
U. S. Naval Academy
Webb Institute (NY)
Wisconsin, U. of

OCCUPATIONAL THERAPY

Boston U. (MA)
Buffalo (SUNY) (NY)
Colorado State
Elizabethtown (PA)
Florida, U. of
Kansas, U. of
Minnesota, U. of
Misericordia, College (PA)
New England, U. of (ME)
New Hampshire, U. of
New York University

North Dakota, U. of
Ohio State
St. Ambrose (IA)
▲ St. Catherine (MN)
San Jose State (CA)
▲ Texas Woman's
Tufts (MA)
Utica College (NY)
Washington U. (MO)
Wayne State (MI)
Western Michigan

PARKS AND RECREATION SERVICES

Arizona State
Aurora (IL)
Ball State (IN)
Bowling Green (OH)
California Poly (Pomona)
California State (Chico)
California State (Fresno)
Catawba (NC)
Clemson (SC)
Colorado State
Delaware, U. of
Florida International
Florida State
Idaho
Illinois, U. of
Indiana U.
Kansas State
Longwood (VA)
Maine, U. of

Michigan State
Minnesota
Montana
North Carolina State
Northern Arizona
Ohio U.
Pennsylvania State
Pepperdine (CA)
Pfeiffer (NC)
Purdue (IN)
Shepherd (WV)
Slippery Rock (PA)
Springfield College (MA)
Texas A&M
Virginia Wesleyan
Western Washington
Wingate (NC)
Winona State (MN)
Wisconsin (Stevens Point)

PHYSICAL EDUCATION

Bemidji State (MN)
California, U. of (Santa Barbara)
Colorado, U. of
Colorado State
Cortland State (NY)
Elon (NC)
Florida State
Iowa, U. of
Ithaca (NY)
Johnson C. Smith (NC)
Linfield (OR)
Maine, U. of
Michigan State

Monmouth (IL)
North Carolina, U. of
Norwich (VT)
Oberlin (OH)
Occidental (CA)
Pacific U. (OR)
Pennsylvania State
Purdue (IN)
Rockford (L)
▲ Simmons (MA)
Slippery Rock (PA)
Springfield (MA)

■ Men Only
▲ Women Only

PHYSICAL EDUCATION. continues next page

PHYSICAL EDUCATION, *continued*

Texas, U. of
Ursinus (PA)
Washington State

Westmont (CA)
William & Mary (VA)
Wisconsin (LaCrosse)

PHYSICAL THERAPY

American International (MA)
Boston U. (MA)
Buffalo (SUNY) (NY)
California State U. (Long Beach)
California State U. (Fresno)
Colorado, U. of
Connecticut, U. of
D'Youville (NY)
Daemen (NY)
Duquesne (PA)
Evansville (IN)
Florida, U. of
Grand Valley (MI)
Hunter (CUNY) (NY)
Ithaca (NY)
Kentucky, U. of
Louisville, U. of (KY)
Marquette (WI)
Maryville (St. Louis) (MO)
Miami, U. of (FL)
Misericordia, College
Montana, U. of
Mt. St. Mary's (CA)
Nebraska, U. of
New England, U. of (ME)
Northeastern (MA)

Northwestern (IL)
Oakland (MI)
Ohio University
Pacific U. (OR)
Philadelphia College of Pharmacy & Science
Pittsburgh, U. of (PA)
Puget Sound (WA)
Quinnipiac (CT)
Rockhurst (MO)
Sage Colleges (NY)
Saint Scholastica (MN)
Scranton, U. of (PA)
Seton Hall (NJ)
▲ Simmons (MA)
Slippery Rock (PA)
Southern Oregon
Southwest Texas State
Springfield College (MA)
Temple (PA)
Texas Tech
▲ Texas Woman's
Vermont, U. of
Washington U. (MO)
Wisconsin, U. of

PRE-VETERINARY

Auburn (AL)
Clemson (SC)
Evansville, U. of (IN)
Fort Lewis (CO)
Humboldt State (CA)
Idaho, U. of
Kansas State
Lawrence (WI)
Loyola (CA)
Maryland, U. of
Michigan State
Minnesota, U. of
Montana, U. of
Moravian (PA)
Muskingham (OH)
Nevada, U. of (Reno)
New Hampshire, U. of
New Mexico State

Northland (WI)
Oklahoma State
Purdue (IN)
▲ Russell Sage (The Sage Colleges) (NY)
▲ Salem (NC)
Southern Mississippi, U. of
Susquehanna (PA)
Tennessee, U. of
Utah State
Virginia Wesleyan
Washington & Jefferson (PA)
Washington State
West Virginia Wesleyan
Wilmington (OH)
Wingate (NC)
Winona State (MN)

■ Men Only
▲ Women Only

SOCIAL AND REHABILITATION SERVICES

Arizona, U. of
Assumption (MA)
Auburn (AL)
Boston U. (MA)
California State (Los Angeles)
Florida State
Gustavus Adolphus (MN)
Iowa, U. of
Louisiana State

Northern Colorado
North Texas
Ohio State
South Florida, U. of
Springfield College (MA)
Texas, U. of (Austin)
Virginia Commonwealth
Wisconsin
Wright State (OH)

SOCIAL WORK

Augsburg (MN)
Baylor (TX)
Bemidji State (MN)
Colorado State
Cornell (NY)
Gordon (MA)
Humboldt State (CA)
Illinois College
Juniata (PA)
Madonna (MI)
Marquette (WI)
Michigan State
Michigan, U. of
New York University
North Carolina State
Penn State

Pittsburgh, U. of (PA)
Radford (VA)
Sacred Heart (CT)
St. Louis (MO)
St. Olaf (MN)
Shepherd (WV)
Shippensburg, U. of (PA)
South Florida, U. of
Tennessee, U. of
Vermont, U. of
Washington U. (MO)
Washington, U. of
Wayne State (MI)
Western New England (MA)
Wisconsin, U. of

SPECIAL EDUCATION

Adelphi (NY)
American International (MA)
Arkansas
Arizona State
Augustana (SD)
Boston U. (MA)
California State (Chico)
California State (Sonoma)
California State (Stanislaus)
Connecticut, U. of
Curry (MA)
Denver, U. of (CO)
Eastern Montana
Flagler (FL)
Florida State
Geneseo (SUNY) (NY)
Hofstra (NY)
Kansas, U. of
Landmark College (VT)
Lenoir-Rhyne (NC)
Lesley (MA)

Loyola (MD)
Maine, U. of (Farmington)
Marygrove (MI)
Maryland, U. of
Muskingum (OH)
Nebraska
Northern Colorado, U. of
Pacific, U. of (CA)
Penn State
Rhode Island College
Rowan (NJ)
▲ Simmons (MA)
Southern Illinois U.
   (Carbondale)
Texas, U. of
Texas Christian
Toledo (OH)
Virginia, U. of
Wisconsin, U. of (Oshkosh)
Wyoming, U. of

■ Men Only
▲ Women Only

SPORTS MEDICINE

Adelphi (NY)
Castleton (VT)
Catawba (NC)
Charleston, U. of (WV)
Colorado State
Denver, U. of (CO)
Guilford (NC)
Heidelberg (OH)
Indiana U.
Manhattan (NY)
Marietta (OH)
Mercyhurst (PA)
New Mexico State
Occidental (CA)

Ohio Northern
Otterbein (OH)
Pacific, U. of the (CA)
Pepperdine (CA)
Radford (VA)
St. Andrews (NC)
Salisbury State (MD)
Sanford (AL)
Springfield (MA)
West Virginia Wesleyan
Wilmington (OH)
Wingate (NC)
Winona State (MN)

SPORTS SCIENCES

Alabama, U. of
Averett (VA)
Bowling Green (OH)
Connecticut, U. of
Denver, U. of (CO)
Florida Southern
Guilford (NC)
Husson (ME)
Incarnate Word (TX)
Indiana U.
Kansas, U. of
Massachusetts, U. of
Mount Union (OH)
Ohio Northern
Pfeiffer (NC)

Robert Morris (PA)
Rutgers (NJ)
Seton Hall (NJ)
Shepherd (WV)
South Carolina, U. of
Springfield (MA)
St. John's (NY)
St. Leo (FL)
St. Thomas U. (FL)
Stetson (FL)
Temple (PA)
Tennessee
Western New England (MA)
Wingate (NC)

URBAN STUDIES

Arizona State
Augburg (MN)
Boston U. (MA)
Brown (RI)
Buffalo (SUNY) (NY)
California (San Diego)
Case Western Reserve (OH)
Columbia (NY)
Cornell (NY)
Evansville (IN)
Georgia State
Lake Forest (IL)
Macalester (MN)
Maryland, U. of
Michigan State
New York U.
North Carolina (Greensboro)
Pennsylvania, U. of

Pittsburgh, U. of
Rockford (IL)
Rutgers (NJ)
St. Louis (MO)
Seattle Pacific (WA)
Shippensburg (PA)
Stanford (CA)
Tennessee (Knoxville)
Trinity (TX)
Virginia Commonwealth
Virginia Poly
Washington U. (MO)
Wayne State (MI)
Western Washington
Wooster (OH)
Worcester State (MA)
Wright State (OH)

■ Men Only
▲ Women Only

WOMEN'S STUDIES

Arizona, U. of	▲ Mt. Holyoke (MA)
Bates (ME)	Northwestern (IL)
Bowling Green (OH)	Pennsylvania, U. of
Brown (RI)	Pitzer (CA)
California, U. of (Berkeley)	Portland State (OR)
California, U. of (Santa Barbara)	Rochester, U. of (NY)
California, U. of (Santa Cruz)	Rollins (FL)
Carleton (MN)	Sarah Lawrence (NY)
Chicago, U. of (IL)	▲ Simmons (MA)
Colorado, U. of	▲ Smith
DePauw (IN)	Southern California
Emory (GA)	▲ Spelman (GA)
Florida, U. of	Stanford (CA)
Goucher (MD)	Tennessee, U. of
Harvard (MA)	Texas, U. of
Hobart & William Smith (NY)	Vanderbilt (TN)
Kalamazoo (MI)	Washington U. (MO)
Macalester (MN)	Washington, U. of
Michigan, U. of	▲ Wellesley (MA)
Middlebury (VT)	Wheaton (MA)
▲ Mills (CA)	Wooster (OH)

■ Men Only
▲ Women Only

SECTION THREE

AVERAGE SAT-1 TOTAL
RECOMMENDED MAJORS

ADELPHI COLLEGE (NY) 1050
Ed, Nurs, Physics

ADRIAN COLLEGE (MI) 1035
Ed, English, Poli Sci, Pre-Law, Soc

AGNES SCOTT COLLEGE (GA) 1160
Art, Econ, English, For Lang, Hist, Pre-Law, Psych

ALABAMA, UNIVERSITY OF (AL) 1065
Bus Admin, Engine, Geol, Hist

ALASKA, UNIVERSITY OF (ANCHORAGE) (AK) 1063
Bus Admin, Ed

ALASKA, UNIVERSITY OF (FAIRBANKS) (AK) 1070
Bus Admin, Drama, Nurs

ALBANY COLLEGE OF PHARMACY (NY) 1140
Pharm, Pre-Law, Pre-Med/Pre-Dental

ALBERTSON COLLEGE (ID) 1135
Bio, Bus Admin, Chem, Ed, Pre-Med/Pre-Dental, Zoo

ALBION COLLEGE (MI) 1185
Econ, English, Hist, Math, Pre-Law

ALBRIGHT COLLEGE (PA) 1060
Biochem, Bio, Bus Admin, Poli Sci, Pre-Law, Pre-Med/Pre-Dental

ALFRED UNIVERSITY (NY) 1190
Bus Admin, Ed, Engine, English, Pre-Law, Psych

ALLEGHENY COLLEGE (PA) 1195
Bio, Comp Sci, Econ, Geol, Hist, Philo, Pre-Law, Pre-Med/Pre-Dental, Psych

ALLENTOWN COLLEGE (PA) 1040
Drama

ALMA COLLEGE (MI) 1170
Art, Bio, Bus Admin, Chem, Comp Sci, Ed, Hist, Pre-Law, Pre-Med/Pre-Dental

AMERICAN ACADEMY OF DRAMATIC ARTS (NY) 1205
Drama

AMERICAN INTERNATIONAL COLLEGE (MA) 1025
Bus Admin, Pre-Med/Pre-Dental, Psych

AMERICAN UNIVERSITY (DC) 1200
Amer St, Bus Admin, Econ, Communic, Math, Poli Sci, Pre-Law

AMHERST COLLEGE (MA) 1365
*Amer St, Bio, Chem, Drama, Econ, English, Geol, Hist, Physics, Poly Sci, Pre-Law,
Pre-Med/Pre-Dental, Psych, Soc*

APPALACHIAN STATE UNIVERSITY (NC) 1099
Bus Admin, Communic, Ed

AQUINAS COLLEGE (MI) **1050**
Psych

ARIZONA, UNIVERSITY OF (AZ) **1100**
*Ag, Amer St, Anthro, Arch, Art, Astro, Bus Admin, Communic, Ed, Engin, English,
Forest, Geol, Pre-Law, Psych*

ARIZONA STATE UNIVERSITY (AZ) **1080**
Arch, Art, Bus Admin, Communic, Comp Sci, Ed, Engine, Home Ec, Math, Nurs, Pre-Med

ARKANSAS, UNIVERSITY OF (AR) **1070**
Ag, Arch, Bus Admin, Communic, Ed, Engine, English, Music, Pre-Law

ART CENTER COLLEGE OF DESIGN (CA) **1100**
Art

ASBURY COLLEGE (KY) **1100**
Bus Admin, Philo, Soc

AUBURN UNIVERSITY (AL) **1170**
Ag, Arch, Art, Ed, Engine, Forest

AUGSBURG COLLEGE (MN) **1040**
Communic, Ed

AUGUSTANA COLLEGE (IL) **1150**
Art, Bus Admin, Ed, Music

AUGUSTANA COLLEGE (SD) **1105**
Ed, Nurs

AUSTIN COLLEGE (TX) **1140**
Bus Admin, Ed, Poly Sci, Pre-Med/Pre-Dental

AVERETT COLLEGE (VA) **1075**
Ed

AZUSA PACIFIC (CA) **925**
Bus Admin, Nurs

BABSON COLLEGE (MA) **1150**
Bus Admin

BAKER UNIVERSITY **1075**
Bus Admin, Psych

BALDWIN-WALLACE COLLEGE (OH) **1075**
Busis Admin, Ed, English, Music, Pre-Law

BARD COLLEGE (NY) **1270**
Art, Drama, English, Music, Pre-Law

BARRY UNIVERSITY (FL) **1115**
Bus Admin, Drama

BATES COLLEGE (ME) **1340**
*Art, Bio, Chem, Econ, Geol, Hist, Math, Philo, Physics, Pre-Law, Pre-Med/Pre-Dental, Psych,
Rel Stu*

BAYLOR UNIVERSITY (TX) 1145
Bus Admin, Chem, Drama, Ed, English, Hist, Nurs, Pre-Law, Pre-Med/Pre-Dental, Reli Stu

BELHAVEN COLLEGE (MS) 1099
Art, Music

BELLARMINE COLLEGE (KY) 1099
Nurs

BELMONT ABBEY COLLEGE (NC) 1099
Bus Admin, Poli Sci, Pre-Law, Soc

BELMONT UNIVERSITY (TN) 1099
Music

BELOIT COLLEGE (WI) 1199
Anthro, Biochem, Classics, Drama, English, For Lang, Geol, Physics, Psych, Soc

BEMIDJI STATE UNIVERSITY (MN) 1035
Communic

BENEDICTINE COLLEGE (KS) 1025
Bus Admin, Soc

BENNETT COLLEGE (NC) 1000
Bus Admin, Ed, Pre-Law, Pre-Med/Pre-Dental

BENNINGTON COLLEGE (VT) 1199
Drama, English, Pre-Law

BENTLEY COLLEGE (MA) 1120
Bus Admin

BEREA COLLEGE (KY) 1050
Ag, Ed, Home Ec, Nurs

BERRY COLLEGE (GA) 1150
Bio, Ed, Forest, Pre-Med/Pre-Dental, Psych

BETHANY COLLEGE (WV) 1099
Bio, Communic, Drama, Ed, For Lang, Music, Pre-Med/Pre-Dental

BETHEL COLLEGE (MN) 1070
Bus Admin, Ed, Nurs, Psych

BIOLA UNIVERSITY (CA) 1090
Philo, Psych, Soc

BIRMINGHAM-SOUTHERN COLLEGE (AL) 1180
Art, Bus Admin, Chem, Ed, English, Hist, Math, Music, Pre-Law, Pre-Med/Pre-Dental, Reli Stu

BLACKBURN COLLEGE (IL) 1000
Bio, Pre-Med/Pre-Dental, Psych

BLOOMSBURG UNIVERSITY (PA) 1085
Art, Ed

BLUFFTON COLLEGE (OH) 1055
Bus Admin

BOSTON COLLEGE (MA) 1270
Bio, Bus Admin, English, For Lang, Hist, Nurs, Philo, Pre-Med/Pre-Dental

BOSTON CONSERVATORY OF MUSIC (MA) 1050
Music

BOSTON UNIVERSITY (MA) 1255
Art, Astro, Bus Admin, Communic, Drama, Econ, Ed, Engine, Hist, Music, Philo, Physics,
Poli Sci, Pre-Law, Psych

BOWDOIN COLLEGE (ME) 1330
Art Hist, Biochem, Bio, Chem, Econ, English, For Lang, Geol, Hist, Math, Music, Philo,
Pre-Law, Pre-Med/Pre-Dental

BOWLING GREEN STATE UNIVERSITY (OH) 1050
Art, Bus Admin, Ed, Music

BRADLEY UNIVERSITY (IL) 1150
Comp Sci, Engine

BRANDEIS UNIVERSITY (MA) 1300
Anthro, Biochem, Bio, Comp Sci, Drama, Econ, English, Hist, Music, Poli Sci, Pre-Law,
Pre-Med/Pre-Dental

BRIGHAM YOUNG UNIVERSITY (UT) 1195
For Lang, Home Ec, Reli Stu

BROWN UNIVERSITY (RI) 1345
Art, Art Hist, Bio, Biochem, Chem, Classics, Comp Sci, Engine, For Lang, Geol, Hist, Poli Sci,
Pre-Law, Pre-Med/Pre-Dental, Reli Stu

BRYANT COLLEGE (RI) 1100
Bus Admin

BRYN MAWR COLLEGE (PA) 1320
Art, Art Hist, Bio, Chem, Classics, Econ, English, For Lang, Geol, Hist, Physics, Pre-Law,
Pre-Med/Pre-Dental, Psych, Soc

BUCKNELL UNIVERSITY (PA) 1265
Bio, Bus Admin, Chem, Ed, Engine, Hist, Math, Music, Philo, Pre-Med/Pre-Dental, Psych, Soc

BUENA VISTA COLLEGE (IA) 1120
Communic, Ed

BUTLER UNIVERSITY (IN) 1135
Bus Admin, Communic, Drama, Ed, Music, Pharm, Pre_Law, Pre-Med/Pre-Dental

CALDWELL COLLEGE (NJ) 1050
Bus Admin, Ed, Psych

CALIFORNIA INSTITUTE OF THE ARTS (CA) 1100
Art, Music

CALIFORNIA INSTITUTE OF TECHNOLOGY (CA) 1480
Astro, Bio, Chem, Engine, Geol, Math, Physics, Pre-Med/Pre-Dental

CALIFORNIA, UNIVERSITY OF, AT
       BERKELEY 1295
       Anthro, Arch, Biochem, Bot, Bus Admin, Chem, Comp Sci, Engine, English,
       For Lang, Forest, Geol, Hist, Math, Music, Philo, Physics, Pre-Law,
       Pre-Med/Pre-Dental, Psych, Reli Stu, Soc, Zoo
       DAVIS 1150
       Ag, Bio, Biochem, Bot, Chem, Engine, English, Geol, Hist, Home, Ec, Poli Sci,
       Pre-Law, Pre-Med/Pre-Dental, Zoo
       IRVINE 1130
       Art, Bio, Comp Sci, Drama, Engine, Math, Physics, Pre-Med/Pre-Dental
       LOS ANGELES 1230
       Art Hist, Astro, Bio, Biochem, Communic, Comp Sci, Drama, Econ, Engine, English,
       For Lang, Geog, Hist, Math, Music, Philo, Poli Sci, Pre-Law, Psych, Soc
       RIVERSIDE 1100
       Art Hist, Biochem, Bio, Bot, Engine, Math Music, Poli Sci, Pre-Law,
       Pre-Med/Pre-Dental, Psych
       SAN DIEGO 1210
       Amer Stu, Biochem, Bio, Chem, Econ, Engine, Math, Music, Physics, Poly Sci,
       Pre-Law,
       Pre-Med/Pre-Dental, Psych
       SANTA BARBARA 1105
       Art, Art Hist, Bus Admin, Classics, Comp Sci, Ed, Engine, For Lang, Geog, Geol,
       Music, Physics, Poli Sci, Pre-Law, Reli Stu, Zoo
       SANTA CRUZ 1150
       Amer Stu, Anthro, Bio, Chem, Math, Music, Physics, Pre-Med/Pre-Dental, Psych

CALIFORNIA MARITIME ACADEMY (CA) 1100
Engine

CALIFORNIA POLYTECHNIC UNIVERSITY AT SAN LUIS OBISPO (CA) 1140
Ag, Arch, Bus Admin, Comp Sci, Communic, Engine, English, Poli Sci

CALIFORNIA STATE UNIVERSITY, AT:
       CHICO 1000
       Comp Sci, Geog, Nurs
       FULLERTON 1000
       Bus Admin, Communic
       LONG BEACH 1000
       Art, Communic
       SAN JOSE 1050
       Art

CALVIN COLLEGE (MI) 1135
Ed, Engine, English, For Lang, Hist, Pre-Law

CANISIUS COLLEGE 1080
Bus Admin, Psych

CAPITAL UNIVERSITY (OH) 1100
Bus Admin, Ed, Music, Nurs

CARLETON COLLEGE (MN) 1335
Bio, Chem, Drama, English, For Lang, Geol, Hist, Math, Physics, Pre-Law, Pre-Med/Pre-Dental

CARNEGIE MELLON UNIVERSITY (PA) 1300
Arch, Art, Bus Admin, Chem, Comp Sci, Drama, Engine, Music, Pre-Med/Pre-Dental, Psych

CARROLL COLLEGE (WI) 1100
Chem, Ed, Nurs, Pre-Med/Pre-Dental, Psych

CARROLL COLLEGE (MT) 1070
Bio, Nurs, Pre-Med/Pre-Dental

CARTHAGE COLLEGE (WI) 1080
Bus Admin, Psych

CASE WESTERN RESERVE UNIVERSITY (OH) 1300
*Art Hist, Astro, Bus Admin, Chem, Comp Sci, Engine, Math, Music, Nurs, Physics,
Pre-Med/Pre-Dental*

CATAWBA COLLEGE (NC) 1000
Bus Admin, Comp Sci, Ed

CATHOLIC UNIVERSITY OF AMERICA (DC) 1160
Arch, Classics, Drama, Engine, For Lang, Music, Nurs, Reli Stu

CEDAR CREST COLLEGE (PA) 1075
Nurs, Psych

CEDARVILLE COLLEGE (OH) 1099
Bus Admin, Ed

CENTENARY COLLEGE OF LOUISIANA (LA) 1140
Bus Admin, Chem, Ed, Geol

CENTRAL COLLEGE OF IOWA (IA) 1120
Comp Sci, Ed, For Lang

CENTRAL FLORIDA, UNIVERSITY OF (FL) 1100
Comp Sci, Communic, Engine

CENTRAL MICHIGAN UNIVERSITY (MI) 1000
Ed, Home Ec

CENTRAL WASHINGTON UNIVERSITY 1000
Music

CENTRE COLLEGE (KY) 1100
Chem, Econ, Physics, Poli Sci, Pre-Law, Pre-Med/Pre-Dental

CHAPMAN UNIVERSITY (CA) 1090
Bus Admin, Communic, Psych

CHARLESTON, COLLEGE OF (SC) 1080
Ed

CHARLESTON, UNIVERSITY OF (WV) 1045
Hist

CHATHAM COLLEGE (PA) 1080
Art, Bus Admin, Poli Sci, Pre-Law

CHESTNUT HILL COLLEGE (PA) 1075
English, Pre-Law

CHICAGO, UNIVERSITY OF (IL) 1340
*Anthro, Art Hist, Bio, Classics, Econ, English, Geog, Geol, Hist, Math, Philo, Physics, Poli Sci,
Pre-Law, Pre-Med/Pre-Dental, Psych, Reli Stu, Soc*

CHRISTIAN BROTHERS COLLEGE (TN) 1105
Bus Admin, Engine

CINCINNATI, UNIVERSITY OF (OH) 1110
Engine, Math

CLAREMONT MCKENNA COLLEGE (CA) 1340
Bio, Bus Admin, Econ, English, Hist, Philo, Poli Sci, Pre-Law, Pre-Med/Pre-Dental, Psych

CLARK UNIVERSITY (MA) 1160
Bus Admin, For Lang, Geog, Music, Pre-Law, Pre-Med/Pre-Dental, Psych

CLARKE COLLEGE (IA) 1115
Comp Sci

CLARKSON UNIVERSITY (NY) 1200
Bus Admin, Engine, Soc

CLEMSON UNIVERSITY (SC) 1110
Ag, Arch, Bus Admin, Comp Sci, Engine, Forest

CLEVELAND INSTITUTE OF MUSIC (OH) 1200
Music

COE COLLEGE (IA) 1155
Bus Admin, Ed, Hist, Music

COLBY COLLEGE (ME) 1290
Bio, Bus Admin, Econ, English, For Lang, Poli Sci, Pre-Law, Pre-Med/Pre-Dental, Psych

COLGATE UNIVERSITY (NY) 1300
*Bio, Chem, English, Geog, Geol, Hist, Math, Philo, Poli Sci, Pre-Law, Pre-Med/Pre-Dental,
Reli Stu*

COLORADO COLLEGE (CO) 1250
Bio, English, Geol, Hist, Philo, Pre-Law, Pre-Med/Pre-Dental

COLORADO, UNIVERSITY OF (CO) 1170
*Anthro, Astro, Biochem, Chem, Communic, Engine, Geog, Geol, Math, Music, Nurs, Physics,
Pre-Med/Pre-Dental*

COLORADO, UNIVERSITY OF (COLORADO SPRINGS) 1060
Bus Admin, Comp Sci, Engine, Physics, Psych

COLORADO, UNIVERSITY OF (DENVER) 1080
Comp Sci, Psych

COLORADO SCHOOL OF MINES (CO) 1270
Comp Sci, Engine, Geol, Physics

COLORADO STATE UNIVERSITY (CO) 1125
Ag, Art, Art Hist, Bot, Bus Admin, Forest, Geol, Psych, Zoo

COLUMBIA UNIVERSITY/BARNARD COLLEGE (NY) 1340/1300
*Anthro, Arch, Art Hist, Biochem, Chem, Classics, Drama, Econ, English, For Lang, Geol,
Hist, Math, Music, Nurs, Philo, Physics, Pre-Law, Reli Stu, Soc*

CONCORDIA COLLEGE-MOORHEAD (MN) 1120
Bio, Bus Admin, Ed, Math, Pre-Med/Pre-Dental, Psych, Soc

CONNECTICUT, UNIVERSITY OF (CT) 1130
Ag, Bio, Bot, Ed, Home Ec, Pharm, Zoo

CONNECTICUT COLLEGE (CT) 1260
Bot, Ed, English, Hist, Music, Philo, Poli Sci, Pre-Law, Psych

CONVERSE COLLEGE (SC) 1105
Art, Ed, Music

THE COOPER UNION (NY) 1400
Arch, Art, Engine

CORNELL COLLEGE (IA) 1150
English, Geol, Philo, Pre-Law, Psych, Soc

CORNELL UNIVERSITY (NY) 1344
*Ag, Arch, Art, Astro, Biochem, Bio, Bot, Comp Sci, Drama, Engine, Hist, Home Ec, Philo,
Physics, Pre-Med/Pre-Dental*

COVENANT COLLEGE (GA) 1150
Hist, Soc

CREIGHTON UNIVERSITY 1145
Bio, Communic, Nurs, Pharm, Poli Sci, Pre-Law, Pre-Med/Pre-Dental

CURTIS INSTITUTE OF MUSIC (PA) 1100
Music

DAEMEN COLLEGE (NY) 1030
Nurs

DALLAS, UNIVERSITY OF (TX) 1225
*Art, Bio, Biochem, Classics, Econ, Ed, English, For Lang, Hist, Pre-Law,
Pre-Med/Pre-Dental*

DARTMOUTH COLLEGE (NH) 1372
*Anthro, Bio, Chem, Comp Sci, Drama, Econ, Engine, English, For Lang, Geog, Geol, Math,
Physics, Poli Sci, Pre-Law, Pre-Med/Pre-Dental, Reli Stu, Soc*

DAVIDSON COLLEGE (NC) 1315
Chem, English, Hist, Math, Philo, Pre-Law, Pre-Med/Pre-Dental, Reli Stu

DAYTON, UNIVERSITY OF (OH) 1160
Engine, Ed

DELAWARE, UNIVERSITY OF (DE) 1150
Art, Art Hist, Bio, Bus Admin, Chem, Communic, Ed, Engine, Home Ec, Nurs, Pre-Med/Pre-Dental

DELAWARE VALLEY COLLEGE (PA) 1000
Ag, Bio, Bus Admin

DENISON UNIVERSITY (OH) 1150
Bio, Biochem, Econ, English, Geol, Hist, Philo, Poli Sci, Pre-Law, Pre-Med/Pre-Dental, Psych

DENVER, UNIVERSITY OF (CO) 1115
Bus Admin, English, Physics, Pre-Law, Psych

DEPAUL UNIVERSITY (IL) 1145
Bus Admin, Communic, Drama, Poli Sci, Pre-Law

DEPAUW UNIVERSITY (IN) 1235
Bus Admin, Music, Nurs

DETROIT MERCY, UNIVERSITY OF (MI) 1100
Engine, Nurs

DICKINSON COLLEGE (PA) 1200
Bio, English, For Lang, Hist, Poli Sci, Pre-Law, Pre-Med/Pre-Dental, Reli Stu

DILLARD UNIVERSITY (LA) 1000
Bus Admin

DOANE COLLEGE (NE) 1080
Bus Admin

DORDT COLLEGE (IA) 1075
Ag, Ed

DRAKE UNIVERSITY (IA) 1150
Bus Admin, Communic, Ed, For Lang, Pharm, Poli Sci, Pre-Law

DREW UNIVERSITY (NJ) 1220
Art, Chem, Drama, For Lang, Hist, Poli Sci, Pre-Law, Psych

DREXEL UNIVERSITY (PA) 1110
Comp Sci, Home Ec

DRURY COLLEGE (MO) 1140
Arch, Music

DUBUQUE, UNIVERSITY OF (IA) 1060
Ed

DUKE UNIVERSITY (NC) 1400
Anthro, Bio, Bot, Chem, Classics, Econ, Engine, English, Hist, Math, Nurs, Philo, Poli Sci, Pre-Law, Pre-Med/Pre-Dental, Psych, Reli Stu

DUQUESNE UNIVERSITY (PA) 1100
Bio, Chem, Communic, Nurs, Pharm, Pre-Med/Pre-Dental

D'YOUVILLE COLLEGE (NY) 1025
Nurs, Soc

EARLHAM COLLEGE (IN) 1180
Bio, Chem, Ed, For Lang, Geol, Math, Pre-Med/Pre-Dental, Psych, Soc

ECKERD COLLEGE (FL) 1170
Bio, Bus Admin, For Lang, Pre-Med/Pre-Dental

ELIZABETHTOWN COLLEGE (PA) 1135
Bus Admin

ELMHURST COLLEGE (IL) 1000
Bio

ELMIRA COLLEGE (NY) 1060
Bus Admin, Ed, Psych

ELON COLLEGE (NC) 1060
Communic

EMERSON COLLEGE (MA) 1130
Drama, English, Pre-Law

EMORY & HENRY COLLEGE (VA) 1050
Bus Admin, For Lang

EMORY UNIVERSITY (GA) 1310
Bio, Bus Admin, Chem, English, For Lang, Hist, Nurs, Poli Sci, Pre-Law, Pre-Med/Pre-Dental, Psych, Reli Stu

ERSKINE COLLEGE (SC) 1100
Bio, Bus Admin, Ed, Hist, Pre-Med/Pre-Dental

EUREKA COLLEGE (IL) 1040
Bus Admin, Comp Sci

EVANSVILLE, UNIVERSITY OF (IN) 1190
Comp Sci, Drama, Nurs, Physics, Pre-Med/Pre-Dental

FAIRFIELD UNIVERSITY (CT) 1155
Bio, Bus Admin, Communic, Math, Nurs, Physics, Pre-Med, Psych

FAIRLEIGH DICKINSON (NJ) 1040
Art, Bus Admin, English, Pre-Law

FERRIS STATE UNIVERSITY (MI) 1000
Bus Admin, Comp Sci, Pharm

FISK UNIVERSITY (TN) 1030
Bus Admin, Math, Pre-Law, Soc

FIVE TOWNS COLLEGE (NY) 1000
Music

FLAGLER COLLEGE (FL) 1099
Communic, Ed

FLORIDA, UNIVERSITY OF (FL) 1225
Ag, Anthro, Arch, Bot, Bus Admin, Communic, English, Forest, Geol, Math, Nurs, Pharm, Philo, Physics, Pre-Law, Soc, Zoo

FLORIDA A&M (FL) 1000
Bus Admin, Ed, Pre-Law, Pre-Med/Pre-Dental

FLORIDA ATLANTIC UNIVERSITY (FL) 1050
Bus Admin, Ed

FLORIDA INSTITUTE OF TECHNOLOGY (FL) 1185
Biochem, Bus Admin, Engine, Psych

FLORIDA INTERNATIONAL UNIVERSITY (FL) 1130
Bus Admin, Psych

FLORIDA STATE UNIVERSITY (FL) 1170
*Art Hist, Bus Admin, Chem, Drama, Ed, Home Ec, Music, Philo, Pre-Med/Pre-Dental,
Psych, Reli Stu*

FLORIDA SOUTHERN COLLEGE (FL) 1085
Communic, Pre-Med/Pre-Dental

FONTBONNE COLLEGE (MO) 1025
Drama, Home Ec, Math

FORDHAM UNIVERSITY (NY) 1160
Classics, English, Philo, Pre-Law, Reli Stu

FORT LEWIS COLLEGE (CO) 1025
English, Geol, Pre-Law

FRANCISCAN UNIVERSITY OF STEUBENVILLE (OH) 1090
Philo, Psych, Reli Stu

FRANKLIN COLLEGE OF INDIANA (IN) 1100
Communic, Drama, Ed

FRANKLIN & MARSHALL COLLEGE (PA) 1250
*Amer Stu, Bio, Bus Admin, Chem, English, Geol, Physics, Poli Sci, Pre-Law,
Pre-Med/Pre-Dental, Soc*

FURMAN UNIVERSITY (SC) 1200
Art, Chem, Comp Sci, Geol, Music, Poli Sci, Pre-Law, Pre-Med/Pre-Dental, Psych, Reli Stu

GANNON UNIVERSITY (PA) 1099
Bus Admin, Engine

GENERAL MOTORS INSTITUTE (MI) 1250
Engine

GENEVA COLLEGE (PA) 1070
Engine

GEORGETOWN UNIVERSITY (DC) 1310
*Amer St, Bio, Bus Admin, English, For Lang, Hist, Nurs, Philo, Poli Sci, Pre-Law,
Pre-Med/Pre-Dental, Reli Stu*

GEORGE FOX COLLEGE (OR) 1065
Ed, Soc

GEORGE MASON UNIVERSITY (VA) 1160
Amer St, Bus Admin, Drama, Econ, English, Nurs, Psych, Pre-Law

GEORGE WASHINGTON UNIVERSITY (DC) 1235
Amer St, Geog, Hist, Philo, Poli Sci, Pre-Law, Psych

GEORGIA, UNIVERSITY OF (GA) 1190
Ag, Bio, Chem, Communic, Ed, English, For Lang, Forest, Home Ec, Pharm, Pre-Law,
Pre-Med/Pre-Dental

GEORGIA INSTITUTE OF TECHNOLOGY (GA) 1293
Arch, Comp Sci, Engine, Physics

GEORGIA SOUTHERN UNIVERSITY (GA) 1040
Ed

GETTYSBURG COLLEGE (PA) 1205
Bio, Bus Admin, English, Hist, Pre-Law, Pre-Med/Pre-Dental, Psych, Soc

GONZAGA UNIVERSITY (WA) 1160
Bus Admin, Communic, English, Pre-Law

GORDON COLLEGE (MA) 1125
Ed, Reli Stu

GOSHEN COLLEGE (IN) 1090
Nurs, Physics

GOUCHER COLLEGE (MD) 1190
Bus Admin, Chem, Comp Sci, Drama, Ed, English, Hist, Pre-Law

GRACELAND COLLEGE (IA) 1040
Bus Admin, Ed, Nurs

GRAND VALLEY STATE UNIVERSITY (MI) 1100
English, Psych, Pre-Law

GREEN MOUNTAIN COLLEGE (VT) 1000
Bus Admin

GRINNELL COLLEGE (IA) 1320
Anthro, Bio, Chem, Comp Sci, English, For Lang, Hist, Physics, Poli Sci, Pre-Law,
Pre-Med/Pre-Dental, Psych

GROVE CITY COLLEGE (PA) 1199
Bus Admin, Engine

GUILFORD COLLEGE (NC) 1150
Bio, Ed, English, Geol, Physics, Pre-Law, Pre-Med/Pre-Dental, Psych

GUSTAVUS ADOLPHUS COLLEGE (MN) 1200
Bus Admin, For Lang, Music, Nurs, Physics, Psych

GWYNEDD-MERCY COLLEGE (PA) 1055
Nurs

HAMILTON COLLEGE (NY) 1200
Bio, Chem, English, Hist, Philo, Poli Sci, Pre-Law, Pre-Med/Pre-Dental, Reli Stu

HAMLINE UNIVERSITY (MN) 1160
Anthro, Art, Bio, Chem, English, Pre-Law, Pre-Med/Pre-Dental, Psych, Soc

HAMPDEN-SYDNEY COLLEGE (VA) 1170
Bio, Classics, English, Hist, Pre-Law, Pre-Med/Pre-Dental

HAMPTON UNIVERSITY (VA) 1020
Bus Admin

HANOVER COLLEGE (IN) 1145
Bus Admin, Communic, Ed, Psych

HARTFORD, UNIVERSITY OF (CT) 1050
Bus Admin, Music

HARTWICK COLLEGE (NY) 1099
Bus Admin, Geol, Music, Nurs, Poli Sci, Pre-Law, Soc

HARVARD/RADCLIFFE COLLEGES (MA) 1435
Amer St, Anthro, Art, Art Hist, Astro, Biochem, Bio, Chem, Classics, Econ, for Lang, Geol, Hist, Math, Music, Philo, Physics, Poli Sci, Pre-Law, Pre-Med/Pre-Dental, Psych

HARVEY MUDD COLLEGE (CA) 1500
Bio, Chem, Engine, Math, Physics, Pre-Med/Pre-Dental

HASTINGS COLLEGE (NE) 1040
Bus Admin

HAVERFORD COLLEGE (PA) 1365
Astro, Bio, Chem, Comp Sci, Econ, English, Hist, Philo, Physics, Pre-Law, Pre-Med/Pre-Dental, Psych, Reli Stu

HAWAII, UNIVERSITY OF (HI) 1080
Ag, Anthro, Art, Astro, Bot, For Lang, Poli Sci, Pre-Law

HAWAII PACIFIC UNIVERSITY (HI) 1110
Bus Admin, Comp Sci

HEIDELBERG COLLEGE (OH) 1000
Bus Admin, Pre-Med

HENDRIX COLLEGE (AR) 1170
Bio, Bus Admin, Chem, Econ, Pre-Med/Pre-Dental, Reli Stu, Soc

HILLSDALE COLLEGE (MI) 1170
Bus Admin, Ed, Hist

HIRAM COLLEGE (OH) 1180
Bio, Chem, Comp Sci, English, Ed, Hist, Math, Pre-Law, Pre-Med/Pre-Dental, Reli Stu

HOBART & WILLIAM SMITH COLLEGE (NY) 1190
Amer Stu, Bio, Chem, Econ, English, Hist, Poli Sci, Pre-Law, Pre-Med/Pre-Dental, Psych

HOFSTRA UNIVERSITY (NY) 1120
Anthro, Art, Bus Admin, Communic, Drama, Music, Poli Sci, Pre-Law, Soc

HOLLINS COLLEGE (VA) 1125
Amer St, Art, Art Hist, English, For Lang, Pre-Law, Psych

HOLY CROSS, COLLEGE OF THE (MA) 1250
Bio, Classics, Econ, English, Hist, Math, Philo, Pre-Law, Pre-Med/Pre-Dental

HOOD COLLEGE (MD) 1000
Bio, Bus Admin, Ed, Home Ec, Philo, Pre-Med/Pre-Dental

HOPE COLLEGE (MI) 1145
Bio, Chem, Geol, Music, Poli Sci, Pre-Law, Pre-Med/Pre-Dental

HOUGHTON COLLEGE (NY) 1150
Art, Bio, Chem, Ed, Pre-Med, Psych, Reli Stu

HOUSTON BAPTIST UNIVERSITY (TX) 1080
Bio, Chem, Pre-Med/Pre-Dental

HOUSTON, UNIVERSITY OF (TX) 1100
Arch, Bus Admin, Engine

HOWARD UNIVERSITY (DC) 1000
Bus Admin, Communic, Nurs, Zoo

HUMBOLDT STATE UNIVERSITY (CA) 1075
Bot, Drama, Forest, Music

HUNTINGDON COLLEGE (AL) 1080
Chem, Ed, Pre-Med/Pre-Dental

IDAHO, UNIVERSITY OF (ID) 1085
Ag, Forest

ILLINOIS, UNIVERSITY OF, AT:
    URBANA-CHAMPAIGN 1230
    Ag, Arch, Anthro, Astro, Bus Admin, Chem, Comp Sci, Ed, Engine, For Lang,
    Home Ec, Math, Music, Pharm, Physics, Pre-Med/Pre-Dental, Psych, Soc
    CHICAGO 1000
    Bus Admin

ILLINOIS COLLEGE (IL) 1100
Communic, Econ, Pre-Law

ILLINOIS INSTITUTE OF TECHNOLOGY (IL) 1160
Arch, Engine, Math

ILLINOIS STATE UNIVERSITY (IL) 1040
Drama, Ed

ILLINOIS WESLEYAN UNIVERSITY (IL) 1245
Bio, Drama, Music, Pre-Med/Pre-Dental

INDIANA STATE UNIVERSITY (IN) 1000
Bus Admin, Ed

INDIANA UNIVERSITY (IN)..1110
Bio, Bus Admin, Chem, Drama, Ed, For Lang, Geog, Geol, Music, Pre-Med/Pre-Dental, Psych, Zoo

INDIANA UNIVERSITY OF PENNSYLVANIA..1100
Bus Admin, Ed, Home Ec

IONA UNIVERSITY (NY)...1000
Bus Admin

IOWA, UNIVERSITY OF...1145
Astro, Biochem, Bus Admin, Communic, Ed, English, For Lang, Music, Nurs, Pre-Law, Pre-Med, Psych, Reli Stu

IOWA STATE UNIVERSITY (IA)...1145
Ag, Comp Sci, Ed, Engine, Forest, Home Ec, Zoo

ITHACA COLLEGE (NY)...1125
Chem, Music, Pre-Med/Pre-Dental

JACKSONVILLE STATE (AL)...1000
Ed

JACKSONVILLE UNIVERSITY (FL)..1050
Art, Bio, Bus Admin, Communic, Drama, Music, Nurs, Physics, Pre-Med/Pre-Dental

JAMES MADISON UNIVERSITY (VA)...1199
Bus Admin, Ed, For Lang, Home Ec, Music

JOHN CARROLL UNIVERSITY (OH)...1160
Bus Admin, Communic

JOHNS HOPKINS UNIVERSITY (MD)...1400
Art Hist, Bio, Chem, Classics, Engine, Geog, Philo, Poli Sci, Pre-Law, Pre-Med/Pre-Dental

JOHNSON C. SMITH (NC)..900
Communic, Soc

JUDSON COLLEGE (AL)...1000
Home Ec, Music, Psych

JULLIARD SCHOOL (NY)...1100
Drama, Music

JUNIATA COLLEGE (PA)...1160
Bio, Bus Admin, Chem, Ed, Pre-Med/Pre-Dental

KALAMAZOO COLLEGE (MI)..1220
Amer St, Bio, Chem, Classics, Econ, English, For Lang, Hist, Physics, Pre-Law, Pre-Med/Pre-Dental, Soc

KANSAS NEWMAN COLLEGE (KS)..1100
Bus Admin, Philo

KANSAS, UNIVERSITY OF (KS)..1105
Anthro, Arch, Art Hist, Astro, Chem, Communic, Drama, Engine, For Lang, Geog, Hist, Pre-Med/Pre-Dental, Zoo

KANSAS STATE UNIVERSITY (KS) 1105
Ag, Arch, Bio, Biochem, Communic, Engine, Home Ec, Math Pre-Law, Pre-Med/Pre-Dental

KEENE STATE COLLEGE (NH) 1000
Art, Ed, Music

KENNESAW STATE COLLEGE (GA) 1045
Bus Admin

KENT STATE UNIVERSITY (OH) 1000
Arch, Art, Communic, Ed, Music

KENTUCKY, UNIVERSITY OF (KY) 1130
Ag, Bus Admin, Communic, Ed, Engine, Hist, Home Ec, Pharm, Pre-Med/Pre-Dental

KENTUCKY WESLEYAN (KY) 1035
Bus Admin

KENYON COLLEGE (OH) 1265
Bio, Chem, Drama, Econ, English, Hist, Math, Philo, Poli Sci, Pre-Law, Pre-Med/Pre-Dental, Psych, Reli Stu

KING COLLEGE (TN) 1090
Reli Stu

KING'S COLLEGE (PA) 1075
Bus Admin

KNOX COLLEGE (IL) 1099
Art, Chem, English, Hist, Math, Poli Sci, Pre-Law, Pre-Med/Pre-Dental

KUTZTOWN UNIVERSITY (PA) 1005
Art, Ed

LAFAYETTE COLLEGE (PA) 1240
Anthro, Art, Bio, Chem, Econ, Engine, English, Geol, Hist, Pre-Law, Pre-Med/Pre-Dental, Psych

LAKE FOREST COLLEGE (IL) 1125
Art, Art Hist, Bio, Chem, Econ, English, Hist, Music, Pre-Law, Pre-Med/Pre-Dental, Psych

LA SALLE UNIVERSITY (PA) 1120
Bus Admin, Comp Sci

LA VERNE, UNIVERSITY OF (CA) 1000
Bus Admin

LAWRENCE UNIVERSITY (WI) 1230
Bio, Chem, English, For Lang, Hist, Music, Physics, Pre-Law, Pre-Med/Pre-Dental, Reli Stu

LEBANON VALLEY COLLEGE (PA) 1105
Bus Admin, Math, Music, Nurs, Psych

LEHIGH UNIVERSITY (PA) 1220
Bus Admin, Engine, Geol

LEMOYNE COLLEGE (NY) 1110
Bus Admin

LENOIR-RHYNE COLLEGE (NC) 1020
Bus Admin, Soc

LESLEY COLLEGE (MA) 1000
Bus Admin, Ed

LETOURNEAU COLLEGE (TX) 1115
Engine

LEWIS & CLARK COLLEGE (OR) 1199
Bio, Biochem, Bus Admin, For Lang, Physics, Pre-Med/Pre-Dental, Soc

LINDENWOOD COLLEGE (MO) 1040
Psych

LINFIELD COLLEGE (OR) 1145
Bio, Bus Admin, Chem, Ed, For Lang, Home Ec

LOCK HAVEN UNIVERSITY (PA) 1060
Ed

LONG ISLAND UNIVERSITY (SOUTHAMPTON) (NY) 1050
Bio

LONGWOOD COLLEGE (VA) 1099
Bus Admin, Ed, Psych

LORAS COLLEGE (IA) 1070
Art, Bio, Bus Admin, Ed, English, Pre-Law

LOUISIANA STATE UNIVERSITY (LA) 1099
Ag, Arch, Astro, Biochem, Chem, Communic, Comp Sci, Geog, Geol, Math, Music, Physics, Pre-Med/Pre-Dental, Psych

LOUISVILLE, UNIVERSITY OF (KY) 1000
Engine

LOWELL, UNIVERSITY OF MASSACHUSETTS AT (MA) 1050
Bus Admin, Engine, Music

LOYOLA COLLEGE (MD) 1175
Bio, Bus Admin, Engine

LOYOLA MARYMOUNT UNIVERSITY (CA) 1110
Bus Admin, Engine, Journal

LOYOLA UNIVERSITY OF CHICAGO (IL) 1105
Bio, Communic, Drama, Nurs, Physics, Pre-Med/Pre-Dental, Psych

LOYOLA UNIVERSITY OF NEW ORLEANS (LA) 1145
Bus Admin, Comp Sci, Communic, Music, Philo, Reli Stu

LUTHER COLLEGE (IA) 1150
Bus Admin, Ed, Music, Nurs, Psych

LYCOMING COLLEGE (PA) 1090
Astro

LYNCHBURG COLLEGE (VA) 1000
Communic, Soc

LYON COLLEGE (AR) 1130
Drama, Ed, Psych

MACALESTER COLLEGE (MN) 1305
Anthro, Art, Bio, Classics, Drama, Econ, English, Geog, Hist, Philo, Poli Sci, Pre-Law, Pre-Med/Pre-Dental, Psych

MacMURRAY COLLEGE (IL) 1035
Nurs

MAINE, UNIVERSITY OF (ME) 1100
Ag, Bot, Engine, Forest, Home Ec

MAINE, UNIVERSITY OF (FARMINGTON) (ME) 1030
Bus Admin

MALONE COLLEGE (OH) 1040
Bus Admin, Math

MANCHESTER COLLEGE (IN) 1030
Bus Admin, Psych

MANHATTAN COLLEGE (NY) 1110
Bus Admin, Ed, Engine

MANHATTANVILLE COLLEGE (NY) 1120
Art, Art Hist, Bus Admin, Ed, Music, Psych

MANHATTAN SCHOOL OF MUSIC (NY) 1100
Music

MANSFIELD UNIVERSITY OF PENNSYLVANIA (PA) 1030
Ed, Geog

MARIETTA COLLEGE (OH) 1115
Art, Bus Admin, English, Pre-Law

MARIST COLLEGE (NY) 1150
Bus Admin, Communic, Psych

MARQUETTE UNIVERSITY (WI) 1140
Bio, Bus Admin, Chem, English, Engine, Hist, Nurs, Poli Sci, Pre-Law, Pre-Med/Pre-Dental

MARY BALDWIN COLLEGE (VA) 1045
Art, Bus Admin, Communic, Psych, Soc

MARYCREST COLLEGE (IA) 1050
Nurs

MARYGROVE COLLEGE (MI) 1000
Comp Sci

MARYLAND INSTITUTE-COLLEGE OF ART (MD) 1130
Art

MARYLAND, UNIVERSITY OF (MD) 1190
Ag, Anthro, Astro, Bot, Bus Admin, Communic, Econ, Ed, Hist, Home Ec, Pharm, Pre-Law, Zoo

MARYLAND, UNIVERSITY OF (BALTIMORE COUNTY) (MD) 1250
Comp Sci, Nurs, Poli Sci, Pre-Law

MARYVILLE UNIVERSITY-ST. LOUIS (MO) 1060
Nurs

MARY WASHINGTON COLLEGE (VA) 1195
Amer St, Bio, Geog, Hist, Pre-Med/Pre-Dental, Psych

MASSACHUSETTS, UNIVERSITY OF (MA) 1120
*Bus Admin, Chem, Communic, Comp Sci, Engine, English, Hist, Home Ec, Nurs, Pre-Law,
Pre-Med/Pre-Dental, Zoo*

MASSACHUSETTS, UNIVERSITY OF (BOSTON) (MA) 1040
Bus Admin, Engine, Music

MASSACHUSETTS, UNIVERSITY OF (DARTMOUTH) (MA) 1070
Art, Nurs, Soc

MASSACHUSETTS COLLEGE OF ART (MA) 1060
Art

MASSACHUSETTS COLLEGE OF PHARMACY (MA) 1000
Pharm

MASSACHUSETTS INSTITUTE OF TECHNOLOGY (MA) 1440
*Arch, Astro, Biochem, Bio, Bus Admin, Chem, Comp Sci, Econ, Geol, Math, Physics, Poli Sci,
Pre-Law, Pre-Med/Pre-Dental*

MASSACHUSETTS MARITIME ACADEMY (MA) 1030
Engine

MASSACHUSETTS STATE COLLEGE SYSTEM (MA) 1040
Ed

MEMPHIS, UNIVERSITY OF (TN) 1040
Music

MERCER UNIVERSITY (GA) 1099
Bus Admin, Pharm

MEREDITH COLLEGE (NC) 1030
Bio, Bus Admin, Home Ec, Music

MERCY COLLEGE (NY) 1000
Nurs

MERCYHURST COLLEGE (PA) 1080
Art, Bus Admin

MERRIMACK COLLEGE (MA) 1060
Bus Admin

MESSIAH COLLEGE (PA) 1150
Art, Ed

MIAMI UNIVERSITY (OH) 1200
Arch, Bot, Bus Admin, Ed, Zoo

MIAMI, UNIVERSITY OF (FL) 1150
Bio, Biochem, Communic, Drama, Hist, Music, Pre-Med/Pre-Dental

MICHIGAN, UNIVERSITY OF (MI) 1260
*Amer St, Anthro, Arch, Art, Art Hist, Astro, Bot, Bus Admin, Classics, Communic, Econ, Ed,
Engine, For Lang, Geog, Music, Nurs, Pharm, Philo, Pre-Law, Pre-Med/Pre-Dental,
Psych, Soc, Zoo*

MICHIGAN, UNIVERSITY OF (DEARBORN) (MI) 1115
Bus Admin, Comp Sci, Engine

MICHIGAN STATE UNIVERSITY (MI) 1100
*Ag, Biochem, Bio, Bot, Bus Admin, Chem, Communic, Econ, Ed, Forest, Geog, Home Ec, Math,
Poli Sci, Pre-Law, Pre-Med/Pre-Dental, Psych, Soc*

MICHIGAN TECHNOLOGICAL UNIVERSITY (MI) 1185
Ag, Engine, Forest, Geol

MIDDLEBURY COLLEGE (VT) 1300
Art, Bio, Classics, Econ, English, For Lang, Geog, Hist, Poli Sci, Pre-Law, Pre-Med/Pre-Dental

MILLERSVILLE UNIVERSITY OF PENNSYLVANIA (PA) 1100
Bus Admin, Hist, Pre-Law

MILLIGAN COLLEGE (TN) 1045
Bus Admin, Philo, Reli Stu

MILLIKIN UNIVERSITY (IL) 1099
Art, Ed

MILLS COLLEGE (CA) 1145
Art, Ed, For Lang, Music, Psych

MILLSAPS COLLEGE (MS) 1190
Bio, Bus Admin, English, Geol, Math, Music, Pre-Law

MILWAUKEE SCHOOL OF ENGINEERING (WI) 1130
Arch, Engine

MINNESOTA, UNIVERSITY OF (MN) 1135
*Ag, Amer St, Art Hist, Bus Admin, Communic, Ed, Engine, Forest, Geol, Home Ec, Nurs,
Poli Sci, Pre-Law, Psych, Soc*

MINNESOTA, UNIVERSITY OF (MORRIS) (MN) 1199
Bio, Chem, Comp Sci, For Lang, Pre-Law, Pre Med/Pre-Dental

COLLEGE MISERICORDIA (PA) 1010
Nurs

MISSISSIPPI COLLEGE (MS) 1060
Bus Admin, Nurs, Reli Stu

MISSISSIPPI STATE UNIVERSITY (MS) 1050
Ag, Ed, Engine

MISSISSIPPI, UNIVERSITY OF (MS) 1099
Bus Admin, Communic, English, Pharm, Physics, Pre-Law

MISSISSIPPI UNIVERSITY FOR WOMEN (MS) 1110
Bus Admin, Nurs

MISSOURI, UNIVERSITY OF (MO) 1140
Ag, Art Hist, Communic, Forest, Hist

MISSOURI, UNIVERSITY OF (KANSAS CITY) (MO) 1015
Art, Music

MISSOURI, UNIVERSITY OF (ROLLA) (MO) 1255
Comp Sci, Engine

MONMOUTH COLLEGE (IL) 1060
Bus Admin, Ed

MONMOUTH UNIVERSITY (NJ) 900
Comp Sci

MONTANA COLLEGE OF MINERAL SCIENCE & TECHNOLOGY (MT) 1120
Comp Sci, Engine

MONTANA, UNIVERSITY OF (MT) 1060
Bot, Classics, Communic, Comp Sci, Forest, Pharm, Zoo

MONTANA STATE UNIVERSITY (MT) 1090
Ag, Arch, Engine, For Lang, Forest

MONTCLAIR STATE (NJ) 1099
Home Ec, Psych

MONTEVALLO, UNIVERSITY OF (AL) 1000
Communic, Ed, English, Home Ec

MONTREAT COLLEGE (NC) 1070
Bus Admin

MORAVIAN COLLEGE (PA) 1135
Art, Bus Admin, Communic, Comp Sci, Ed, Soc

MOREHOUSE COLLEGE (GA) 1099
Bus Admin, Comp Sci

MORNINGSIDE COLLEGE (IA) 1060
Bio, Communic, Nurs, Pre-Med/Pre-Dental

MOUNT HOLYOKE COLLEGE (MA) 1225
Art Hist, Biochem, Bio, Chem, Drama, Econ, English, For Lang, Hist, Math, Poli Sci, Pre-Law,
Pre-Law, Pre-Med/Pre-Dental, Psych

MOUNT MERCY COLLEGE (IA) 1050
Bus Admin, Nurs

MOUNT ST. JOSEPH (OH) 1040
Art, Bus Admin, Ed, Nurs

MOUNT ST. MARY'S COLLEGE (NY) 1040
Nurs

MOUNT ST. MARY'S COLLEGE (MD) 1050
Bus Admin, Poli Sci, Pre-Law, Pre-Med/Pre-Dental

MOUNT ST. MARY'S COLLEGE (CA) 1060
Bio, Bus Admin, Nurs

MOUNT UNION COLLEGE (OH) 1099
Bus Admin, Comp Sci

MUHLENBERG COLLEGE (PA) 1160
Art, Bio, Biochem, Bus Admin, Communic, Drama, Hist, Math, Philo, Pre-Law,
Pre-Med/Pre-Dental

MUSKINGUM COLLEGE (OH) 1180
Bus Admin, Comp Sci, Ed

NAZARETH COLLEGE OF ROCHESTER (NY) 1135
Bus Admin, Ed

NEBRASKA, UNIVERSITY OF (NE) 1080
Ag, Arch, Bus Admin, Communic, Home Ec

NEBRASKA WESLEYAN UNIVERSITY (NE) 1110
Bio, Pre-Med/Pre-Dental

NEVADA, UNIVERSITY OF, AT:
    LAS VEGAS 1000
    Arch, Engine
    RENO 1050
    Ag, Communic, Ed

NEW COLLEGE OF THE UNIVERSITY OF SOUTH FLORIDA (FL) 1270
Anthro, Bio, Chem, Math, Philo, Physics, Pre-Med/Pre-Dental, Psych

NEW ENGLAND CONSERVATORY (MA) 1100
Music

NEW HAMPSHIRE, UNIVERSITY OF (NH) 1150
Ag, Bio, Chem, Communic, English, Pre-Med/Pre-Dental, Pre-Law

NEW JERSEY INSTITUTE OF TECHNOLOGY (NJ) 1145
Engine

NEW JERSEY, COLLEGE OF (NJ) 1240
Art, Ed, Engine, Math, Philo, Pre-Law, Pre-Med/Pre-Dental, Reli Stu

NEW MEXICO INSTITUTE OF MINING (NM) 1160
Engine, Geol, Physics

NEW MEXICO STATE UNIVERSITY (NM) 1040
Ag, Anthro, Engine

NEW MEXICO, UNIVERSITY OF (NM) 1060
Anthro, Art, For Lang, Hist, Pharm

NEW ORLEANS, UNIVERSITY OF (LA) 1050
Bus Admin, Engine

NEW YORK, CITY UNIVERSITY OF, AT
      BARUCH COLLEGE 1000
      Bus Admin
      BROOKLYN COLLEGE 1040
      Geol, Physics
      CITY COLLEGE 1050
      Arch, Ed, Physics
      HERBERT LEHMAN COLLEGE 1000
      Home Ec, Psych
      HUNTER COLLEGE 1030
      Art, Art Hist, Communic, Comp Sci, Ed, English, Nurs, Pre-Law, Psych
      QUEENS COLLEGE 1020
      Anthro, Ed, Psych

NEW YORK, STATE UNIVERSITY OF, AT
      ALBANY 1160
      Bio, Bus Admin, English, Geol, Pre-Law, Psych
      BINGHAMTON 1230
      Biochem, Bus Admin, Math, Nurs, Physics, Pre-Law, Pre-Med/Pre-Dental, Psych
      BROCKPORT, COLLEGE AT 1040
      Bus Admin
      BUFFALO 1200
      Amer Stu, Anthro, Arch, Bus Admin, Ed, Engine, Geog, Pharm, Pre-Law,
      Pre-Med/Pre-Dental
      FREDONIA, COLLEGE AT 1115
      Bus Admin, Ed, Music
      GENESEO, COLLEGE AT 1220
      Biochem, Bus Admin, Geol, Music, Physics, Pre-Med/Pre-Dental
      NEW PALTZ, COLLEGE AT 1120
      Bus Admin, Ed, Psych
      ONEONTA, COLLEGE AT 1110
      Econ, Home Ec, Pre-Law
      OSWEGO, COLLEGE AT 1120
      Bus Admin, Home Ec, Psych
      PLATTSBURGH, COLLEGE AT 1100
      Bus Admin
      POTSDAM, COLLEGE AT 1100
      Comp Sci, Math, Music
      PURCHASE, COLLEGE AT 1060
      Drama, English, Music, Pre-Law, Psych

STONY BROOK 1110
Biochem, Bio, Chem, Comp Sci, English, Geo, Philo, Physics, Pre-Med/Pre-Dental, Psych, Reli Stu

NEW YORK UNIVERSITY (NY) 1215
Art, Art Hist, Bus Admin, Classics, Drama, For Lang, Math, Music, Nurs, Philo, Pre-Med/Pre-Dental

NIAGARA UNIVERSITY (NY)..1040
Bus Admin, Drama, English, Pre-Law

NORTH CAROLINA SCHOOL OF THE ARTS (NC) 1030
Drama

NORTH CAROLINA, UNIVERSITY OF, AT
      ASHEVILLE...1145
      Ed, Hist, Soc, Psych
      CHAPEL HILL 1205
      Amer St, Art Hist, Astro, Bus Admin, Chem, Classics, Communic, Drama, Ed, English, For Lang, Hist, Pharm
      CHARLOTTE 1040
      Bus Admin, Nurs, Pre-Med/Pre-Dental, Pre-Law, Psych, Zoo
      GREENSBORO 1050
      Art, Bus Admin, Communic, Home Ec, Nurs
      WILMINGTON 1050
      Bus Admin, English, Pre-Law, Soc, Psych

NORTH CAROLINA STATE UNIVERSITY (NC) 1160
Ag, Arch, Econ, Engine, Forest, Math, Pre-Law, Zoo

NORTH CENTRAL COLLEGE (IL)..1125
Bio, Communic, Comp Sci, Poli Sci, Pre-Med/Pre-Dental, Pre-Law

NORTH DAKOTA STATE UNIVERSITY (ND)..1100
Ag, Engine, Pharm

NORTH DAKOTA, UNIVERSITY OF (ND) 1100
Bus Admin, Ed

NORTH FLORIDA, UNIVERSITY OF (FL) 1125
Bus Admin, Ed, Music

NORTH GEORGIA COLLEGE (GA) 1000
Bus Admin

NORTH TEXAS, UNIVERSITY OF (TX) 1080
Music

NORTHEASTERN UNIVERSITY (MA) 1105
Bus Admin, Engine

NORTHEAST LOUISIANA UNIVERSITY (LA) 1000
Bus Admin, Nurs, Pharm

NORTHERN ARIZONA (AZ) 1025
Ed, Forest, Psych

NORTHERN COLORADO UNIVERSITY 1050
Soc

NORTHERN ILLINOIS UNIVERSITY (IL) 1090
Bus Admin, Nurs

NORTHERN IOWA, UNIVERSITY OF (IA) 1090
Art, Bus Admin, Ed

NORTHLAND COLLEGE (WI) 1080
Bio

NORTHWESTERN COLLEGE (IA) 1075
Drama, Ed

NORTHWESTERN COLLEGE (MN) 1090
Ed

NORTHWESTERN UNIVERSITY (IL) 1340
Anthro, Astro, Chem, Communic, Drama, Econ, Engine, English, Hist, Math, Music, Poli Sci,
Pre-Med/Pre-Dental, Pre-Law, Soc

NORTHWOOD INSTITUTE (MI) 1000
Bus Admin

NOTRE DAME, UNIVERSITY OF (IN) 1300
Arch, Bus Admin, Chem, Engine, Poli Sci, Pre-Med/Pre-Dental, Pre-Law

NOVA SOUTHEASTERN UNIVERSITY (FL) 1020
Bus Admin

OAKLAND UNIVERSITY (MI) 1045
Comp Sci, Engine

OBERLIN COLLEGE (OH) 1310
Art Hist, Chem, English, Music, Philo, Pre-Med/Pre-Dental, Pre-Law, Reli Stu, Soc

OCCIDENTAL COLLEGE (CA) 1200
Bio, Chem, Econ, Ed, Math, Physics, Poli Sci, Pre-Med/Pre-Dental, Pre-Law, Psych, Reli Stu

OGLETHORPE UNIVERSITY (GA) 1199
Bus Admin, Poli Sci, Pre-Law

OHIO NORTHERN UNIVERSITY (OH) 1115
Bio, Chem, Pharm

OHIO STATE UNIVERSITY (OH) 1085
Ag, Arch, Art/Studio, Bus Admin, Drama, Engine, Geog, Home Ec, Nurs, Pharm, Physics,
Pre-Med/Pre-Dental

OHIO UNIVERSITY (OH) 1115
Art, Bus Admin, Communic, Drama, Ed, Engine, English, Hist, Math, Music, Pre-Law,
Psych, Zoo

OHIO WESLEYAN UNIVERSITY (OH) 1185
Bio, Bot, Chem, Communic, Econ, Poli Sci, Pre-Med/Pre-Dental, Pre-Law, Psych, Zoo

OKLAHOMA BAPTIST UNIVERSITY (OK) **1099**
Ed

OKLAHOMA CITY UNIVERSITY (OK) **1100**
Bus Admin

OKLAHOMA, UNIVERSITY OF (OK) **1115**
Arch, Astro, Engine, English, Geol, Hist, Pre-Law, Zoo

OKLAHOMA STATE UNIVERSITY (OK) **1100**
Ag, Bus Admin, Drama, Engine

OLD DOMINION UNIVERSITY (VA) **1050**
Art, Bus Admin

OREGON, UNIVERSITY OF (OR) **1140**
Anthro, Arch, Art Hist, Bus Admin, Chem, Comp Sci, Ed, Geog, Math, Psych

OREGON STATE UNIVERSITY (OR) **1040**
Ag, Biochem, Bot, Forest, Home Ec, Physics

OTIS ART INSTITUTE/PARSONS (CA) **1000**
Art

OTTERBEIN COLLEGE (OH) **1090**
Drama, Psych

OZAKRS, COLLEGE OF THE (MO) **1050**
Bus Admin, Ed, Psych

PACE UNIVERSITY (NY) **1070**
Bus Admin, Nurs, Psych

PACIFIC LUTHERAN UNIVERSITY (WA) **1115**
Bus Admin, For Lang

PACIFIC UNIVERSITY (OR) **1110**
Bus Admin, For Lang

PACIFIC, UNIVERSITY OF THE (CA) **1080**
Engine, Music, Pharm

PALM BEACH ATLANTIC COLLEGE (FL) **1040**
Psych

PARSONS SCHOOL OF DESIGN (NY) **1070**
Art

PENNSYLVANIA, UNIVERSITY OF (PA) **1340**
Amer St, Anthro, Art, Art Hist, Astro, Biochem, Bus Admin, Classics, Econ, Engine, English, For Lang, Geol, Hist, Nurs, Philo, Poli Sci, Pre-Law, Psych, Soc

PENNSYLVANIA STATE UNIVERSITY (PA) **1195**
Ag, Arch, Biochem, Bot, Bus Admin, Chem, Comp Sci, Ed, Engine, Forest, Geog, Home Ec, Nurs, Pre-Med/Pre-Dental

PEPPERDINE UNIVERSITY (CA) 1155
Bus Admin, Communic, Comp Sci, For Lang

PERU STATE COLLEGE (NE) 1000
Ed

PHILADELPHIA COLLEGE OF ART (PA) 1000
Art

PHILADELPHIA COLLEGE OF PHARMACY AND SCIENCE (PA) 1130
Pharm

PHILADELPHIA COLLEGE OF TEXTILES AND SCIENCE (PA) 1050
Bus Admin

PITTSBURGH, UNIVERSITY OF (PA) 1130
Anthro, Bio Chem, Bus Admin, Engine, English, Nurs, Philo, Pre-Med/Pre-Dental, Pre-Law, Psych

PITTSBURGH, UNIVERSITY OF (BRADFORD) (PA) 1040
Comp Sci

PITTSBURGH, UNIVERSITY OF (JOHNSTOWN) (PA) 1100
Comp Sci, Engine

PITZER COLLEGE (CA) 1200
Anthro, Psych, Soc

POINT LOMA (CA) 1000
Bus Admin, Home Ec, Nurs

POINT PARK COLLEGE (PA) 1000
Drama

POLYTECHNIC UNIVERSITY OF NEW YORK (NY) 1195
Engine

POMONA COLLEGE (CA) 1400
Amer St, Anthro, Bio, Chem, Econ, English, For Lang, Geol, Hist, Math, Philo,
Pre-Med/Pre-Dental, Pre-Law, Reli Stu

PORTLAND, UNIVERSITY OF (OR) 1120
Engine

PRATT INSTITUTE (NY) 1040
Arch

PRESBYTERIAN COLLEGE (SC) 1110
Bio, Bus Admin, English, Poli Sci, Pre-Med/Pre-Dental, Pre-Law

PRINCETON UNIVERSITY (NJ) 1430
Arch, Art Hist, Bio, Biochem, Chem, Classics, Drama, Econ, Engine, English, For Lang, Geol,
Hist, Math, Music, Philo, Physics, Poli Sci, Pre-Med/Pre-Dental, Pre-Law, Reli Sci

PRINCIPIA COLLEGE (IL) 1100
Art, Bus Admin, Ed, English, Pre-Law

PROVIDENCE COLLEGE (RI) 1165
Bus Admin, Poli Sci, Pre-Law

PUERTO RICO, UNIVERSITY OF (PR) 1100
Bus Admin, Ed

PUERTO RICO, UNIVERSITY OF (CAYEY) (PR) 1000
Bio, Bus Admin, Ed

PUGET SOUND, UNIVERSITY OF (WA) 1170
Bus Admin, English, Pre-Law

PURDUE UNIVERSITY (IN) 1120
Ag, Biochem, Bot, Bus Admin, Chem, Engine, Forest, Geol, Home Ec, Pharm

QUEENS COLLEGE (NC) 1150
Bus Admin, English, Hist, Pre-Law

QUINCY COLLEGE (IL) 1090
Bus Admin, Soc

QUINNIPIAC COLLEGE (CT) 1099
Bus Admin, Comp Sci

RADFORD UNIVERSITY (VA) 1000
Bus Admin, Ed, Geog, Poli Sci, Pre-Law

RANDOLPH-MACON COLLEGE (VA) 1143
Bio, Econ, English, Poli Sci, Pre-Law, Pre-Med/Pre-Dental, Psych

RANDOLPH-MACON WOMAN'S COLLEGE (VA) 1143
Art, Bio, Classics, Communic, English, Pre-Law, Pre-Med/Pre-Dental, Psych

REDLANDS, UNIVERSITY OF (CA) 1120
Art, Bus Admin, Ed, English, Music, Poli Sci, Pre-Law

REED COLLEGE (OR) 1300
Bio, Chem, English, Hist, Philo, Physics, Pre-Law, Pre-Med/Pre-Dental, Psych

REGIS UNIVERSITY (CO) 1050
Bus Admin, Communic, Comp Sci, Ed, Philo, Pre-Med/Pre-Dental, Psych, Reli Stu

RENSSELAER POLYTECHNIC INSTITUTE (NY) 1240
Arch, Bus Admin, Comp Sci, Engine, Math, Physics

RHODE ISLAND SCHOOL OF DESIGN (RI) 1100
Arch, Art

RHODE ISLAND, UNIVERSITY OF (RI) 1080
Comp Sci, Engine, English, Nurs, Pharm, Poli Sci, Pre-Law

RHODES COLLEGE (TN) 1260
Bio, Econ, English, Hist, Poli Sci, Pre-Law, Pre-Med/Pre-Dental, Psych

RICE UNIVERSITY (TX) 1405
Anthro, Arch, Biochem, Bio, Chem, Comp Sci, Engine, Hist, Math, Music, Physics,
Pre-Med/Pre-Dental

RICHMOND, UNIVERSITY OF (VA) 1270
Bus Admin, English, Pre-Law

RIDER COLLEGE (NJ) 1015
Comp Sci, Music

RIPON COLLEGE (WI) 1125
Bio, Biochem, Bus Admin, Chem, Econ, English, Poli Sci, Pre-Law, Pre-Med/Pre-Dental

ROANOKE COLLEGE (VA) 1150
Art, Bio, Bus Admin, Psych, Pre-Law, Reli Stu, Soc

ROCHESTER, UNIVERSITY OF (NY) 1210
Art, Art Hist, Biochem, Bio, Chem, Comp Sci, Econ, English, For Lang, Geol, Music, Nurs, Philo, Poli Sci, Pre-Law, Pre-Med/Pre-Dental

ROCHESTER INSTITUTE OF TECHNOLOGY (NY) 1170
Comp Sci, Engine

ROCKFORD COLLEGE (IL) 1010
Art, Drama, English, Pre-Law

ROCKHURST COLLEGE (MO) 1115
Bus Admin, Chem, Home Ec

ROGER WILLIAMS UNIVERSITY (RI) 1000
Arch

ROLLINS COLLEGE (FL) 1170
Classics, Drama, English, Physics, Psych

ROOSEVELT UNIVERSITY (IL) 1000
Bus Admin

ROSARY COLLEGE (IL) 1040
Home Ec

ROSE-HULMAN INSTITUTE OF TECHNOLOGY 1275
Engine

ROSEMONT COLLEGE (PA) 1100
Art, Art Hist

ROWAN COLLEGE OF NEW JERSEY (NJ) 1140
Bus Admin, Home Ec, Music

RUSSELL SAGE COLLEGE (THE SAGE COLLEGES) (NY) 1050
Nurs

RUTGERS UNIVERSITY (NJ) 1200
Ag, Biochem, Bio, Chem, Ed, Engine, English, For Lang, Pharm, Pre-Law, Pre-Med/Pre-Dental

RUTGERS UNIVERSITY (CAMDEN) (NJ) 1160
Comp Sci, English, Hist, Pre-Law

SACRED HEART UNIVERSITY (CT) 1010
Biochem, Bus Admin, Psych

ST. AMBROSE COLLEGE (IA) 1050
Communic, Comp Sci

ST. ANDREWS PRESBYTERIAN COLLEGE (NC) 1060
Biochem, Bus Admin, Philo

ST. ANSELM COLLEGE (NH) 1099
Econ, Nurs, Pre-Law, Soc

ST. BONAVENTURE UNIVERSITY (NY) 1025
Bus Admin, Communic, Philo, Poli Sci, Pre-Law, Reli Stu

ST. CATHERINE, COLLEGE OF (MN) 1040
Music, Nurs, Reli Stu, Soc

ST. FRANCIS COLLEGE (NY) 1000
Bus Admin

ST. JOHN FISHER COLLEGE (NY) 1080
Bus Admin, Communic

ST. JOHN'S UNIVERSITY (NY) 1045
Bus Admin, Pharm

SAINT JOHN'S UNIVERSITY/COLLEGE OF SAINT BENEDICT (MN) 1110
Bio, Bus Admin, Chem, Econ, Physics, Physics, Poli Sci, Pre-Law, Pre-Med/Pre-Dental

SAINT JOSEPH'S COLLEGE (CT) 1000
Ed

ST. JOSEPH'S COLLEGE (IN) 1040
Ed, Psych

ST. JOSEPH'S COLLEGE (ME) 1005
Ed, Nurs

SAINT JOSEPH'S UNIVERSITY (PA) 1135
Bus Admin

ST. LAWRENCE UNIVERSITY (NY) 1190
Econ, English, Geol, Poli Sci, Pre-Law, Psych, Soc

ST. LOUIS COLLEGE OF PHARMACY (MO) 1115
Pharm, Pre-Med/Pre-Dental

SAINT LOUIS UNIVERSITY (MO) 1135
Bio, Chem, Nurs, Philo

SAINT MARY COLLEGE (KS) 1000
English

SAINT MARY'S COLLEGE (IN) 1115
Bus Admin, Ed, English, Nurs, Pre-Law

SAINT MARY'S COLLEGE OF CALIFORNIA (CA) 1120
Bus Admin, Ed, Soc

ST. MARY'S COLLEGE OF MARYLAND (MD) 1250
Bio, Math, Music, Pre-Med/Pre-Dental, Psych

ST. MARY'S COLLEGE OF MINNESOTA (MN) 1030
Bus Admin, Communic, Drama, Ed, Hist

ST. MARY'S UNIVERSITY OF SAN ANTONIO (TX) 1050
Bus Admin, Poli Sci, Pre-Law, Soc

SAINT MICHAEL'S COLLEGE (VT) 1100
Bus Admin, Chem, Communic, Ed

ST. NORBERT COLLEGE (WI) 1120
Bus Admin

ST. OLAF COLLEGE (MN) 1200
*Amer St, Art, Bio, Chem, Econ, English, Home Ec, Math, Music, Nurs, Philo, Pre-Law,
Pre-Med/Pre-Dental, Psych*

SAINT ROSE, COLLEGE OF (NY) 1060
Bus Admin, Ed

SAINT SCHOLASTICA, COLLEGE OF (MN) 1075
Nurs

SAINT THOMAS, UNIVERSITY OF (MN) 1099
Bus Admin

SAINT THOMAS, UNIVERSITY OF (TX) 1135
Pre-Med/Pre-Dental

ST. VINCENT COLLEGE (PA) 1090
Bio, Pre-Med/Pre-Dental, Psych

SALEM COLLEGE (NC) 1135
Art, Art Hist, Bus Admin, Econ, English, Pre-Law, Soc

SALEM STATE COLLEGE (MA) 1000
Geog

SALISBURY STATE UNIVERSITY (MD) 1150
Ed, Psych

SAMFORD UNIVERSITY (AL) 1115
Bus Admin, Communic, Nurs, Pharm

SAN DIEGO STATE UNIVERSITY (CA) 1000
Bus Admin, Communic

SAN DIEGO, UNIVERSITY OF (CA) 1125
Bus Admin, Nurs, Reli Stu

SAN FRANCISCO CONSERVATORY OF MUSIC (CA) 1120
Music

SAN FRANCISCO, UNIVERSITY OF (CA) 1100
Bus Admin, Nurs, Psych

SAN FRANCISCO STATE UNIVERSITY (CA) 1020
Drama, English, Pre-Law, Soc

SANTA CLARA UNIVERSITY (CA) 1175
Bus Admin, Comp Sci, Music, Pre-Law

SANTA FE, COLLEGE OF (NM) 1010
Art, Communic, Drama

SARAH LAWRENCE COLLEGE (NY) 1200
Drama, English, Pre-Law

SCHREINER COLLEGE (TX) 1070
Bus Admin

SCRANTON, UNIVERSITY OF (PA) 1170
Bio, Bus Admin, Communic, *Pre-Med/Pre-Dental*

SCRIPPS COLLEGE (CA) 1200
Art, Bio, Drama, English, Pre-Law, Pre-Med/Pre-Dental

SEATTLE UNIVERSITY (WA) 1099
Bus Admin, Nurs

SEATTLE PACIFIC UNIVERSITY (WA) 1100
Engine, Home Ec, Nurs

SETON HALL UNIVERSITY (NJ) 1060
Bus Admin, Communic, Psych

SETON HILL COLLEGE (PA) 1040
Art, Drama, Home Ec, Music

SHAW UNIVERSITY (NC) 1010
Bus Admin

SHEPHERD COLLEGE (WV) 1180
Art, Bus Admin, Ed, Music, Psych

SHIPPENSBURG UNIVERSITY (PA) 1120
Bus Admin, Ed

SIENA COLLEGE (NY) 1120
Bus Admin, Poli Sci, Pre-Law, Pre-Med/Pre-Dental

SIMMONS COLLEGE (MA) 1100
Bus Admin, Communic, Math, Nurs, Psych

SIMPSON COLLEGE (IA) 1080
Bus Admin, Ed

SKIDMORE COLLEGE (NY) 1200
Amer St, Anthro, Art, Art Hist, Bio, Biochem, Bus Admin, Chem, Drama, Ed, English, For Lang, Music, Philo, Pre-Law, Pre-Med/Pre-Dental

SMITH COLLEGE (MA) **1270**
*Amer St, Anthro, Art, Art Hist, Bio, Econ,English, For Lang, Hist, Music, Philo, Physics,
Poli Sci, Pre-Law, Pre-Med/Pre-Dental, Psych*

SONOMA STATE UNIVERSITY (CA) **1020**
Bus Admin, Psych

SOUTH, UNIVERSITY OF THE (TN) **1200**
Anthro, Bio, Econ, English, for Lang, Hist, Poli Sci, Pre-Law, Pre-Med/Pre-Dental, Reli Stu

SOUTH CAROLINA, UNIVERSITY OF (SC) **1070**
Bus Admin, Communic, Engine, Phar

SOUTH DAKOTA, UNIVERSITY OF (SD) **1050**
Bus Admin, Nurs

SOUTH DAKOTA SCHOOL OF MINES (SD) **1135**
Engine

SOUTHERN CALIFORNIA, UNIVERSITY OF (CA) **1190**
Arch, Bus Admin, Communic, Engine, Math, Music, Pharm, Psych

SOUTHERN ILLINOIS UNIVERSITY (CARBONDALE) (IL) **1020**
Bus Admin, Zoo

SOUTHERN MAINE, UNIVERSITY OF (ME) **1060**
Engine, Nurs

SOUTH FLORIDA, UNIVERSITY OF (FL) **1099**
Amer St, Bus Admin, Drama, For Lang, Nurs

SOUTHERN METHODIST UNIVERSITY (TX) **1180**
Art, Art Hist, Bus Admin, Drama, Communic, Reli Stu

SOUTHERN MISSISSIPPI, UNIVERSITY OF (MS) **1040**
Bus Admin

SOUTHWEST MISSOURI STATE UNIVERSITY (MO) **1080**
Ed, Math

SOUTHERN OREGON STATE COLLEGE (OR) **1040**
Ed, For Lang

SOUTHWEST BAPTIST UNIVERSITY (MO) **1050**
Ed, Music, Reli Stu

SOUTHWESTERN UNIVERSITY (TX) **1205**
*Art, Bio, Bus Admin, Chem, Communic, Drama, English, For Lang, Hist, Music, Poli Sci,
Pre-Law, Pre-Med/Pre-Dental, Psych, Soc*

SOUTHWEST TEXAS STATE UNIVERSITY (TX) **1010**
Bus Admin

SPELMAN COLLEGE (GA) **1050**
Bio, Chem, Comp Sci, English, Poli Sci, Pre-Law, Pre-Med/Pre-Dental, Soc

SPRING HILL COLLEGE (AL) 1100
Bio, Bus Admin, Chem, Communic, English, Hist, Poli Sci, Pre-Law, Pre-Med/Pre-Dental

STANFORD UNIVERSITY (CA) 1390
Amer St, Anthro, Bio, Chem, Classics, Communic, Comp Sci, Econ, Engine, English, Hist, Math, Physics, Poli Sci, Pre-Law, Pre-Med/Pre-Dental, Psych, Reli Stu, Soc

STEPHAN F. AUSTIN STATE UNIVERSITY (TX) 1000
Forest

STETSON UNIVERSITY (FL) 1120
Bus Admin, Chem, Ed, English, Hist, Math, Music, Pre-Law, Pre-Med/Pre-Dental, Psych

STEVENS UNIVERSITY OF TECHNOLOGY (NJ) 1250
Engine

STOCKTON STATE (RICHARD STOCKTON COLLEGE OF NEW JERSEY) (NJ) 1140
Bus Admin

STONEHILL COLLEGE (MA) 1100
Bus Admin, Poli Sci, Pre-Law, Psych

SUNY COLLEGE OF ENVIRONMENTAL SCIENCE & FORESTRY (NY) 1200
Forestry

SUSQUEHANNA UNIVERSITY (PA) 1150
Bus Admin, Communic

SWARTHMORE COLLEGE (PA) 1375
Art Hist, Biochem, Bio, Classics, Econ, Ed, Engine, English, Hist, Philo, Physics, Poli Sci, Pre-Law, Pre-Med/Pre-Dental, Psych

SWEET BRIAR COLLEGE (VA) 1140
Art Hist, For Lang, Math, Psych

SYRACUSE UNIVERSITY (NY) 1199
Arch, Art, Bus Admin, Communic, Forest, Poli Sci, Pre-Law, Psych, Soc

TAMPA, UNIVERSITY OF (FL) 1070
Bus Admin, Communic, Music

TAYLOR UNIVERSITY (IN) 1099
Psych, Reli Stu

TEMPLE UNIVERSITY (PA) 1099
Art, Biochem, Bio, Chem, English, Drama, Pharm, Pre-Law, Pre-Med/Pre-Dental, Soc

TENNESSEE, UNIVERSITY OF (TN) 1099
Ag, Anthro, Bot, Bus Admin, Ed, English, Pre-Law, Zoo

TEXAS, UNIVERSITY OF, AT
    ARLINGTON 1030
      Arch, Bus Admin, Engine
    AUSTIN 1180
      Amer St, Arch, Astro, Bot, Bus Admin, Comp Sci, Drama, Ed, For Lang, Geog, Geol, Hist, Journal, Math, Pharm, Physics, Psych

SAN ANTONIO 950
Bus Admin

TEXAS A&M (TX) 1155
Ag, Arch, Bus Admin, Chem, Ed, Engine, Forest, Geol, Pre-Med/Pre-Dental, Zoo

TEXAS A&M AT GALVESTON (TX) 1100
Bus Admin

TEXAS CHRISTIAN UNIVERSITY (TX) 1140
Bus Admin, Communic, Drama, Geol, Hist, Nurs, Reli Stu

TEXAS TECH UNIVERSITY (TX) 1060
Ag, Ed, Home Ec, Math

TEXAS WESLEYAN COLLEGE (TX) 1020
Bus Admin, Communic, Ed

THOMAS MORE COLLEGE (KY) 1080
Bio, Bus Admin, Pre-Med/Pre-Dental

TOLEDO, UNIVERSITY OF (OH) 1099
Bus Admin, Econ, Pharm

TOUGALOO COLLEGE (MS) 1000
Bio, Ed

TOWSON STATE (MD) 1070
Bus Admin

TRANSYLVANIA UNIVERSITY (KY) 1170
Bus Admin, Comp Sci, Pre-Med/Pre-Dental

TRINITY COLLEGE (CT) 1255
Bio, Bus Admin, Econ, Engine, Math, Philo, Pre-Law, Pre-Med/Pre-Dental, Reli Stu

TRINITY COLLEGE (DC) 1115
Bus Admin, For Lang, Math, Poli Sci, Pre-Law, Soc

TRINITY UNIVERSITY (TX) 1270
Art, Chem, Communic, Econ, Ed, English, Hist, Philo, Poli Sci, Pre-Law, Pre-Med/Pre-Dental

TRUMAN STATE UNIVERSITY (MO) 1180
Bio, Bus Admin, Chem, Ed, For Lang, Nurs, Pre-Med/Pre-Dental

TUFTS UNIVERSITY (MA) 1295
Bio, Chem, Classics, Drama, Ed, Engine, English, Hist, Poli Sci, Pre-Law, Pre-Med/Pre-Dental, Psych

TULANE UNIVERSITY (LA) 1250
Amer St, Arch, Bio, Biochem, Bus Admin, Drama, Engine, For Lang, Hist, Math, Philo, Pre-Med/Pre-Dental, Psych

TULSA, UNIVERSITY OF (OK) 1185
Anthro, Communic, Engine, Geol, Psych

TUSKEGEE INSTITUTE (AL) **1000**
Ag, Arch, Engine, Nurs

UNION COLLEGE (NY) **1240**
Bio, Chem, Engine, Hist, Math, Poli Sci, Pre-Law, Pre-Med/Pre-Dental, Psych

U. S. AIR FORCE ACADEMY (CO) **1265**
Bus Admin, Engine

U. S. COAST GUARD ACADEMY (CT) **1260**
Engine

U. S. MILITARY ACADEMY (NY) **1260**
Engine

U. S. NAVAL ACADEMY (MD) **1285**
Engine

URSINUS COLLEGE (PA) **1170**
Bio, Bus Admin, Chem, Econ, Ed, Physics, Poli Sci, Pre-Law, Pre-Med/Pre-Dental

UTAH, UNIVERSITY OF (UT) **1115**
Comp Sci, Drama, Engine, English, For Lang, Pre-Law

UTAH STATE UNIVERSITY (UT) **1040**
Ag, Ed, Forest

UTICA COLLEGE OF SYRACUSE UNIVERSITY (NY) **1070**
Bus Admin

VALPARAISO UNIVERSITY (IN) **1180**
Bus Admin, Math, Nurs

VANDERBILT UNIVERSITY (TN) **1300**
Anthro, Econ, Ed, Engine, English, Hist, Nurs, Pre-Law, Pre-Med, Psych

VASSAR COLLEGE (NY) **1300**
Art Hist, Bio, Drama, English, Hist, Music, Pre-Law, Psych

VERMONT, UNIVERSITY OF (VT) **1150**
Ag, Bio, Bot, Bus Admin, Chem, For Lang, Geog, Geol, Hist, Physics, Poli Sci, Pre-Law, Pre-Med/Pre-Dental, Zoo

VILLANOVA UNIVERSITY (PA) **1205**
Astro, Bio, Bus Admin, Communic, Engine, Nurs, Pre-Med/Pre-Dental

VIRGINIA COMMONWEALTH UNIVERSITY (VA) **1040**
Art, Drama, Pharm, Pre-Law, Psych, Reli Stu

VIRGINIA, UNIVERSITY OF (VA) **1285**
Amer St, Arch, Art, Astro, Bio, Bus Admin, Econ, English, Hist, Nurs, Reli Stu

VIRGINIA MILITARY INSTITUTE (VA) **1150**
Bus Admin, Econ, Engine, Pre-Law

VIRGINIA POLYTECHNIC INSTITUTE (VA) **1165**
Ag, Arch, Biochem, Bus Admin, Engine, Forest, Psych

VIRGINIA WESLEYAN UNIVERSITY (VA) 1050
Bus Admin, Poli Sci, Pre-Law, Psych, Soc

WABASH COLLEGE (IN) 1220
Bio, Hist, Math, Poli Sci, Pre-Law, Pre-Med/Pre-Dental, Psych

WAGNER COLLEGE (NY) 1090
Bus Admin, Ed, Soc

WAKE FOREST UNIVERSITY (NC) 1310
*Bio, Bus Admin, Econ, English, For Lang, Hist, Physics, Pre-Law, Pre-Med/Pre-Dental, Psych,
Reli Stu*

WARTBURG COLLEGE (IA) 1099
Bio, Ed, Pre-Med/Pre-Dental

WASHINGTON COLLEGE (MD) 1150
Amer St, Bio, Hist, Pre-Med/Pre-Dental, Psych

WASHINGTON & JEFFERSON COLLEGE (PA) 1100
Art, Bio, Bus Admin, Chem, Econ, Ed, English, Pre-Law, Pre-Med/Pre-Dental, Psych

WASHINGTON & LEE UNIVERSITY (VA) 1325
Bus Admin, Econ, English, For Lang, Geol, Hist, Poli Sci, Pre-Law

WASHINGTON UNIVERSITY (MO) 1315
*Anthro, Arch, Art, Art Hist, Bio, Bus Admin, Comp Sci, Engine, English, For Lang, Geol, Math,
Physics, Pre-Law, Pre-Med/Pre-Dental*

WASHINGTON, UNIVERSITY OF (WA) 1145
*Anthro, Art, Bot, Bus Admin, Chem, Comp Sci, Drama, Econ, Ed, Engine, Forest, Geol, Math,
Nurs, Pre-Law, Pre-Med/Pre-Dental, Psych, Zoo*

WASHINGTON STATE UNIVERSITY (WA) 1075
Ag, Anthro, Bus Admin, Econ, Engine, Pharm, Zoo

WAYNE STATE UNIVERSITY (MI) 1000
Engine, For Lang, Nurs, Pharm, Pre-Med/Pre-Dental

WEBSTER UNIVERSITY (MO) 1080
Drama, Psych

WELLESLEY COLLEGE (MA) 1340
*Art, Art Hist, Bio, Chem, Econ, Ed, English, For Lang, Hist, Math, Physics, Poli Sci, Pre-Law,
 Pre-Med/Pre-Dental, Reli Stu*

WELLS COLLEGE (NY) 1160
Amer St, Bus Admin, Ed, English, For Lang, Hist, Pre-Law, Psych, Soc

WESLEYAN COLLEGE (GA) 1135
Art, Bus Admin

WESLEYAN UNIVERSITY (CT) 1350
*Amer St, Art, Astro, Bio, Chem, Drama, Econ, English, Hist, Math, Pre-Law,
Pre-Med/Pre-Dental, Psych, Reli Stu*

WEST CHESTER UNIVERSITY (PA) 1040
Bus Admin, Music

WESTERN CONNECTICUT STATE UNIVERSITY (CT) 1000
Bus Admin, Nurs

WESTERN KENTUCKY (KY) 1000
Ed, Nurs

WESTERN MARYLAND COLLEGE (MD) 1190
Bio, Bus Admin, Ed, Pre-Med/Pre-Dental, Soc

WESTERN MICHIGAN UNIVERSITY (MI) 1100
Ag, Bus Admin, Drama, Ed, Psych

WESTERN NEW ENGLAND COLLEGE (MA) 1025
Bus Admin, Engine, Psych

WESTERN WASHINGTON UNIVERSITY (WA) 1100
Art, Communic, Ed, Home Ec, Soc

WESTFIELD STATE COLLEGE (MA) 1010
Ed

WEST FLORIDA, UNIVERSITY OF (FL) 1099
Bus Admin, Comp Sci, Ed

WESTMINSTER COLLEGE (MO) 1140
Econ, Pre-Law, Psych

WESTMONT COLLEGE (CA) 1130
Econ, Pre-Law, Pre-Med/Pre-Dental, Psych, Reli Stu

WEST VIRGINIA UNIVERSITY (WV) 1050
Bus Admin, Communic, Drama, Forest, Music

WEST VIRGINIA WESLEYAN COLLEGE (WV) 1040
Art, Comp Sci, Ed

WHEATON COLLEGE (IL) 1265
*Bio, Chem, Communic, Ed, English, Math, Music, Philo, Physics, Pre-Law,
Pre-Med/Pre-Dental, Reli Stu. Soc*

WHEATON COLLEGE (MA) 1160
*Art, Art Hist, Bio, Drama, Econ, English, For Lang, Poli Sci, Pre-Law,
Pre-Med/Pre-Dental, Psych, Soc*

WHEELOCK COLLEGE (MA) 1000
Ed

WHITMAN COLLEGE (WA) 1250
*Bio, Chem, Drama, Econ, English, For Lang, Hist, Math, Music, Philo, Physics, Poli Sci,
Pre-Law, Pre-Med/Pre-Dental, Psych, Soc*

WHITTIER COLLEGE (CA) 1050
Bus Admin, Chem, Econ, Ed, English, Poli Sci, Pre-Law

WHITWORTH COLLEGE (WA) 1130
Art, Ed, Music, Reli Stu

WIDENER UNIVERSITY (PA) 1060
Bus Admin, Nurs

WILBERFORCE UNIVERSITY (OH) 1000
Bus Admin, Poli Sci, Pre-Law

WILLAMETTE UNIVERSITY (OR) 1200
Bio, Chem, Econ, English, Math, Music, Poli Sci, Pre-Law, Pre-Med/Pre-Dental, Psych

WILLIAM JEWELL COLLEGE (MO) 1115
Bus Admin, Ed, Music, Nurs

WILLIAM & MARY, COLLEGE OF (VA) 1310
*Amer St, Bio, Bus Admin, Comp Sci, Drama, Ed, Geol, Hist, Physics, Pre-Med/Pre-Dental,
Reli Stu*

WILLIAMS COLLEGE (MA) 1390
*Amer St, Art, Art Hist, Astro, Chem, Classics, Comp Sci, Econ, English, Hist, Poli Sci,
Pre-Med/Pre-Dental, Psych*

WILMINGTON COLLEGE (OH) 1000
Ag

WILSON COLLEGE (PA) 1063
Econ, Pre-Law, Soc

WINONA STATE UNIVERSITY (MN) 1050
Communic, Soc

WISCONSIN, UNIVERSITY OF, AT
      LA CROSSE 1080
      Comp Sci
      MADISON 1199
      *Ag, Anthro, Biochem, Bot, Bus Admin, Communic, Comp Sci, Ed, Engine, English,
      For Lang, Forest, Geol, Hist, Home Ec, Math, Nurs, Physics, Psych, Soc*
      MILWAUKEE 1050
      Ed, English, Nurs, Pre-Law

WITTENBERG UNIVERSITY (OH) 1170
*Art, Bio, Bus Admin, Ed, English, Geog, Hist, Music, Poli Sci, Pre-Law, Pre-Med/Pre-Dental,
Psych*

WOFFORD COLLEGE (SC) 1175
*Bio, Chem, Comp Sci, Econ, Ed, English, For Lang, Hist, Math, Philo, Pre-Law,
Pre-Med/Pre-Dental, Psych*

WOODBURY UNIVERSITY (CA) 1000
Arch, Bus Admin

WOOSTER, COLLEGE OF (OH) 1165
*Art Hist, Bio, Chem, Drama, Econ, Geol, Hist, Math, Music, Pre-Law, Pre-Med/Pre-Dental,
Reli Stu, Soc*

WORCESTER POLYTECHNIC INSTITUTE (MA) **1250**
Comp Sci, Engine, Physics

WYOMING, UNIVERSITY OF (WY) **1070**
Ag, Astro, Bot, Bus Admin, Chem, Econ, Engine, Geol, Pharm, Physics, Pre-Law,
Pre-Med/Pre-Dental, Psych

XAVIER UNIVERSITY (OH) **1090**
Bus Admin, Communic

XAVIER UNIVERSITY OF LOUISIANA (LA) **1020**
Bio, Bus Admin, Chem, Pharm, Pre-Med/Pre-Dental, Psych

YALE UNIVERSITY (CT) **1405**
Amer St, Anthro, Arch, Art, Art Hist, Biochem, Bio, Classics, Drama, Econ, English, For Lang,
Hist, Math, Music, Philo, Poli Sci, Pre-Law, Pre-Med/Pre-Dental, Psych, Reli Stu

YESHIVA UNIVERSITY (NY) **1240**
Bio, Bus Admin, Comp Sci, Hist, Physics, Poli Sci, Pre-Med/Pre-Dental, Psych

YORK COLLEGE OF PENNSYLVANIA (PA) **1105**
Ed, Nurs

SECTION FOUR

APPENDICES

APPENDIX A
The 760 Colleges Used In This Study

A   **Adelphi University**
Garden City, NY 11530

Adrian College
Adrian, Michigan 49221

◆ **Agnes Scott College**
Decatur, Georgia 30030

◆ **Alabama, University of**
Tuscaloosa, Alabama 35487

Alaska, University of
Fairbanks, Alaska 99775

Alaska, University of
Anchorage, Alaska 99508

Albany College of Pharmacy (Union College)
Schenectady, New York 12308

Albertson College
Caldwell, Idaho 83605

◆ **Albion College**
Albion, Michigan 49224

Albright College
Reading, Pennsylvania 19612

Alfred University
Alfred, New York 14802

◆ **Allegheny College**
Meadville, Pennsylvania 16335

Allentown College of St. Francis De Sales
Center Valley, Pennsylvania 18034

◆ **Alma College**
Alma, Michigan 48801

American Academy of Dramatic Arts
New York, New York 10016

American International College
Springfield, Massachusetts 01109

◆ **American University**
Washington, DC 20016

◆ **Amherst College**
Amherst, Massachusetts 01002

Appalachian State University
Boone, North Carolina 28608

Aquinas College
Grand Rapids, Michigan 49506

◆ **Arizona, University of**
Tucson, Arizona 85721

◆ **Arizona State University**
Tempe, Arizona 85287

◆ **Arkansas, University of**
Fayetteville, Arkansas 72701

Art Center College of Design
Pasadena, California 91103

Asbury College
Wilmore, Kentucky 40390

Auburn University
Auburn University, Alabama 36849

Augsburg College
Minneapolis, Minnesota 55454

◆ **Augustana College**
Rock Island, Illinois 61201

Augustana College
Sioux Falls, South Dakota 57197

Austin College
Sherman, Texas 75091

Averett College
Danville, Virginia 24541

B   **Babson College**
Wellesley, Massachusetts 02157

Baker University
Baldwin City, Kansas 66006

Baldwin-Wallace College
Berea, Ohio 44017

Bard College, Annandale-on-Hudson
New York 12504

Barry University
Miami Shores, Florida 33161

◆ **Bates College**
Lewiston, Maine 04240

◆ **Baylor University**
Waco, Texas 76798

Belhaven College
Jackson, Mississippi 39202

Bellarmine College
Louisville, Kentucky 40205

Belmont Abbey College
Belmont, North Carolina 28012

Belmont University
Nashville, Tennessee 37212

◆ **Beloit College**
Beloit, Wisconsin 53511

Bemidji State University
Bemidji, Minnesota 56601

Benedictine College
Atchison, Kansas 66002

◆ Phi Beta Kappa Schools   ■ Predominantly African-American Institution

■ **Bennett College**
Greensboro, North Carolina 27401

Bennington College
Bennington, Vermont 05201

Bethel College
St. Paul, Minnesota 55112

Bentley College
Waltham, Massachusetts 02254

Berea College
Berea, Kentucky 40404

Berry College
Rome, Georgia 30149

Bethany College
Bethany, West Virginia 26032

Biola University
La Mirada, California 91720

◆ **Birmingham-Southern College**
Birmingham, Alabama 32254

Bloomsburg University
Bloomsburg, Pennsylvania 17815

Bluffton College
Bluffton, Ohio 45817

◆ **Boston College**
Chestnut Hill, Massachusetts 02167

Boston Conservatory
Boston, Massachusetts 02215

◆ **Boston University**
Boston, Massachusetts 02215

◆ **Bowdoin College**
Brunswick, Maine 04011

◆ **Bowling Green State University**
Bowling Green, Ohio 43403

Bradley University
Peoria, Illinois 61625

◆ **Brandeis University**
Waltham, Massachusetts 02250

Brigham Young University
Provo, Utah 84602

◆ **Brown University**
Providence, Rhode Island 02912

Bryant College
Smithfield, Rhode Island 02917

Bryn Mawr College
Bryn Mawr, Pennsylvania 19010

◆ **Bucknell University**
Lewisburg, Pennsylvania 17837

Buena Vista College
Storm Lake, Iowa 50588

Butler University
Indianapolis, Indiana 46208

C **Caldwell College**
Caldwell, New Jersey 07006

California Institute of the Arts
Valencia, California 91355

California Institute of Technology
Pasadena, California 91125

California, University of, at
◆ **Berkeley**, California 94720
◆ **Davis**, California 95616
◆ **Irvine**, California 92664
◆ **Los Angeles**, California 90024
◆ **Riverside**, California 92521
◆ **San Diego**, California 92093
◆ **Santa Barbara**, California 93106
◆ **Santa Cruz**, California 95064

California Maritime Academy
Vallejo, California 94590

California Polytechnic State University
San Luis Obispo, California 93407

California Polytechnic State University
Pomona, California 91768

◆ **California State University**
Chico, California 95926

California State University
Long Beach, California 90840

Calvin College
Grand Rapids, Michigan 49506

Capital University
Columbus, Ohio 43209

◆ **Carleton College**
Northfield, Minnesota 55057

◆ **Carnegie Mellon University**
Pittsburgh, Pennsylvania 15213

Carroll College
Helena, Montana 59601

Carroll College
Waukesha, Wisconsin 53186

Carthage College
Kenosha, Wisconsin 53141

◆ **Case Western Reserve University**
Cleveland, Ohio 44106

Catawba College
Salisbury, North Carolina 28144

Catholic University of America
Washington, DC 20064

Cedar Crest College
Allentown, Pennsylvania 18104

◆ Phi Beta Kappa Schools   ■ Predominantly African-American Institution

Cedarville College
Cedarville, Ohio 45314

Centenary College of Louisiana
Shreveport, Louisiana 71135

Central Florida, University of
Orlando, Florida 32816

Central Michigan University
Mount Pleasant, Michigan 48859

Central College
Pella, Iowa 50219

◆ **Centre College**
Danville, Kentucky 40422

Chapman College
Orange, California 92666

College of Charleston
Charleston, South Carolina 29424

Charleston, University of
Charleston, West Virginia 25304

◆ **Chatham College**
Pittsburgh, Pennsylvania 15232

Chestnut Hill College
Philadelphia, Pennsylvania 19118

◆ **Chicago, University of**
Chicago, Illinois 60637

Christian Brothers College
Memphis, Tennessee 38104

◆ **Cincinnati, University of**
Cincinnati, Ohio 45221

◆ **Claremont McKenna College**
Claremont, California 91711

◆ **Clark University**
Worcester, Massachusetts 01610

Clarke College
Dubuque, Iowa 52001

Clarkson University
Potsdam, New York 13676

Clemson University
Clemson, South Carolina 29634

Cleveland Institute of Music
Cleveland, Ohio 44106

◆ **Coe College**
Cedar Rapids, Iowa 52402

◆ **Colby College**
Waterville, Maine 04901

◆ **Colgate University**
Hamilton, New York 13346

◆ **Colorado College**
Colorado Springs, Colorado 80903

◆ **Colorado, University of**
Boulder, Colorado 80309

Colorado, University of
Colorado Springs, Colorado 80933

Colorado, University of
Denver, Colorado 80208

Colorado School of Mines
Golden, Colorado 80401

◆ **Colorado State University**
Fort Collins, Colorado 80523

◆ **Columbia University**
New York, New York 10027
    ◆ **Barnard College**, New York, NY 10027

Concordia College
Moorhead, Minnesota 56560

◆ **Connecticut, University of**
Storrs, Connecticut 06268

◆ **Connecticut College**
New London, Connecticut 06320

Converse College
Spartanburg, South Carolina 29301

Cooper Union College, The
New York, New York 10003

◆ **Cornell College**
Mount Vernon, Iowa 52314

◆ **Cornell University**
Ithaca, New York 14853

Covenant College
Lookout Mountain, Georgia 30750

Creighton University
Omaha, Nebraska 68178

Curtis Institute of Music
Philadelphia, Pennsylvania 19103

D **Daemen College**
Amherst, New York 14226

◆ **Dallas, University of**
Irving, Texas 75062

◆ **Dartmouth College**
Hanover, New Hampshire 03755

◆ **Davidson College**
Davidson, North Carolina 28036

Dayton, University of
Dayton, Ohio 45469

◆ **Delaware, University of**
Newark, Delaware 19716

Delaware Valley College
Doylestown, Pennsylvania 18901

◆ Phi Beta Kappa Schools   ▮ Predominantly African-American Institution

◆ **Denison University**
Granville, Ohio 43023

◆ **Denver, University of**
Denver, Colorado 80208

DePaul University
Chicago, Illinois 60604

◆ **DePauw University**
Greencastle, Indiana 46135

Detroit Mercy, University of
Detroit, Michigan 48221

◆ **Dickinson College**
Carlisle, Pennsylvania 17013

■ **Dillard University**
New Orleans, Louisiana 70122

Doane College
Crete, Nebraska 68333

Dordt College
Sioux Center, Iowa 51250

◆ **Drake University**
Des Moines, Iowa 50311

◆ **Drew University**
Madison, New Jersey 07940

Drexel University
Philadelphia, Pennsylvania 19104

Drury College
Springfield, Missouri 65802

◆ **Duke University**
Durham, North Carolina 27706

Duquesne University
Pittsburgh, Pennsylvania 15219

D'Youville College
Buffalo, New York 14201

E ◆ **Earlham College**
Richmond, Indiana 47374

Eckerd College
St. Petersburg, Florida 33733

Elizabethtown College
Elizabethtown, Pennsylvania 17022

Elon College
Elon College, North Carolina 27244

◆ **Elmira College**
Elmira, New York 14901

Emerson College
Boston, Massachusetts 02116

Emory and Henry College
Emory, Virginia 24327

◆ **Emory University**
Atlanta, Georgia 30322

Erskine College
Due West, South Carolina 39639

Eureka College
Eureka, Illinois 61530

Evansville, University of
Evansville, Indiana 47722

F ◆ **Fairfield University**
Fairfield, Connecticut 06430

Fairleigh Dickinson University
Rutherford, New Jersey 07070

Ferris State University
Big Rapids, Michigan 49307

◆■ **Fisk University**
Nashville, Tennessee 37203

Five Towns College
Dix Hills, New York 11746

Flagler College
St. Augustine, Florida 32085

◆ **Florida, University of**
Gainesville, Florida 32611

■ **Florida A&M University**
Tallahassee, FL 32307

Florida Atlantic University
Boca Raton, Florida 33431

Florida Institute of Technology
Melbourne, Florida 32901

Florida International University
Miami, Florida 33199

◆ **Florida State University**
Tallahassee, Florida 32306

Florida Southern College
Lakeland, Florida 33801

Fontbonne College
St. Louis, Missouri 63105

Franklin College of Indiana
Franklin, Indiana 46131

◆ **Fordham University**
Bronx, New York 10458

Fort Lewis College
Durango, Colorado 81301

Franciscan University of Steubenville
Steubenville, Ohio 43952

◆ **Franklin & Marshall College**
Lancaster, Pennsylvania 17604

◆ **Furman University, Greenville**
South Carolina 29613

◆ Phi Beta Kappa Schools   ■ Predominantly African-American Institution

G   **Gannon University, Erie**
Pennsylvania 16541

Geneva College
Beaver Falls, Pennsylvania 15010

General Motors Inst.
Flint, MI 48504

Geneva College
Beaver Falls, Pennsylvania 15010

◆ **Georgetown University**
Washington, DC 20057

George Fox College
Newberg, Oregon 97132

George Mason University
Fairfax, Virginia 22030

◆ **George Washington University**
Washington, DC 20052

◆ **Georgia, University of**
Athens, Georgia 30602

Georgia Institute of Technology
Atlanta, Georgia 30332

Georgia Southern University
Statesboro, Georgia 30460

◆ **Gettysburg College**
Gettysburg, Pennsylvania 17325

Gonzaga University
Spokane, Washington 99258

Gordon College
Wenham, Massachusetts 01984

Goshen College
Goshen, Indiana 46526

◆ **Goucher College**
Towson, Maryland 21204

Graceland College
Lamoni, Iowa 50140

Grand Valley State University
Allendale, Michigan 49401

◆ **Grinnell College**
Grinnell, Iowa 50112

Grove City College
Grove City, Pennsylvania 16127

Guilford College
Greensboro, North Carolina 27410

◆ **Gustavus Adolphus College**
St. Peter, Minnesota 56082

H ◆ **Hamilton College**
Clinton, New York 13323

◆ **Hamline University**
St. Paul, Minnesota 55104

◆ **Hampden-Sydney College**
Hampden-Sydney, Virginia 23943

▮ **Hampton University**
Hampton, Virginia 23668

Hanover College
Hanover, Indiana 47243

Hartford, University of
Hartford, Connecticut 06117

Hartwick College
Oneonta, New York 13820

◆ **Harvard/Radcliffe Colleges**
Cambridge, Massachusetts 02138

Harvey Mudd College
Claremont, California 91711

Hastings College
Hastings, Nebraska 68901

◆ **Haverford College**
Haverford, Pennsylvania 19041

Hawaii Pacific University
Honolulu, Hawaii 96813

◆ **Hawaii, University of**
Manoa, Honolulu, Hawaii 96822

Heidelberg College
Tiffin, Ohio 44883

Hendrix College
Conway, Arkansas 72032

Hillsdale College
Hillsdale, Michigan 49242

◆ **Hiram College**
Hiram, Ohio 44234

◆ **Hobart & William Smith Colleges**
Geneva, New York 14456

◆ **Hofstra University**
Hempstead, New York 11550

◆ **Hollins College**
Roanoke, Virginia 24020

◆ **Holy Cross, College of the**
Worcester, Massachusetts 01610

Hood College
Frederick, Maryland 21701

◆ **Hope College**
Holland, Michigan 49423

Houghton College
Houghton, New York 14744

Houston Baptist University
Houston, Texas 77074

◆ Phi Beta Kappa Schools   ▮ Predominantly African-American Institution

Houston, University of
Houston, Texas 77004

◆▮ **Howard University**
Washington, DC 20059

Humboldt State University
Arcata, California 95521

Huntingdon College
Montgomery, Alabama 36194

▮ ◆ **Idaho, University of**
Moscow, Idaho 83843

Illinois, University of, at
◆ **Urbana-Champaign**, Illinois 61801
◆ **Chicago**, Illinois 60680

◆ **Illinois College**
Jacksonville, Illinois 62650

Illinois Institute of Technology
Chicago, Illinois 60616

Illinois State University
Normal, Illinois 61761

Illinois Wesleyan University
Bloomington, Illinois 61701

Indiana State University
Terre Haute, Indiana 47809

◆ **Indiana University**
Bloomington, Indiana 47401

Indiana University of Pennsylvania
Indiana, Pennsylvania 15705

Iona College
New Rochelle, New York 10801

◆ **Iowa, University of**
Iowa City, Iowa 52242

◆ **Iowa State University of Science & Technology**
Ames, Iowa 50011

Ithaca College
Ithaca, New York 14850

J **Jacksonville State University**
Jacksonville, Alabama 36265

Jacksonville University
Jacksonville, Florida 32211

James Madison University
Harrisonburg, Virginia 22807

John Carroll University
Cleveland, Ohio 44118

◆ **Johns Hopkins University**
Baltimore, Maryland 21218

Johnson C. Smith University
Charlotte, North Carolina 28216

Judson College
Marion, Alabama 36756

Juilliard School
New York, New York 10023

Juniata College
Huntingdon, Pennsylvania 16652

K ◆ **Kalamazoo College**
Kalamazoo, Michigan 49007

Kansas Newman College
Wichita, Kansas 67213

◆ **Kansas, University of**
Lawrence, Kansas 66045

◆ **Kansas State University**
Manhattan, Kansas 66506

Keene State College
Keene, New Hampshire 03431

Kennesaw State College
Marietta, Georgia 30061

◆ **Kent State University**
Kent, Ohio 44242

◆ **Kentucky, University of**
Lexington, Kentucky 40506

Kentucky Wesleyan College
Owensboro, Kentucky 42301

◆ **Kenyon College**
Gambier, Ohio 43022

King College
Bristol, Tennessee 37620

King's College
Wilkes-Barre, Pennsylvania 18711

◆ **Knox College**
Galesburg, Illinois 61401

Kutztown University
Kutztown, Pennsylvania 19530

L ◆ **Lafayette College**
Easton, Pennsylvania 18042

◆ **Lake Forest College**
Lake Forest, Illinois 60045

LaSalle University
Philadelphia, Pennsylvania 19141

La Verne, University of
La Verne, California 91750

◆ **Lawrence University**
Appleton, Wisconsin 54912

Lebanon Valley College
Annville, Pennsylvania 17003

◆ Phi Beta Kappa Schools   ▮ Predominantly African-American Institution

◆ **Lehigh University**
Bethlehem, Pennsylvania 18015

LeMoyne College
Syracuse, New York 13214

Lenoir Rhyne College
Hickory, North Carolina 28603

Lesley College
Cambridge, Massachusetts 02138

Letourneau College
Longview, Texas 75607

Lewis & Clark College
Portland, Oregon 97219

Lindenwood College
St. Charles, Missouri 63301

Linfield College
McMinnville, Oregon 97128

Lock Haven University of Pennsylvania
Lock Haven, Pennsylvania 17745

Long Island University-Southampton College
Southampton, New York 11968

Longwood College
Farmville, Virginia 23909

Loras College
Dubuque, Iowa 52001

◆ **Louisiana State University**
Baton Rouge, Louisiana 70802

Louisville, University of
Louisville, Kentucky 40292

Lowell, University of
Lowell, Massachusetts 01854

◆ **Loyola College**
Baltimore, Maryland 21210

◆ **Loyola Marymount University**
Los Angeles, California 90045

◆ **Loyola University of Chicago**
Chicago, Illinois 60611

Loyola University
New Orleans, Louisiana 70118

◆ **Luther College**
Decorah, Iowa 52101

Lycoming College
Williamsport, Pennsylvania 17701

Lynchburg College
Lynchburg, Virginia 24501

Lyon College
Batesville, Arkansas 72501

M ◆ **Macalester College**
St. Paul, Minnesota 55105

MacMurray College
Jacksonville, Illinois 62650

Maine, University of
Farmington, Maine 04938

◆ **Maine, University of**
Orono, Maine 04469

Malone College
Canton, Ohio 44709

Manchester College
Manchester, Indiana 46962

◆ **Manhattan College**
Riverdale, New York 10471

Manhattan School of Music
New York, New York 10027

Manhattanville College
Purchase, New York 10577

Mansfield University of Pennsylvania
Mansfield, Pennsylvania 16933

◆ **Marietta College**
Marietta, Ohio 45750

Marist College
Poughkeepsie, NY 12601

◆ **Marquette University**
Milwaukee, Wisconsin 53233

◆ **Mary Baldwin College**
Staunton, Virginia 24401

Marycrest College
Davenport, Iowa 52804

Marygrove College
Detroit, Michigan 48221

Maryland Institute-College of Art
Baltimore, Maryland 21217

Maryland, University of Baltimore County
Baltimore, Maryland 21228

◆ **Maryland, University of**
College Park, Maryland 20742

Maryville University-Saint Louis
St. Louis, Missouri 63141

◆ **Mary Washington College**
Fredericksburg, Virginia 22401

Massachusetts College of Art
Boston Massachusetts 02215

◆ **Massachusetts, University of**
Amherst, Massachusetts 01003

Massachusetts, University of
Boston, Massachusetts 02125

◆ Phi Beta Kappa Schools   ▮ Predominantly African-American Institution

Massachusetts, University of
Lowell, Massachusetts 01854

Massachusetts, University of
North Dartmouth, Massachusetts 02747

◆ Massachusetts Institute of Technology
Cambridge, Massachusetts 02139

Massachusetts Maritime Academy
Buzzards Bay, Massachusetts 02532

Memphis, University of
Memphis, Tennessee 38152

Mercer University
Macon, Georgia 31207

Mercy College
Dobbs Ferry, New York 10522

Mercyhurst College
Erie, Pennsylvania 16546

Meredith College
Raleigh, North Carolina 27607

Merrimack College
No. Andover, Massachusetts 01845

Messiah College
Grantham, Pennsylvania 17027

◆ Miami University
Oxford, Ohio 45056

◆ Miami, University of
Coral Gables, Florida 33124

◆ Michigan, University of
Ann Arbor, Michigan 48109

Michigan, University of
Dearborn, Michigan 48128

◆ Michigan State University
East Lansing, Michigan 48824

Michigan Technological University
Houghton, Michigan 49931

◆ Middlebury College
Middlebury, Vermont 05753

Millersville University of Pennsylvania
Millersville, Pennsylvania 17551

Milligan College
Milligan College, Tennessee 37682

Millikin University
Decatur, Illinois 62522

◆ Mills College
Oakland, California 94613

◆ Millsaps College
Jackson, Mississippi 39210

Milwaukee School of Engineering
Milwaukee, Wisconsin 53201

◆ Minnesota, University of
Minneapolis, Minnesota 55455

Minnesota, University of
Morris, Minnesota 56267

Misericordia, College
Dallas, Pennsylvania 18612

Mississippi College
Clinton, Mississippi 39058

Mississippi State University
Mississippi State, Mississippi 39762

Mississippi, University of
University, Mississippi 38677

Mississippi University for Women
Columbus, Mississippi 39701

◆ Missouri, University of
Columbia, Missouri 65201

Missouri, University of
Kansas City, Missouri 64110

Missouri, University of
Rolla, Missouri 65401

Monmouth College
Monmouth, Illinois 61462

Monmouth University
West Long Branch, New Jersey 07764

Montana College of
Mineral Science & Technology
Butte, Montana 59701

Montana, University of
Missoula, Montana 59812

Montana State University
Bozeman, Montana 59717

Montevallo, University of
Montevallo, Alabama 35115

Montclair State College
Upper Montclair, New Jersey 07043

Montreat College
Montreat, North Carolina 28757

Moore College of Art
Philadelphia, Pennsylvania 19103

Moravian College
Bethlehem, Pennsylvania 18018

◆ ■Morehouse College
Atlanta, Georgia 30314

Morningside College
Sioux City, Iowa 51106

◆ Mount Holyoke College
South Hadley, Massachusetts 01075

Mount Mercy College
Cedar Rapids, Iowa 52402

Mount St. Joseph
Cincinnati, Ohio 45233

Mount St. Mary's College
Emmitsburg, Maryland 21727

Mount St. Mary's College
Newburgh, New York, 12550

Mount St. Mary's College
Los Angeles, California 90049

Mount Union College
Alliance, Ohio 44601

◆ **Muhlenberg College**
Allentown, Pennsylvania 18104

Mundelein College
Chicago, Illinois 60660

Muskingum College
New Concord, Ohio 43762

N **Nazareth College of Rochester**
Rochester, New York 14610

◆ **Nebraska, University of**
Lincoln, Nebraska 68588

Nebraska Wesleyan University
Lincoln, Nebraska 68504

Nevada, University of, at
Las Vegas, Nevada 89154
Reno, Nevada 89557

New College of U.S.F.
Sarasota, Florida 34243

New England Conservatory of Music
Boston, Massachusetts 02115

◆ **New Hampshire, University of**
Durham, New Hampshire 03824

New Jersey, College of
Trenton, New Jersey 08650

New Jersey Institute of Technology
Newark, New Jersey 07102

New Mexico Institute of Mining and Technology
Socorro, New Mexico 87801

New Mexico State University
Las Cruces, New Mexico 88003

◆ **New Mexico, University of**
Albuquerque, New Mexico 87131

New Orleans, University of
New Orleans, Louisiana 70148

New York, City University of
◆ **Baruch College**, New York, NY 10010
◆ **Brooklyn College**, Brooklyn, NY 11210
◆ **City College**, New York, New York 10031

◆ **Herbert H. Lehman College**, Bronx, NY 10468
◆ **Hunter College**, New York, NY 10021
◆ **Queens College**, Flushing, NY 11367

New York, State University of, at
◆ **Albany**, New York 12222
◆ **Binghamton**, New York 13901
Brockport, New York 14420
◆ **Buffalo**, New York 14214
Fredonia, New York 14063
Geneseo, New York 1445
New Paltz, New York 12561
Oneonta, New York 13820
Oswego, New York 13126
Plattsburgh, New York 12901
Potsdam, New York 13676
Purchase, New York 10577
◆ **Stony Brook**, New York 11794

◆ **New York University**
New York, New York 10011

Niagara University
Niagara Falls, New York, 14109

North Carolina School of the Arts
Winston-Salem, North Carolina 27117

North Carolina, University of, at
Asheville, North Carolina 28804
◆ **Chapel Hill**, North Carolina 27514
Charlotte, North Carolina 28223
◆ **Greensboro**, North Carolina 27412
Wilmington, North Carolina 28403

◆ **North Carolina State University**
Raleigh, North Carolina 27650

North Central College
Naperville, Illinois 60566

North Dakota State University
Fargo, North Dakota 58105

◆ **North Dakota, University of**
Grand Forks, North Dakota 58201

North Florida, University of
Jacksonville, Florida 32216

North Georgia College
Dahlonega, Georgia 30597

North Texas, University of
Denton, Texas 76203

Northeastern University
Boston, Massachusetts 02115

Northern Arizona University
Flagstaff, Arizona 86011

Northern Colorado University
Greeley, Colorado 80639

Northern Illinois University
DeKalb, Illinois 60115

◆ Phi Beta Kappa Schools   ∎ Predominantly African-American Institution

Northern Iowa, University of
Cedar Falls, Iowa 50614

Northwestern College
Orange City, Iowa 51041

Northwestern College
St. Paul, Minnesota 55113

◆ **Northwestern University**
Evanston, Illinois 60201

Northwood Institute
Midland, Michigan 48640

◆ **Notre Dame, University of**
Notre Dame, Indiana 46556

Nova Southeastern University
Ft. Lauderdale, Florida 33314

O **Oakland University**
Rochester, Michigan 48309

◆ **Oberlin College**
Oberlin, Ohio 44074

◆ **Occidental College**
Los Angeles, California 90041

Oglethorpe University
Atlanta, Georgia 30319

◆ **Ohio University**
Athens, Ohio 45701

Ohio Northern University
Ada, Ohio 45810

◆ **Ohio State University**
Columbus, Ohio 43210

◆ **Ohio Wesleyan University**
Delaware, Ohio 43015

Oklahoma Baptist University
Shawnee, Oklahoma 74801

Oklahoma City University
Oklahoma City, Oklahoma 73106

◆ **Oklahoma, University of**
Norman, Oklahoma 73069

Oklahoma State University
Stillwater, Oklahoma 74078

Old Dominion University
Norfolk, Virginia 23529

◆ **Oregon, University of**
Eugene, Oregon 97403

Oregon State University
Corvallis, Oregon 97331

Otis Art Institute of Parsons School of Design
Los Angeles, California 90057

Otterbein College
Westerville, Ohio 43081

Ozarks, College of the
Point Lookout, Missouri 65726

P **Pace University**
New York, New York 10038

Pacific Lutheran University
Tacoma, Washington 98447

Pacific, U. of the
Stockton, California 95211

Pacific University
Forest Grove, Oregon 97116

Palm Beach Atlantic College
West Palm Beach, Florida 33416

Parsons School of Design
New York, New York 10011

◆ **Pennsylvania, University of**
Philadelphia, Pennsylvania 19104

◆ **Pennsylvania State University**
University Park, Pennsylvania 16802

Pepperdine University
Malibu, California 90265

Philadelphia College of Pharmacy and Science
Philadelphia, Pennsylvania 19104

Philadelphia College of Textiles & Sciences
Philadelphia, Pennsylvania 19144

Pittsburgh, University of
Johnstown, Pennsylvania 15904

Pittsburgh, University of
Bradford, Pennsylvania 16701

◆ **Pittsburgh, University of**
Pittsburgh, Pennsylvania 15260

Pitzer College
Claremont, California 91711

Point Loma Nazarene College
San Diego, California 92106

Point Park College
Pittsburgh, Pennsylvania 15222

Polytechnic Institute of New York
Brooklyn, New York 11201

◆ **Pomona College**
Claremont, California 91711

Portland, University of
Portland, Oregon 97203

Pratt Institute
Brooklyn, New York 11205

Presbyterian College
Clinton, South Carolina 29325

◆ Phi Beta Kappa Schools ▮ Predominantly African-American Institution

◆ **Princeton University**
Princeton, New Jersey 08544

Principia College
Elsah, Illinois 62028

Providence College
Providence, Rhode Island 02918

Puerto Rico, University of
CAYEY Puerto Rico 00633

Puerto Rico, University of
Rio Piedras, Puerto Rico 00931

◆ **Puget Sound, University of**
Tacoma, Washington 98416

◆ **Purdue University**
W. Lafayette, Indiana 47907

Q **Queens College**
Charlotte, North Carolina 28274

Quincy College
Quincy, Illinois 62301

Quinnipiac College
Hamden, Connecticut 06518

R **Radford University**
Radford, Virginia 24142

◆ **Randolph-Macon College**
Ashland, Virginia 23005

◆ **Randolph-Macon Woman's College**
Lynchburg, Virginia 24503

◆ **Redlands, University of**
Redlands, California 92373

◆ **Reed College**
Portland, Oregon 97202

Regis University
Denver, Colorado 80221

Rensselaer Polytechnic Institute
Troy, New York 12180

Rhode Island School of Design
Providence, Rhode Island 02903

◆ **Rhode Island, University of**
Kingston, Rhode Island 02881

◆ **Rhodes College**
Memphis, Tennessee 38112

◆ **Rice University**
Houston, Texas 77251

◆ **Richmond, University of**
Richmond, Virginia 23173

Rider College
Lawrenceville, New Jersey 08648

◆ **Ripon College**
Ripon, Wisconsin 54971

Roanoke College
Salem, Virginia 24153

◆ **Rochester, University of**
Rochester, New York 14627

Rochester Institute of Technology
Rochester, New York 14623

◆ **Rockford College**
Rockford, Illinois 61108

Rockhurst College
Kansas City, Missouri 64110

Roger Williams University
Bristol, Rhode Island 02809

Rollins College
Winter Park, Florida 32789

Roosevelt University
Chicago, Illinois 60605

Rosary College
River Forest, Illinois 60305

Rose-Hulman Institute of Technology
Terre Haute, Indiana 47803

Rosemont College
Rosemont, Pennsylvania 19010

Rowan College of New Jersey
Mahwah, New Jersey 08028

◆ **Rutgers University**
New Brunswick, New Jersey 08903

Rutgers University
Camden, New Jersey 08102

S **Sacred Heart University**
Fairfield, Connecticut 06432

Sage Colleges
Troy, New York 12180

St. Ambrose University
Davenport, Iowa 52803

St. Andrews Presbyterian College
Laurinburg, North Carolina 28352

St. Anselm College
Manchester, New Hampshire 03102

St. Bonaventure University
St. Bonaventure, New York 14778

◆ **St. Catherine, College of**
St. Paul, Minnesota 55105

St. Francis College
Brooklyn, New York 11201

St. John Fisher College
Rochester, New, York 14618

◆ Phi Beta Kappa Schools ■ Predominantly African-American Institution

St. John's University
Jamaica, New York 11439

Saint John's University/College of Saint Benedict
Collegeville, Minnesota 56321

Saint Joseph's College
W. Hartford, Connecticut 06117

St. Joseph's College
Rensselaer, Indianna 47978

St. Joseph's College
Standish, Maine 04084

Saint Joseph's University
Philadelphia, Pennsylvania 19131

◆ St. Lawrence University
Canton, New York 13617

St. Louis College of Pharmacy
St. Louis, Missouri 63110

◆ Saint Louis University
St. Louis, Missouri 63103

Saint Mary's College
Notre Dame, Indiana 46556

Saint Mary's College of California
St. Mary's College, California 94575

St. Mary's College of Maryland
St. Mary's City, Maryland 20686

St. Mary's College of Minnesota
Winona, Minnesota 55987

St. Mary's University of San Antonio
San Antonio, Texas 78228

Saint Michael's College
Winooski Park, Colchester, Vermont 05439

St. Norbert College
DePere, Wisconsin 54115

◆ St. Olaf College
Northfield, Minnesota 55057

Saint Rose, College of
Albany, New York 12203

Saint Scholastica, College of
Duluth, Minnesota 55811

Saint Thomas, University of
St. Paul, Minnesota 55105

Saint Thomas, University of
Houston, Texas 77006

St. Vincent College
Latrobe, Pennsylvania 15650

Salem College
Winston-Salem, North Carolina 27108

Salem State College
Salem, Massachusetts 01970

Salisbury State University
Salisbury, Maryland 21801

Samford University
Birmingham, Alabama 35229

◆ San Diego State University
San Diego, California 92182

San Diego, University of
San Diego, California 92110

San Francisco Conservatory of Music
San Francisco, California 94122

San Francisco, University of
San Francisco, California 94117

◆ San Francisco State University
San Francisco, California 94132

◆ Santa Clara University
Santa Clara, California 95053

Santa Fe, College of
Santa Fe, New Mexico 87501

Sarah Lawrence College
Bronxville, New York 10708

Schreiner College
Kerrville, Texas 78028

Scranton, University of
Scranton, Pennsylvania 18510

◆ Scripps College
Claremont, California 91711

Seattle University
Seattle, Washington 98122

Seattle Pacific University
Seattle, Washington 98119

Seton Hall University
South Orange, New Jersey 07079

Seton Hill College
Greensburg, Pennsylvania 15601

▌ Shaw University
Raleigh, North Carolina 27611

Shepherd College
Shepherdstown, West Virginia 25443

Shippensburg University
Shippensburg, Pennsylvania 17257

Siena College
Loudonville, New York 12211

Simmons College
Boston, Massachusetts 02115

Simpson College
Indianola, Iowa 50125

◆ Phi Beta Kappa Schools   ▌ Predominantly African-American Institution

◆ **Skidmore College**
Saratoga Springs, New York 12866

◆ **Smith College**
Northampton, Massachusetts 01063

Sonoma State University
Rohnert Park, California 94928

◆ **South, University of The**
Sewanee, Tennessee 37375

◆ **South Carolina, University of**
Columbia, South Carolina 29208

◆ **South Dakota, University of**
Vermillion, South Dakota 57069

South Dakota School of Mines
Rapid City, South Dakota 57701

◆ **Southern California, University of**
Los Angeles, California 90007

Southern Illinois University
Carbondale, Illinois 62901

Southern Maine, University of
Portland, Maine 04103

◆ **Southern Methodist University**
Dallas, Texas 75275

Southern Oregon State College
Ashland, Oregon 97520

South Florida, University of
Tampa, Florida 33620

Southwest Baptist University
Bolivar, Missouri 65613

Southwest Texas State University
San Marcos, Texas 78666

◆ **Southwestern University**
Georgetown, Texas 78626

▮ **Spelman College**
Atlanta, Georgia 30314

Spring Hill College
Mobile, Alabama 36608

◆ **Stanford University**
Stanford, California 94305

Stephen F. Austin State University
Nagogdoches, Texas 75962

◆ **Stetson University**
Deland, Florida 32720

Stevens Institute of Technology
Hoboken, New Jersey 07030

Stockton State
Pomona, New Jersey 08240

Stonehill College
North Easton, Massachusetts 02357

Susquehanna University
Selinsgrove, Pennsylvania 17870

◆ **Swarthmore College**
Swarthmore, Pennsylvania 19081

◆ **Sweet Briar College**
Sweet Briar, Virginia 24595

◆ **Syracuse University**
Syracuse, New York 13210

T   **Tampa, University of**
Tampa, Florida 33606

Taylor University
Upland, Indiana 46989

◆ **Temple University**
Philadelphia, Pennsylvania 19122

◆ **Tennessee, University of**
Knoxville, Tennessee 37916

Texas, University of, at
Arlington, Texas 76019
◆ Austin, Texas 78712
San Antonio, Texas 78249

Texas A & M
College Station, Texas 77843

Texas A & M at Galveston
Galveston, Texas 77553

◆ **Texas Christian University**
Fort Worth, Texas 76129

Texas Tech University
Lubbock, Texas 79409

Thomas More College
Crestview Hills, Kentucky 41017

Toledo, University of
Toledo, Ohio 43606

Texas Wesleyan College
Fort Worth, Texas 76105

▮ **Tougaloo College**
Tougaloo, Mississippi 39174

Towson State University
Towson, Maryland 21204

Transylvania University
Lexington, Kentucky 40508

◆ **Trinity College**
Hartford, Connecticut 06106

◆ **Trinity College**
Washington, DC 20017

◆ **Trinity University**
San Antonio, Texas 78284

◆ Phi Beta Kappa Schools   ▮ Predominantly African-American Institution

Truman State University
Kirksville, Missouri 63501

◆ Tufts University
Medford, Massachusetts 02155

◆ Tulane University
New Orleans, Louisiana 70118

❙ Tuskegee University
Tuskegee, Alabama 36088

◆ Tulsa, University of
Tulsa, Oklahoma 74104

U ◆ Union College
Schenectady, New York 12308

U.S. Air Force Academy
Colorado Springs, Colorado 80840

U.S. Coast Guard Academy
New London, Connecticut 06320

U.S. Military Academy
West Point, New York 10996

U.S. Naval Academy
Annapolis, Maryland 21402

◆ Ursinus College
Collegeville, Pennsylvania 19426

◆ Utah, University of
Salt Lake City, Utah 84112

Utah State University
Logan, Utah 84322

Utica College of Syracuse University
Utica, New York 13502

V Valparaiso University
Valparaiso, Indiana 46383

◆ Vanderbilt University
Nashville, Tennessee 37235

◆ Vassar College
Poughkeepsie, New York 12601

◆ Vermont, University of
Burlington, Vermont 05401

◆ Villanova University
Villanova, Pennsylvania 19085

◆ Virginia, University of
Charlottesville, Virginia 22903

Virginia Commonwealth University
Richmond, Virginia 23284

Virginia Military Institute
Lexington, Virginia 24450

◆ Virginia Polytechnic Institute
Blacksburg, Virginia 24061

Virginia Wesleyan College
Norfolk, Virginia 23502

W ◆ Wabash College
Crawfordsville, Indiana 47933

Wagner College
Staten Island, New York 10301

◆ Wake Forest University
Winston-Salem, North Carolina 27109

Wartburg College
Waverly, Iowa 50677

Washington College
Chestertown, Maryland 21620

◆ Washington & Jefferson College
Washington, Pennsylvania 15301

◆ Washington & Lee University
Lexington, Virginia 24450

◆ Washington University
St. Louis, Missouri 63130

◆ Washington, University of
Seattle, Washington 98195

◆ Washington State University
Pullman, Washington 99164

◆ Wayne State University
Detroit, Michigan 48202

Webster University
Lows, Missouri 63119

◆ Wellesley College
Wellesley, Massachusetts 02181

◆ Wells College
Aurora, New York 13026

Wesleyan College
Macon, Georgia 31297

◆ Wesleyan University
Middletown, Connecticut 06457
West Chester University
West Chester, Pennsylvania 19383

Western Connecticut State University
Danbury, Connecticut 06810

Western Kentucky University
Bowling Green, Kentucky 42101

◆ Western Maryland College
Westminster, Maryland 21157

Western Michigan University
Kalamazoo, Michigan 49008

Western New England College
Springfield, Massachusetts 01119

Western Washington University
Bellingham, Washington 98225

◆ Phi Beta Kappa Schools   ❙ Predominantly African-American Institution

Westfield State College
Westfield, Massachusetts 01086

West Florida, University of
Pensacola, FL 32514

Westminster College
Fulton, Missouri 65251

Westminster College
Wilmington, Pennsylvania 16172

Westmont College
Santa Barbara, California 93108

◆ **West Virginia University**
Morgantown, West Virginia 26506

West Virginia Wesleyan
Buckhannon, West Virginia 26201

Wheaton College
Wheaton, Illinois 60187

◆ **Wheaton College**
Norton, Massachusetts 02766

Wheelock College
Boston, Massachusetts 02215

◆ **Whitman College**
Walla Walla, Washington 99362

Whittier College
Whittier, California 90608

Whitworth College
Spokane, Washington 99251

Widener University
Chester, Pennsylvania 19013

■ **Wilberforce University**
Wilberforce, Ohio 45384

William Jewell College
Liberty, Missouri 64068

◆ **William & Mary, College of**
Williamsburg, Virginia 23185

◆ **Williams College**
Williamstown, Massachusetts 01267

Willamette University
Salem, Oregon 97301

Wilmington College
Wilmington, Ohio 45177

◆ **Wilson College**
Chambersburg, Pennsylvania 17201

Winona State University
Winona, Minnesota 55987

◆ **Wisconsin, University of, at**
   LaCrosse, Wisconsin 5460
   ◆ **Madison,** Wisconsin 53706
   ◆ **Milwaukee,** Wisconsin 53201

◆ **Wittenberg University**
Springfield, Ohio 45501

◆ **Wofford College**
Spartanburg, South Carolina 29301

Woodbury University
Burbank, California 91510

◆ **Wooster, College of**
Wooster, Ohio 44691

Worcester Polytechnic Institute
Worcester, Massachusetts 01609

◆ **Wyoming, University of**
Laramie, Wyoming 82071

X **Xavier University**
Cincinnati, Ohio 45207

■ **Xavier University of Louisiana**
New Orleans, Louisiana 70125

Y ◆ **Yale University**
New Haven, Connecticut 06520

✿ **Yeshiva University**
New York, New York 10033

York College of Pennsylvania
York, Pennsylvania 17403

APPENDIX B
The Miscellaneous Majors Colleges Used In This Study

Antioch College
Yellow Springs, OH 45387

Assumption College
Worcester, MA 01609

Atlantic, College of the
Bar Harbor, ME 04609

Aurora University
Aurora, Il 60506

Berklee College of Music
Boston, MA 02215

Bluefield College
Bluefield, VA 24605

Boise State University
Boise, ID 83725

Brooks Institute of Photography
Santa Barbara, CA 93108

California Institute of the Arts
Valencia, CA 91355

California Polytechnic State University
Pomona, CA 91768

California State University
Bakersfield, CA 93311
Fresno, CA 93740
Los Angeles, CA 90032
Northridge, CA 91330
Sacramento, CA 95819
(Sonoma) Rohnert Park, CA 94928
(Stanislaus) Turlock, CA 95380

California University of Pennsylvania
California, PA 15419

Castleton State College
Castleton, VT 05735

Centenary College
Hackettstown, NJ 07840

▌**Cheyney University of Pennsylvania**
Cheyney, PA 19319

Cleveland State University
Cleveland, OH 44115

Cornish College of the Arts
Seattle, WA 98102

Cortland State College
Cortland, NY 13045

Curry College
Milton, MA 02186

Daemen College
Amherst, NY 14226

Deep Springs College
Deep Springs Via Dyer, NV 89010

▌ Predominantly African-American Institution

East Carolina University
Greenville, NC 27858

Eastern Kentucky University
Richmond, KY 40475

Eastern Montana College
Billings, MT 59101

Eugene Lang College (New School Social Research)
New York, NY 11743

Findlay, University of
Findlay, OH 45840

Fitchburg State College
Fitchburg, MA 01420

Georgia State University
Atlanta, GA 30303

Hampshire College
Amherst, MA 01002

Husson College
Bangor, ME 04401

Kansas City Art Institute
Kansas City, MO 64111

Kean College of New Jersey
Union, NJ 07083

Kendall College of Art and Design
Grand Rapids, MI 49503

Lake Erie College
Painesville, OH 44077

Landmark College
Putney, VT 05346

Lesley College
Cambridge, MA 02138

Long Island University
Southampton Center, NY 11968

Lyndon State College
Lyndonville, VT 05851

Madonna University
Livonia, MI 48150

Marist College
Poughkeepsie, NY 12601

Massachusetts State College
Westfield, MA 01085

Memphis College of Art
Memphis, TN 38112

Metropolitan State College
Denver, CO 80204

University of New England
Biddeford, ME 04005

New Hampshire College
Manchester, NH 03104

North Carolina Wesleyan College
Rocky Mount, NC 27804

North Dakota State University
Fargo, ND 58105

Northeastern Louisiana University
Monroe, LA 71209

Parks College of St. Louis University
Cahokia, IL 62206

Pfeiffer College
Misenheimer, NC 28109

Portland State University
Portland, OR 97207

Ramapo College of New Jersey
Mahwah, NJ 07430

Rhode Island College
Providence, RI 02908

Ringling School of Art & Design
Sarasota, FL 34234

Robert Morris College
Coraopolis, PA 15108

Rowan College of New Jersey
Glassboro, NJ, 08028

St. Edward's University
Austin, TX 78704

Saint John's College
Annapolis, MD 21404

Saint Leo College
Saint Leo, FL 33574

Saint Thomas University
Miami, FL 33054

Salve Regina-The Newport College
Newport, RI 02840

San Jose State University
San Jose, CA 95152

Shenandoah University
Winchester, VA 22601

Simon's Rock College of Bard
Great Barrington, MA 01230

Slippery Rock University
Slippery Rock, PA 16057

Springfield College
Springfield, MA 01109

Stephens College
Columbia, MO 65215

Texas Woman's University
Denton, TX 76204

United States Merchant Marine Academy
Kings Point, NY 11024

Webb Institute
Glen Cove, NY 11542

William Woods University
Fulton, MO 65251

Wingate College
Wingate, NC 28174

Wisconsin, University of
Oshkosh, WI 54901

Wisconsin, University of
Stevens Point, WI 54481

Wisconsin, (Stout) University of
Menomonie, WI 54751

Worcester State College
Worcester, MA 01602

Wright State University
Dayton, OH 45435

Youngstown State University
Youngstown, OH 44555

APPENDIX C
Single Sex Colleges Included In This Study

WOMEN'S COLLEGES

Agnes Scott College (GA)
Bennett College (NC)
Bryn Mawr College (PA)
Cedar Crest College (PA)
Chatham College (PA)
Chestnut Hill (PA)
Converse College(SC)
Hollins College (VA)
Hood College (MD)
Judson College (AL)
Lesley (MA)
Mary Baldwin College (VA)
Meredith College (NC)

Mills College (CA)
Mount Holyoke College (MA)
Randolph-Macon Woman's Coll. (VA)
Rosemont College (PA)
St. Catherine, College of (MN)
Salem College (NC)
Scripps College (CA)
Seton Hill (PA)
Simmons College (MA)
Smith College (MA)
Spelman College (GA)
Saint Joseph's (CT)
Saint Mary's College (IN)

Sweet Briar College (VA)
Texas Woman's College
Trinity College (DC)
Wellesley College (MA)
Wesleyan College (GA)
Wheelock (MA)
Wilson College (PA)

MEN'S COLLEGES

Hampden-Sydney College (VA)
Morehouse College (GA)
Wabash College (IN)

APPENDIX D

Anyone who has been touched by the problem of alcohol or substance abuse, or who has worked with those struggling in recovery, knows that higher education will increasingly have to meet the needs of these persons. The colleges listed below are trying to address the needs of these students. The Wellness Institute at Ball State has published this list of wellness dorms. I cannot vouch personally for the level or quality of services here. I can only state that they do exist and that parents requiring such services would do well to contact colleges on their selection lists to determine the availability of such accommodations. More may indeed exist.

Respectfully submitted,
Joseph W. Streit
Secondary School Counselor in New Jersey

INSTITUTIONS OFFERING WELLNESS RESIDENCE HALLS

ALABAMA

University of Alabama/Tuscaloosa	Yoland Reese, Health Educator	205/348-3878
University of Montevallo	Freida Shivers, Director or Housing	205/665-2988

ARIZONA

Arizona State University	Tamra Summers, Asst. Director, Student Services	602/965-8900

ARKANSAS

John Brown University	G. Robert Burns, Chair, Health Promotion	501/524-2000
University of Arkansas	Jim Conneeley, Director, Residence Life	501/575-5000

CALIFORNIA

California Poly State Univ./Pomona	Ali Mossares-Rahmani, Director of Housing	909/869-3306
University of California/Irvine	E. Ellen Thomas, Director, Health Education	714/824-5806
University of California/Los Angeles	Alan Hanson, Director, Residence Life	310/825-3066
University of California/Santa Barbara	Wilfred Brown, Director of Housing	805/893-4155

COLORADO

Fort Lewis College	Bill Bolden, Director, Residence Life	970/247-7503
Regis University	Diane Cooper, Asst. Director, Residence Life	303/458-3505
University of Northern Colorado	Andy Blank, Director of Housing	970/351-2721

CONNECTICUT

Wesleyan University	Patricia Houmiel, Director, Residential Life	860/865-2222

DELAWARE

University of Delaware	Dave Buttler, Executive Director, Housing	302/831-6573

FLORIDA

Florida State University	Dr. Rita Moser, Director, University Housing	904/644-2860
Stetson University	Michelle Espinosa, Director, Residence Life	904/822-7201
University of Miami	Loreto Jackson, Director of Wellness	305/284-3253
University of North Florida	Doreen Perez, Director, Student Health	904/646-2900
University of Tampa	Monnie Huston, Director, Residence Life	813/253-6239

GEORGIA
Georgia Institute of Technology	Terry Sichta, Director of Housing	404/894-2486

ILLINOIS
Illinois State University	Linda Sorrells, Director, Wellness Program	309/438-7003
Northern Illinois University	Chika Nnamani, Exec. Director, Student Housing	815/753-9607
Northwestern University	Bill Tempelmeyer, Director, University Housing	708/491-7564
University of Illinois/Urbana-Champaign	Rosanne Proite, Assoc. Director of Housing	217/333-0770

INDIANA
Ball State University	Neil Schmottlach, Director, Fisher Institute	888/935-5278
Indiana University	Bruce Jacobs, Director, Residence Life	812/855-1764
Manchester College	Charlie Mackey, Director, Residence Life	219/982-5000
Purdue University	Tom Paczolt, Manager, Shreve Hall	317/494-2569
Valparaiso University	Christopher Rasmussen, Asst. Dean of Students	219/464-5413

IOWA
Iowa State University	Charles Frederiksen, Director, Residence Life	515/294-5636
University of Northern Iowa	Bob Hartman, Director, Dept. of Residence	319/273-2333

KENTUCKY
Centre College	Sherry Raitiere, Nurse, Wellness Center	606/238-5330
Northern Kentucky University	Patty Hayden, Director, Residence Life	606/572-5448
University of Kentucky	Melanie Tyner-Wilson, Director, Residence Life	606/257-4783

MAINE
University of Maine/Machias	Peter Schmidt, Coordinator, Residential Life	207/255-3313

MARYLAND
Coppin State College	Linda Dark, Director, Health Promotion	410/383-5859
Loyola College	Kathy Clark-Petersen, Director, Student Life	410/617-2488

MASSACHUSETTS
Boston University	Celine McNelis-Kline, Director, Wellness Center	617/353-3698
Framingham State College	Joe Onofrietto, Director, Residence Life	508/626-4632

MICHIGAN
Oakland University	Eleanor Reynolds, Director, Residence Halls	810/370-3570
Northern Michigan University	Mary McDonald, RD, Director, Residence Life	906/227-2396
Western Michigan University	Julie Gerard, Director, Residence Hall Life	616/387-4460

MINNESOTA
Augsburg College	Denise Anderson-Diffenbach, Hall Director	612/330-1109
Bemidji State University	Dale Ladig, Director, Residence Life	218/755-3750
Macalester College	Ann Bolger, Director, Residence Life	612/696-6215
University of Minnesota	David Golden, Director, Health Education	612/626-6738

MISSOURI
Central Missouri State University	Lisa Schulte, Director of Housing	816/543-4515, 4164

| University of Missouri | Janet Snook, Coordinator for Fitwell | 314/882-2066 |
| Webster University | Sandra Henkes, Director, Residence Life | 314/968-7030 |

MONTANA

| Montana State University/Billings | Gina Swartz, Director of Housing | 406/657-2376 |

NEW HAMPSHIRE

| Plymouth State College | Time Keefe, Director, Residential Life | 603/535-2260 |

NEW JERSEY

| Rutgers University | Roselle Wilson, Vice President, Student Affairs | 908/932-7255 |

NEW YORK

Binghamton University	Jeanne Mathias, Wellness Coordinator	607/777-2594
SUNY/Coll. of Tech./Delhi	John Leddy, Director, Residence Life	607/746-4632
SUNY/Cortland	Michael Holland, Director, Residential Services	607/753-2095
SUNY/Oswego	Marie Driscoll, Assistant Director, Housing	315/341-3039
SUNY/Potsdam	John Horan, Director, Residence Halls	315/267-2305
SUNY/Stony Brook	Andre Serrano, Residence Hall Director	516/632-2910

NORTH CAROLINA

| Elon College | Alice Ledford, Director, Residential Life | 910/584-2218 |
| Univ. of North Carolina/Chapel Hill | Wayne T. Kunel, Director of Housing | 919/962-5405 |

OHIO

| Capital University | Ronald Bell, Director, Residence Life | 614/236-6811 |
| Miami University | Kim Rovansek, Director, Student Housing | 513/529-5000 |

PENNSYLVANIA

Bucknell University	Kari Conrad, Director, Residence Life	717/524-1195
Dickinson College	Tom Matoua, Director of Housing	717/245-1555
Duquesne University	Sharon Goedert, Director, Residence Life	412/396-5028
Muhlenberg College	Scott Salsberry, Director, Residence Life	610/821-3167
Pennsylvania State University	Gail Hurley, Director, Residence Life	814/863-1710
Susquehanna University	Donald Hamum, Athletic Director	717/372-4271
University of Scranton	Fr. Reusseau, Assistant Director, Residence Life	717/941-6226

RHODE ISLAND

Bryant College	Doris Helmich, Health Educator	401/232-6703
Roger Williams University	Richard Stegman, Director, Student Life	401/254-3161
University of Rhode Island	Lester Yuesan, Director, Residential Life	401/874-5374

TENNESSEE

| David Lipscomb University | Donna White, Director of Housing | 615/269-1000 X2218 |

TEXAS

St. Mary's University	Lisa McDouglas, Director, Residence Life	210/436-3714
Southern Methodist University	Dr. Michael Lawrence, Director of Housing	214/768-2422
West Texas A&M University	John Davis, Director, Residence Life	806/656-3000

UTAH

Brigham Young University	David Hunt, Housing Services Director	801/378-2611

VERMONT

Lyndon State College	Lorraine Matteis, Director, Health Services	802/626-6440

WASHINGTON

The Evergreen State College	Mike Segawa, Housing Director	360/866-6000 X6132
Washington State University	Health and Wellness Services	509/335-3528
Western Washington University	Kay Rich, Director, University Residence	360/650-2960

WISCONSIN

Cardinal Stritch College	Janet Callender, Director, Residence Life	414/352-5400 X471
University of Wisconsin/Oshkosh	Jim Chitwood, Director, Residence Life	414/424-3212
University of Wisconsin/Stevens Point	John Munson, Assoc. Dean, Professional Studies	719/346-4614

CANADA

University of Calgary	Kelly Weltanffee, Director of Housing	403/220-5312

INSTITUTIONS REQUIRING UNDERGRADUATE WELLNESS COURSES

Albertson College	Dennis Freeburn, Dean of Student Affairs	208/459-5508
The **American** University	Stephanie F. Franchi, President	202/885-6282
Anderson University	Rebecca A. Hull, Department Chair	317/649-9071
Ball State University	Dr. Neil Schmottlach, Director	317/285-8529
Bellin College Nursing	Vicki A. Moss, Associate Professor	414/433-3409
Black Hills State University	Dr. Rob L. Schurrer, Assistant Professor	605/642-6169
Brigham Young University	Dr. Larry A. Tucker, Director of Health	801/378-4927
Bucks County Community College	Dr. Barry Sysler, Professor	251/968-8455
California State University	Sam J. Gitchel, Health Educator	209/278-2734
California State University	Nancy E. Shanfeld, Health Promotion Coordinator	818/885-3693
Capital University	Barbara A. Nash, Co-Director	614/236-6114
University of **Central Arkansas**	Dr. Arvil Burks, Department Chair	501/450-3191
Coastal Carolina College	Dr. Marshall E. Parker, Assistant Dean	803/349-2810
University of **Dayton**	Dr. Lloyd. L. Laubach, Wellness Program Director	513/229-4205
University of **Delaware**	Joyce L. Walter, Coordinator	302/457-8992
Delgado Community College	Jimmie R. Singeton, Director of Fitness Center	504/483-4255
Delta College	Sandy L. Wright, Health Service Director	504/483-4255
Dickinson College	Dr. Judith M. Vorio, Director, Truly Living Program	717/245-1525
East Los Angeles College	Dr. Sharon Deny, WPE Department Chair	213/265-8917
Eastern Montana College	Kamette C. Butterfield, Program Technician	406/657-2214
Elon College	Robert D. Pelley, Assistant Dean of Student Affairs	919/584-2218
Emporia State University	Dr. Darrell A. Lang, Director, Health Promotion	316/343-5929
Essex Community College	Thomas D. Kemp, Director, Health Fitness Lab	301/522-1415
Fayetteville State University	Dr. Nosa O'Bannor, Assistant Professor	919/486-1524, 1115
Fort Valley State College	Gwendolyn D. Reeves, Wellness Coordinator	912/825-9207
Gateway Community College	Sue Butler, Fitness Coordinator	Phoenix, AZ 85034
Georgia Insitute of Technology	Jami L. Fraze, Director, Wellness Center	404/853-0074
Georgia Southern University	Dr. Jerry E. Lafferty, Dean, Health & Prof, Stu.	912/681-5322

University of **Georgia**	Dr. Harry P. Duval, Associate Professor	404/542-4395
Gordon College	Dr. Peter W. Iltis, Associate Professor	508/927-2300, 4324
Goshen College	Willard S. Krabill, Director of Student Health	219/535-7474
Goucher College	Sally J. Baum, Assoc. Dir., Phys. Ed. Wellness Co.	301/337-6383
Hanover College	William D. Tereshko, Department Chairman	812/866-7375
Henderson University	Dr. Tom E. Ward, Associate Professor	501/246-5511, 3552
Hope College	Donna S. Eaton, Director, Health Dynamics	616/394-7693
Jacksonville State University	Dr. John B. Hammett, Coordinator, Wellness Center	205/782-5114
James Madison University	Nancy O. Grembi, Assistant Director	703/568-6177
Kalamazoo Valley Community College	Allan R. Thompson, Department Chair	616/372-5392
Kennesaw State College	Susan O. Bulter, Wellness Coordinator	401/423-6394
Lake Michigan College	Donald E. Alsbro, Instructor	616/927-3571, X330
Lane Community College	Sandra L. Ing, Director, Special Student Services	503/747-4501, 2666
University of **Maine**	Donna L. Duley, P.E. Lecturer and Women's Coach	207/255-3313, X352
Memphis State University	Dr. David J. Anspaugh, Professor, Division Head	901/678-2323
Millersville University	Dr. William V. Kahler, Chairperson	717/872-3674
Missouri Southern State College	Charles M. Conklin, Faculty Wellness Coordinator	417/625-9713
Montana State University	Dr. Gary F. Evans, Director of Employee Wellness	406/994-4001
University of **Montevallo**	Dr. J. W. Tishler, Professor of Health & P. E.	205/665-6587
Montgomery College	Karen M. Thomas, Assistant Professor	301/251-7582
Muhlenberg College	Connie R. Kunda, Wellness Director	215/821-3393
Murray State University	Dr. Pamela L Rice, Associate Professor	502/762-6826
Northeast Louisiana University	Dr. Luke E. Thomas, Professor	318/342-1310
University of **Northern Iowa**	Kathy M. Gulick, Director, Wellness Promo. Prog.	319/273-6921
Northern Kentucky University	Wiley T. Piazza, Wellness Coordinator	606/572-5684
Northern Michigan University	Dr. Harvey A. Wallace, CHES, Coor. HL Ed.	906/227-1135
Northwestern College	Ev Otten, Director of Health Services	712/737-4821, X251
University of **Wisconsin**/Superior	Dr. Barbara P. Hamann, Program Coord., Health	715/394-8273
University of **Wyoming**	Annette K. Tommerdahl, Director, Cardiac Rehab	307/766-5423

APPENDIX E

A Simplified Timetable and Checklist for Seniors Planning on College

SEPTEMBER - OCTOBER	Write for college catalogs, applications, financial aid information and pick up a financial aid booklet.
SEPTEMBER - OCTOBER	Inquire at your high school Guidance Office about upcoming college nights.
SEPTEMBER - NOVEMBER	Continue campus visits as senior year academic commitments permit.
LATE SEPTEMBER	Deadline for mailing in the late October or early November National College Exam Forms.
OCTOBER	Think about which two teachers you will ask to write college recommendations for you.
LATE OCTOBER	Deadline for mailing in the December National College Exam Forms.
NOVEMBER	Prepare a final list of colleges.
NOVEMBER 1-15	Many early applications due.
NOVEMBER OR DECEMBER	Attend, with your parents, a local financial aid night given by an area high school.
NOVEMBER - DECEMBER	Apply to colleges.
EARLY DECEMBER	Last call for mailing in the National College Exam Forms.
DECEMBER 15	Profile of Financial Aid Form (Step 1) due to College Scholarship Service (CSS).
JANUARY	Fill out the Financial Aid Form (FAF/FAFSA/PROFILE) or Family Financial Statement. Your counselor has it. This form will probably help you get a good deal of your total scholarships, jobs, and loans. It is the big one.
JANUARY - FEBRUARY	Send mid-year reports to colleges.
FEBRUARY 1	Profile application (Step 2) to College Scholarship Service (CSS).
MARCH	Local scholarship forms available in the guidance office.
EARLY APRIL	All colleges will notify you by this time if they will accept you or not. The more competitive colleges usually deliberate longer and many of these top schools wait until April 5th to notify you.
MID-APRIL	If unhappy with the financial aid package at any of the colleges where you have been accepted, call that office and discuss it.
LATE APRIL	Send deposit to selected college.
MAY 1	Inform all colleges which accepted you whether or not you plan to attend.
MAY 1	Notify Guidance Office of your choice of college.
MAY - JUNE	Apply for summer jobs so that you can meet summer earnings expectations. Don't forget to graduate from high school!
SUMMER	Attend college orientation.

NOTE: Before your senior year, prepare preliminary list of colleges you're interested in and those you would like to visit.

APPENDIX F
The Get-Going Form

A simple, useful form to use with the college-bound to get them started applying to colleges.
The student and/or counselor and/or parent should fill in four colleges below, complete with address and zip codes.

Dear Student:

Within the next two weeks, please write to the Director of Admissions at the schools listed below, requesting information. A sample letter is included at the bottom of the page.

1. _____
   _____
   _____

2. _____
   _____
   _____

3. _____
   _____
   _____

4. _____
   _____
   _____

SAMPLE LETTER

Date

Director of Admissions
Name of College
Address of College and Zip Code

Dear Director:

I am a student of Foxborough High School in Foxborough, Massachusetts and expect to graduate in June, 1996.

I am interested in your school and would appreciate your sending me an application for admission and information concerning your financial aid program, and your _____ program of studies. Thank you.

Very truly yours,

Your signature
Your Name
Your Address and Zip Code

APPENDIX G

Fred Rugg's One Hundred Colleges ... Just Darn Good Schools

"I Hear More Nice Things About These Schools Than Any Others"

The most valuable list in this book. Places where students maximize their education.

Alfred (NY)
Allegheny (PA)
Auburn (AL)
Austin (TX)
Barnard (NY)
Bates (ME)
Beloit (WI)
Bemidji State (MN)
Berry (GA)
Bethany (WV)
Biola (CA)
Buffalo (SUNY)
Butler (IN)
California, U. of (Davis)
California, U. of (Riverside)
Claremont McKenna (CA)
Colorado Mines
Creighton (NB)
Dayton (OH)
Denison (OH)
DePaul (IL)
Drake (IA)
Earlham (IN)
Edinboro (PA)
Evansville (IN)
Georgia Institute of Technology
Grinnell (IA)
Guilford (NC)
Hanover (IN)
Harvard (MA)
Haverford (PA)
Heidelberg (OH)
Hendrix (AR)
Hiram (OH)
Hollins (VA)
Humboldt State (CA)

Idaho, U. of
Illinois, U. of
Illinois Wesleyan
Indiana University
Juniata (PA)
Kansas, U. of
Kansas State
Keene State (NH)
Kentucky, U. of
Lawrence (WI)
LeMoyne (NY)
Lesley (MA)
Macalester (MN)
Maine, U. of (Farmington)
Marquette (WI)
Michigan State
Michigan Tech
Minnesota (Morris)
Minnesota, U.of
Montana State
Montana, U. of
Moravian (PA)
Muskingum (OH)
North Carolina State
Northern Michigan
Northern Arizona
Ohio University
Ohio Wesleyan
Pennsylvania, U. of
Pittsburgh, U. of
Portland, U. of (OR)
Purdue (IN)
Radford (VA)
Regis (CO)
Rhodes (TN)
Roanoke (VA)

Rochester Institute of Tech. (NY)
Rockhurst (MO)
St. Andrews (NC)
St. Anselm (NH)
St. Joseph's (ME)
Saint Mary's (CA)
St. Mary's (IN)
St. Norbert (WI)
St. Olaf (MN)
Santa Clara (CA)
Sonoma State (CA)
Southwestern (TX)
Spring Hill (AL)
Stanford (CA)
Susquehanna (PA)
Tennessee, U. of
Texas A&M
Virginia Wesleyan
Wabash (IN)
Washington & Jefferson (PA)
Washington Col. (MD)
Washington, U. of
Wesley (DE)
Western Connecticut
Western Maryland
Westminster (MO)
West Virginia Wesleyan
Wheaton (MA)
Williams (MA)
Wingate (NC)
Winona State (MN)
Wisconsin, U. of
Wittenberg (OH)
Wofford (SC)
Wooster (OH)
Wyoming, U. of

Over 900 Secondary School Counselors responded to the question, "What colleges do you believe offer students the best opportunity to maximize their education?" The list is above. Please don't count the colleges in this list. There's actually a little over 100. I just couldn't get it down to the magic number.

COUNSELOR'S NOTES

COUNSELOR'S NOTES

COUNSELOR'S NOTES

COUNSELOR'S NOTES

ABOUT THE AUTHOR

Frederick E. Rugg

Frederick E. Rugg is a nationally known expert on college admissions. He is the author of *Rugg's Recommendations on the Colleges*, an annual guide to quality colleges. Unlike virtually all other college guidebook authors, Rugg is one of the true professionals, having directed secondary college counseling programs for 20 years in all types of communites. A 1967 Applied Math graduate from Brown, Rugg is the holder of advanced degrees and has written extensively in professional journals. He worked his way through Ivy League Brown, and was the only member of his class to enter public school teaching. Offering dozens of workshops yearly from coast to coast, Fred is an animated and humorous speaker, and has become well-known for giving the most practical college seminars around. He has lived and worked just about everywhere in America, has two daughters in their mid-twenties, has been married for 30 years, and, for over a decade, was a college basketball referee around the country. He can be found several Saturdays during the year at two-year Cuesta College, where he teaches "How to Find Your College and Pay for It."

✄ **PLEASE CLIP AND MAIL TO:** ✄

Rugg's Recommendations • 7120 Serena Court • Atascadero, CA 93422

Please send me _____ copies of *Rugg's Recommendations on the Colleges* at $19.95 (plus $4 S & H) each.

I have enclosed my check in the amount of $ _____

Name _____

Address _____

City _____ State _____ Zip _____

For additional information call 805/462-2503 or 805/462-9019.
Other products and resources from Rugg's appear on pages 162-164.

FROM RUGG'S RECOMMENDATIONS...

INFORMATION THAT IS TO THE POINT, THAT YOU CAN USE IMMEDIATELY

**Saving the college counselor enormous time with lists and answers found nowhere else—
presented from the secondary school point of view!**

---

1. THE BOOK: *RUGG'S RECOMMENDATIONS ON THE COLLEGES 14th Ed.*
Locating Quality Undergraduate Colleges For Counselors, Parents & Students.
ISBN #1-883062-14-4 • LC89-062896 • $19.95 • ©1997 by Frederick E. Rugg

★ Over 750 Entry Changes PLUS New Recentered Scores ★

Rugg's Recommendations on the Colleges has been recommended by dozens of publications, including *USA Today*, *The L.A. Times*, *The Cleveland Plain Dealer*, *College Bound*, *The Boston Globe*, *The Midwest Book Review*, *The Atlanta Constitution*, and *The American Library Association's Booklist*. Rugg's 14th edition is available listing 5,300 quality departments at 760 quality colleges. The guidebook has recently been designated nationally as "a revered staple, the book parents and students must start with" in the search for a college to attend. The 14th edition is the accumulation of 25 years of work in the undergraduate college admissions process, and as always, *Rugg's* is independent of the colleges. There are over 750 entry changes since the 13th edition, 80 majors, 103 recommended departments per major.

"A Revered Staple." —West Coast Library Reviewer

"This is a unique reference and a valuable one." —Kliatt Paperback Book Guide

"A gem." —College Bound, Evanston, Illinois

"A treasure trove of input." —Diane C. Donovan, The MidWest Book Review

"Thank you. It is a valuable resource in our Career Center." —Phyllis Kerr, Career Information Coordinator, Maryland

---

2. THE SPECIAL REPORT: *TWENTY MORE TIPS ON THE COLLEGES, REVISED*
Twenty new behind the scenes tips. Ideal for counselors, parents, and students.
ISBN #1-883062-18-7 • $8.95 • ©January 1997

This Special Report, *Twenty More Tips on the Colleges*, offers insights into assessing a college or university from the first "hello." Author Rugg succinctly presents 20 key tips to assist counselors, parents and students in selecting the best college for a student. Rugg honestly assesses the value of several college rating and reference books. Tips include colleges with high success rates for medical school acceptance, and what to consider before deciding to attend a military school. Overlooked state institutions, as well as other important and helpful comments, are included. The college search and selection process is incomplete without reading the valuable information contained within this Special Report.

"Information for our top students and is up to the minute. Information you can get nowhere else." —Tim Norris, Dir. College Counseling, Proctor (NH) Academy

"...provides a wealth of information on college choices, from differences between the Ivy League colleges to getting financial aid." —The Book Watch, San Francisco, CA

"I have used your information for years. It is a wonderful resource." —Harriet Gershman, Academic Counseling Services, Evanston, IL

---

3. *FORTY TIPS ON THE COLLEGES* : THE REVISED SPECIAL REPORT
For all college bound students, parents, and their counselors. 16 pages.
ISBN # 1-883062-19-5 • $9.95 (money back guarantee) • Revised January 1997

Get the "insider's" advice on college admissions. In *Forty Tips on the Colleges*, author Rugg shares with the reader 40 key tips on the college admissions process. Rugg spent in excess of 1500 hours visiting with over 3500 secondary school counselors in 40 states, to compile the information contained in this transcript. These insightful suggestions provide the reader with some of the unwritten do's and don'ts in the college admissions process. Rugg presents his 40 tips, accompanied by his personal observations of the campuses, with honesty and a sense of humor. *Forty Tips on the Colleges* offers straight talk about selecting a college and gaining admission. The transcript contains helpful advice for the student, parent and school counselor alike. Topics include previously unpublished tips on which colleges really care about their students; colleges with good learning disabilities programs; and how to choose a college where the student "fits in." The tips also contain helpful information concerning financial aid, college applications and SAT/ACT scores. Throughout this transcript, Rugg cites several helpful reference books. This ***must read*** is our most popular transcript.

*"After attending Fred's workshop in Bar Harbor, Maine, I was very eager to buy his special report, 40 **Tips on the Colleges**. This report is as 'on-target' as his workshop. I've used the report in English classes with juniors, in parent meetings, and in faculty meetings. Each time the response has been overwhelmingly positive. 'Finally, someone is telling it as it is!' is a common response. No glossy advertising or slick words, just honest, accurate information".* —Beulah J. Grant, Dean of Students, George Stevens Academy, Blue Hill, ME

"Our parents and students have really enjoyed and learned from your reports...keep up the great work—sure makes our job easier." —Ned Nemacheck, College Counselor, Homestead (WI) H.S.

---

4. THE SPECIAL REPORT: *THIRTY QUESTIONS ON THE COLLEGES, REVISED*
For all college bound students, parents and their counselors. 23 pages.
ISBN # 1-883062-20-9 • $9.95 • Revised 1997

Get straight and informative answers on 30 of the most frequently asked questions on colleges. This special report provides the answers to questions that students, parents, and counselors are asking about colleges. Rugg shares this "inside information" gathered through his extensive research, conversations with counselors and admissions personnel, and many campus visits. Even Deans of Admissions cannot give you some of the answers found here. The report provides answers to questions such as: Which state university should all others visit and copy? – At which 125 colleges can Afro-American students maximize their education? – How do top colleges really view community college graduates at transfer time? – What are the best of the journalism schools? and much, much more.

"For all Counselors, veterans and non-veterans —important and new college information—a beautiful piece of work!" —Hoover Sutton, Director of College Counseling, St. Andrews School, Middletown, DE, 1984-1993; Ind. Educational Consultant, Hanover, NH, 1993-Present